In Me, you are made worthy

I am worthy because of His blood

I am worthy because of I have been chosen by the Father

I am worthy because, [before time began. He knew me

I am His daughter and He cherishes me.

Am I perfect? No by any means! But I am pressing forward in the lord Jesus Christ.

"Come sit with Me awhile" says Jesus.

Daily Beauty Treatments

for the

BRIDE

~ a one year Devotional

by

Christine Beadsworth

Published by Christine Beadsworth,
Fresh Oil Releases

The author may be contacted at freshoil@polka.co.za

Fresh Oil Releases
41 Tharina Road
Somerset west
7130

Other writings and books are available at:
https://freshoilreleases.wordpress.com/

To my parents,

who taught me to

passionately love the Lord

and pursue Truth

Introduction

Welcome! Your name has been entered in the Holy Spirit's appointment book and you will be receiving a year's course of spiritual beauty treatments, concentrating on small doses of Light therapy and gentle applications of the oil of the sevenfold Holy Spirit. Just relax and allow His Word to do its marvelous work!

It has never been more important for the Bride of Christ to get herself ready and make the necessary changes and preparations to ensure that she is not taken by surprise when she hears the sound of the shofar announcing her Bridegroom's imminent arrival. In a world that grows increasingly dark with each passing day, we cannot look to the world for wisdom in making life-changing decisions. We must seek the face of Him Who is Wisdom and learn daily by the light of the seven lamps before the throne. This One Year Devotional deals with heart issues and the role of the Bride of Christ as the light of the world in an hour in which she is desperately needed to stand up and be all God intended her to be. It is my prayer that as you journey through the days of this year, you may experience an ever-deepening revelation of your Bridegroom and His glorious purpose for you in the earth. As you see Him more and more clearly, so too you will be changed from glory to glory. Your life will display an increasing measure of His beauty as you drink of the water of Life that is offered so freely to all who thirst!

Rev 22:17 AMP The Holy Spirit and the bride (the church, the true Christians) say, Come! And let him who is listening say, Come! And let everyone come who is thirsty [who is painfully conscious of his need of those things by which the soul is refreshed, supported, and strengthened]; and whoever [earnestly] desires to do it, let him come, take, appropriate, and drink the water of Life without cost.

Contents

January 1st

Rev 19:7 Let us be glad and rejoice, and give honor to him: for the marriage of the Lamb is come, and his wife has made herself ready.

The wife of the Lamb has a responsibility – to make herself ready! At first glance this seems to imply much strenuous activity – and so it is for an earthly bride. But the Bride of Christ is not fleshly nor made ready by either earthly means nor the good ideas of man. She is a spirit company, governed and led by the wind of the Spirit. His ways are not our ways and His thoughts are not our thoughts. Rushing around in the spirit of Martha trying to do as much as one can for the Kingdom before the Bridegroom comes is not the recommended way to make yourself ready! Rather, like Mary, choose the good portion of sitting at His feet and allow the Holy Spirit to guide your preparations.

Prayer: Today, Lord, grant me discernment to distinguish the ways of man entwined within my thought processes. Use the plaited whip of your 3-fold Truth to drive every fleshly way of serving you from this temple. Overturn the tables that have held the self-serving ideologies of man and restore Your Truth in my inmost parts. Amen.

January 2nd

Rev 21:2 And I, John saw the holy city, new Jerusalem, coming down from God out of heaven, prepared as a bride adorned for her husband.

This holy Bride descends from Heaven, the place where she has been prepared and adorned. Is this not why we are urged to fix our minds on heavenly things? For how can we make ourselves ready if our minds are continually filled with things which will pass away and are of no eternal value? No wonder John received the call to 'come up here' when receiving the Revelation of Christ! It is only as we ascend to a heavenly way of thinking and receive a fresh revelation of Christ by the Spirit, gazing upon His beauty, that we are transformed from glory to glory, becoming a Bride fit for the King of Glory. Let us gaze intently into the perfect Law of Liberty and be made into His image and likeness. The work is accomplished in our heart and the fruit seen outwardly.

Prayer: Father, send Your light to the eyes of my heart that I may see my Bridegroom the way You see Him. Lift me up to view all from the perspective of Heaven so that my priorities are forever changed. Adorn me with revelation of the risen and reigning Christ within me. Amen

January 3rd

Rev 18:16 *Woe to the great city which was clothed in fine linen and purple and scarlet, and adorned with gold and precious stones and pearls!*

There is a counterfeit spiritual city, the great harlot, which attempts to build according to man's ways in order to reach Heaven. With its linen, gold and precious stones it looks quite similar to the Holy City being formed above. Sensuality is often mistaken for spirituality in today's Church. We have been beguiled and blinded so that we can no longer distinguish that which emanates from the soul and that which has its origin in the Spirit of God.

There is a call to come out of this harlot city masquerading as the Bride that we may not participate in her sins or share the plagues appointed her. To do so, we need salve for our eyes that we can find our way back to the place from which we have fallen. Each of us must make a personal journey with the Holy Spirit, seizing and casting away every harlot's way within us as our vision progressively clears.

Prayer: Lord, show me again what You call good and what is inherently evil. I want no part in spiritual harlotry. Apply Your salve to the eyes of my heart - restore clear discernment regarding spiritual things. I choose this day to come out of that counterfeit city. Amen.

January 4th

Son 2:10 My Beloved spoke, and said to me, Rise up, My love, My beautiful one, and come away.

As we come out of Babylon, we do not journey alone. There is a call that lingers in the breeze century after century. It is the voice of the Bridegroom urging us to come away with Him. It is a call away from the known and the familiar and there is always an element of fear as we contemplate leaving the security of our present spiritual position. After all, we know the way things work here in the spiritual lowlands! Yet the wooing of the Spirit is unceasing and where else can we go? He has the words of eternal Life.

Don't let fear of the unknown keep you shackled. Move beyond the wall of your own mindsets. Rise up and follow wherever He leads you. If you trusted Him to pay the Bridal price for you in

His own Blood, you can trust Him to lead you safely through anything else.

Prayer: Lord, forgive me for not trusting You with my safety. You hold the map and have all the provisions we need. I want to come away with You. I want to be moved by the wind of Your Spirit. Take me wherever You desire us to go, amen

January 5th

'Come away with me from Lebanon, my promised bride, come with me. Descend from the top of Amana, from the peak of Senir and Hermon..... Songs 4:8

Lebanon speaks of the heart. This is a heart issue; it is not about doing something you fully understand with your head. The Lord is asking for a response of the heart. From the heart flow the issues of life. 'Amana' means 'covenant, faithfulness'. This is the place you are launching forth from - God is saying He is a God of covenant, He is faithful, you can trust Him.

'Hermon' comes from the root word meaning 'to seclude and devote to religious purposes, to consecrate'. Here the fallen angels covenanted to defile the DNA of the daughters of men. So we must come away from here, put a distance between you and sources of defilement. The Lord is calling us to a deeper consecration to Himself. He is asking for a deliberate setting apart of your heart in betrothal to this Groom, forsaking all others. This not a joining to a pastor or a fellowship or any other human agent, but a choice to take the journey He has mapped out for you which will prepare you as a Bride for your Bridegroom, the Lamb that was slain.

Prayer; Lord, forgive me for always wanting to know where I am going before I am willing to take the first step of the journey. I choose to trust Your wisdom, amen.

January 6th

'Come away with me ...from the lion's dens, from the mountain of the leopards' Songs 4:8

He is calling you to descend, away from the places of the lions' dens and the leopards. The word 'lion' in Hebrew means ' to pluck and pierce'. So God is calling you to follow and come away from those things in your life that pierce and hurt you.

The Hebrew word for 'leopard' means 'to spot and stain by dripping'. The Lord wants you to move away from the things that mark and stain your garment of pure white. If you will respond to Him and go with trust in your heart, He will move you away from this place you have been in that has been damaging to your soul and testimony.

Prayer: Lord, sometimes I do not recognize the lions and leopards in my life. Lead me out of this place in whatever way You choose. Help me to be obedient even when I do not understand Your methods, amen.

January 7th

Rev 12:12 Therefore rejoice, O heavens, and those dwelling in them. Woe to the inhabitants of the earth and in the sea! For the Devil came down to you, having great wrath, knowing that he has but a little time.

Those who make the Heavenly realms their dwelling place in these tumultuous days are assured safety and can rejoice. How different the fate of those bound to the earthly realm! Man-made systems of government are being severely shaken and people's hearts are beginning to fail them for fear. The wisdom of man is progressively coming to nothing.

It is imperative that those who are truly Christ's now learn how to DWELL in the secret place of the Most High. This is the place of safety and immunity. Visiting it once a week is no longer an option. Adjust your schedules, burn your bridges, do whatever you need to do but move your place of residence as a matter of urgency!

Prayer: Father, forgive me for finding shelter in the shaky lean-to's of man. They will never stand in the coming shakings. Help me to travel light and leave what is unnecessary behind. Holy Spirit, teach me how to abide in the secret place, in Christ. Amen.

January 8th

Joh 3:12 If I have told you earthly things and you do not believe, how shall you believe if I tell you heavenly things?

There are heavenly things to be heard. The sevenfold Holy Spirit desires to reveal to us the deep things of God. Just as John the Baptist prepared the way for the coming Jesus, so the Holy Spirit is given the task of preparing the Bride for her Groom. The seven lamps of fire burning before the throne are the seven Spirits of God. The more time we spend absorbing the light and warmth of these lamps, the greater our revelation of Christ will be. Instead of just receiving second-hand revelation from someone else who has been at the throne, let us press in for ourselves.

The atmosphere around the throne is charged with lightnings (strikes of revelation), thunderings (the voice of wisdom following the revelation just as thunder follows lightening) and voices (the speech of the seven Spirits of God). Worshiping and waiting in His presence will open our spiritual eyes and ears to all these good things which God has prepared for those who love Him.

Prayer: Father, as I worship You today, may Your sevenfold Spirit minister to me. Give me eyes that see and ears that hear and a heart that understands. Let me see Your lightnings and hear Your thunderings. Holy Spirit, show me heavenly things, the deep things of God, in Jesus Name, amen.

January 9th

Psa 133:1 A Song of degrees; of David. Behold, how good and how pleasant it is for brothers to dwell together in unity!

'Dwelling together in unity' - the Hebrew word translated 'unity' actually means 'to become one, as one unit'. This psalm is not about getting along with one another but rather holds an important key for understanding how and where God wants His Bride to be positioned in order to access the continuing flow of strengthening life from Him. It is the Bride that 'DWELLS' for this word in Hebrew also means 'to settle down, to marry'.

The anointing, presence and blessing of God is not to be found at particular geographical locations, this meeting or that conference. So where is it that we are to gather as one unit? Where is this 'assembly of the Church of the First-Born'? The flow of His continual resurrection life is tapped in to when we are in the right <u>spiritual</u> position, on Mount Zion, abiding and dwelling in Christ. Those who dwell as one Body, one unit, on Mount Zion are positioned in the right place to receive His blessing. This is not about earthly unity at all! The emphasis on unity horizontally in the Body of Christ needs to be replaced with emphasis on becoming one (in union or unity) with Him.

Prayer; Lord, so much of what I understand comes from the wrong understandings of men. This year as I meditate upon Your Word, I ask Your Holy Spirit to lead me into complete truth and show me where my beliefs are not in line with Truth. I don't want to feed on the letter which kills but on the Spirit-quickened Word which is true meat and brings life, amen.

January 10th

Psa 133:2 It is like the precious ointment upon the head, that ran down upon the beard, even Aaron's beard: that went down to the skirts of his garments;

In the Old Testament, the anointing was the portion of the priest. It was applied to his head and then flowed to and saturated his garments. In other words, the anointing was attached to his office, his garment. The oil did not touch his body. When he left the temple and went home, he wore ordinary clothes and did not function in his calling. His calling was attached to a building made with hands.

However, we are of a different dispensation. We are <u>not</u> the Body of Aaron – we are the Body of Christ. He, as the Head, is continually anointed and we are partakers in that anointing because we are one with Him. Our anointing is not designated to function in a particular building on particular days of the week. WE are His temple and as such, the anointing abides within us as long as we <u>abide</u> in Him and do not try to function as part of a dispensation which is obsolete.

Prayer: Father, deliver me once and for all of a Levitical mindset. You are in me and I am in You. The anointing is within me and does not need to be poured upon me. Help me to get hold of this truth, amen.

January 11th

*Psa 133:3 As the dew of Hermon, and as the dew that descended upon the mountains of Zion: for **there** the LORD commanded the blessing, even life for evermore.*

The dew of Hermon is the dew of consecration and devotion because this is what Hermon means. As we consecrate ourselves to Christ, we are positioned on Mount Zion with the Church of the First-Born. This is where our names are recorded, not in any earthly register or membership list. It is HERE, on Mount Zion, that the Lord commands a blessing, not when we get along with each other as many have taught.

Let us no longer keep gathering at Mount Sinai, waiting for the man of God to come down to us from a higher level with a word from God. We are not children of the covenant of Hagar which produces bondage. Our mother is Jerusalem above, which is free and we are to dwell on Mount Zion and not return to the weak and beggarly things which enslave us and cannot bring us to maturity! We have come to become part of the Church of the First Born and are registered as citizens in Heaven.

Prayer: Lord, I started out in the Spirit but I seem to so easily gravitate to the flesh and the Old Covenant way of doing things. Renew my mind so that I can discern Your good and perfect will for me. Help me to disentangle my thought processes from jail-house ways. It was for freedom You set me free, amen.

January 12th

*Psa 133:3 As the **dew** of Hermon, and as the **dew** that descended upon the mountains of Zion: for there the LORD commanded the blessing, even life for evermore.*

What is the blessing that is commanded when we DWELL in the spiritual position purchased for us? It is everlasting life or continually flowing life. The key here is that it is delivered like <u>dew</u> that descends on mount Zion. Dew falls daily in the evening, which is the beginning of God's day. It will accumulate on anything and everything that is <u>motionless</u> and at a cool enough temperature.

This is why we are urged to strive to enter into the Sabbath <u>rest</u>. This is the place where our own human religious labors and strivings have ceased and we become still and know that He is God. The Sabbath rest is the place of the Bride, those who has become one with Him and are still enough within so that the dew of Heaven can settle upon their hearts. When we are restless and busy with our own so-called spiritual efforts, we cannot receive the daily endowment of eternal life which is appointed us. Then we end up carrying out a lot of religious behavior which does not bring forth any fruit.

Prayer: Lord, why am I so much more comfortable with being Martha rather than Mary? Deliver me from the need to perform for other's approval or jump through the hoops of the Religious Spirit or even to satisfy my own list of spiritual aspirations. Bring me to Sabbath rest deep within, amen.

January 13th

Exo 16:14 And when the layer of dew had gone up, behold, there was a small round thing upon the face of the wilderness, small as the hoar-frost upon the ground.

It is the dew that falls on Mount Zion which carries within it all that we need to sustain us for the day ahead, just as the dew which fell in the wilderness brought the manna to the Israelites. As the Bride flees into the wilderness to escape the serpent (Rev 12), she is sustained and nourished, neither by the hand of man nor the doctrines of man. She is daily strengthened and energized by the impartation carried within the dew of Heaven.

The whole of Israel received as much manna as they could gather daily. In the same way, the whole of mount Zion is covered evenly with dew. It does not fall in some areas and not others because ALL of Mount Zion is a place of rest. There is dew for you, your own portion. It falls without any effort from you. All you need to do is be still in His presence and open your heart to receive it.

Prayer: Lord, may your dew be heavy upon my branch just like it did for Job before his trial. I still my restless heart and mind and I wait in anticipation for the manna the falling dew brings. I will not continue with today's demands until I have absorbed the nourishment You've sent. Amen.

Christine Beadsworth

January 14th

*Exo 16:31 And the house of Israel called the name of it Manna. And it was like coriander seed, white. And **the taste of it was like wafers with honey**.*
*Num 11:8 And the people went about, and gathered it, and ground it in mills, or beat it in a mortar, and baked it in pans, and made cakes of it: and **the taste of it was as the taste of fresh oil***

This daily manna tasted both like honey and fresh oil. Honey represents revelation. Fresh oil represents anointing. But revelation of what? ...and anointing for what purpose?

This manna was called bread from Heaven. Jesus said HE was the true Bread from Heaven. So the manna brought by the dew of Heaven is actually the **revelation** of Christ and the **anointing** which resides in Him as the Anointed One. Remember Paul prayed that the eyes of our hearts would be 'enlightened' (Eph 1). To 'enlighten' means 'to bring revelation, understanding or more light to an area'. Paul was praying for us to receive the dew of Heaven! Prayer: Father, enlighten the eyes of my heart that I may know the hope to which I am called. Give me deeper and fuller understanding of all that You have deposited within me because Christ is in me. Let the entrance of Your Word bring light to me, amen.

January 15th

Isa 26:19 Your dead ones shall live, together with my dead body they shall arise. Awake and sing, you who dwell in the dust; for your dew is as the dew of lights, and the earth shall cast out the dead.

When the dew of Heaven alights on your heart, it not only brings light, it also carries within it resurrection power which causes that which is dead within you to live. Those who have been dwelling in the dust of 'hope deferred' awaken and begin to sing for joy because that which was dead, now lives. That which was lost, is found! Words from God which seemed to have fallen to the ground and died, now spring up and begin to bring forth fruit.

The atmosphere of Heaven is pulsating resurrection life and power and Paul says in Ephesians 1 that it is available to us as believers – if only our hearts can be enlightened to see it! The very same power that raised Christ from the dead is available to us – do we grasp this phenomenal Truth? We are intended to be vessels which impart Life, unquenchable transforming Life.

Prayer: Lord, send out Your Light and Truth as laser beams to bombard my heart. Let every dead place within me awaken and sing! Cause every long-forgotten seed You planted in the soil of my heart to NOW spring up and begin to grow and bear the fruit You intended, in Jesus Name, amen.

January 16th

Son 5:2 I sleep, but my heart is awake. It is the sound of my Beloved that knocks, saying, Open to Me, My sister, My love, My dove, My undefiled; for My head is filled with dew, My locks with the drops of the night.

The knock of the Lord upon the door of our hearts comes often in the night hours. Are we willing to get up and just be with him, forgoing sleep and comfort? Do we sleep with alert hearts, sensitive for the sound of His voice? He comes with His head drenched with dew; dew that brings revelation and anointing for us. Yet so often at the sound of the Beloved, we turn over and descend back into sleep, robbing ourselves of the very things we have been asking Him to give us.

Is our hunger for His voice and presence strong enough to overcome the passivity of our flesh? An hour of lost sleep is nothing compared to the rich deposit which we will receive from our Bridegroom if we can manage to get out of bed!

Prayer: Lord, forgive me for the times I have ignored Your nudge in the night hours. I don't want to sow to the flesh but to the spirit. Help me to respond; shake me and wake me fully so that I may absorb all You come to impart. I look forward expectantly to the sound of Your knock, amen.

January 17th

Joh 17:20,21 And I do not pray for these alone, but for those also who shall believe on Me through their word, that they all may be one, <u>as You, Father, are in Me, and I in You</u>, that they also may be one in Us, so that the world may believe that You have sent Me.

'That they all may be one AS...' – this small word 'as' is a word of explanation, meaning 'in just the same way'. The prayer of Jesus was <u>not</u> a prayer for us to be in unity on a horizontal human level; although it is good to be at peace with one another - this was <u>not</u> what He was asking for. He was very specific when He prayed this prayer. He explained clearly what He meant. The oneness He was requesting for us was the SAME oneness, the same unity He had with the Father – You in Me and I in You!

Only as we daily live in this oneness with the Father and the Son will the world believe! In a marriage, two become one flesh. In the relationship between Christ and His Church, the two become one spirit (1 Cor 6:17) and out of this intimate relationship, much fruit is borne.

It is only as we are one with Christ that we then experience oneness of spirit with one another as believers. Every other soulish effort in the Church to produce unity on an earthly plane, through uniformity of location or goal, will eventually fall to the ground from which it came.
Prayer: Lord, I need a mind renewal here. I want to focus on You in me and me in You, so that my life will cause the world to believe that You came. Amen.

January 18th

*Joh 17:22 And I have given them the **glory** which You have given Me, that they may be one, even as We are one*

The glory which the Father gave Jesus was that He could be one with the Father. Another word for 'glory' in this case is 'honor'. Jesus said in this verse that He had already given His disciples the honor, the glory, of being able to have this same relationship with the Father as He had.

We too have this glory at our disposal. We can have exactly the same relationship with the Father that Jesus has. We are able to hear what the Father is saying and then share it. We can see in the spirit what the Father is doing and do likewise. This is how Jesus functioned on earth. He did nothing of His own accord but worked 'hand in glove' with the Father. This is God's intention for us too.

Prayer: Thank you Lord that I can have this glorious relationship with You. Sharpen my awareness of Your continual presence within me and open my spiritual eyes and eyes as never before that I may co-labor with You in bringing forth Your purposes in the earth, amen.

January 19th

*Joh 17:23 I in them, and You in Me, that they may be made **perfect** in one; and that the world may know that You have sent Me and have loved them as You have loved Me.*

The purpose for this relationship where the Father and Jesus dwell within us is that we may be made 'perfect in one'. This word 'perfect' comes from a root word meaning 'completeness, of full age, manhood'. It is only through this oneness with Jesus and the Father that we come to maturity as sons of God; so we fully express Christ in the earth.

It is one thing for the world to know that Jesus Christ, the Beloved Son, once walked the earth. They also need to see for themselves that God has many sons whom He loves as much as He loved the Firstborn. They need to see we have been with the Father - and the only way they know this is if the life and power of God is flowing from our lives.

Prayer: Father, I know that abiding in the vine is the secret to having Your life flowing through me. Show me the things in my life that draw me away from a vital connection with You. Give me the strength and courage to turn away from them and cleave to You, in Jesus Name, amen.

January 20ᵗʰ

*Joh 17:24 Father, I desire that those whom You have given Me, that they may be with Me where I am, that they may **behold** My glory which You have given Me, for You have loved Me before the foundation of the world.*

We are those the Father has given Jesus – this prayer is about us. Jesus asked that we could be with Him where He is, in order to 'behold' this glory or honor He has. Where is He? He is continually in the presence of the Father. This is where He wants us to be! Why? So that we may behold His glory. The word 'behold' means 'to discern, to experience, to see'. Our beloved Jesus requested that we would be able to experience and see the honor He has of being hidden in the Father, surrounded and immersed in His presence continually.

Christ wants this to be our personal experience ALL THE TIME. Not once a week; not once a day but ALL the time! For a moment, just sit still and allow yourself to become aware of the presence of the Father this morning. Experience His presence, soak it in. Be continually aware that you are IN the Father.

Prayer: Father, I know You heard this prayer 2000 years ago. I come now to receive what Jesus requested for me. May You remove from every blockage, spiritual, mental or emotional, which prevents me from dwelling consciously in the continual glory of Your enveloping permeating presence. Don't let me miss out on anything bought for me by Your precious Blood, in Jesus wonderful Name, amen.

17

Christine Beadsworth

January 21st

*1Jo 1:3 that which we have **seen** and **heard** we declare unto you, so that you also may have fellowship along with us. And truly our fellowship is with the Father and with His Son Jesus Christ.*

Just as the first disciples could only declare or share that which they had seen and heard, so we too can only impart that which we glean from our fellowship with the Father and the Son. Sometimes we forget the Father and focus only upon Jesus. However, they are inseparable. Jesus is in the Father and the Father is in Jesus. We can converse with both of them and both the Father and the Son have things they want to impart to us.

There are things to be seen and heard, not only for our own edification but so that we can declare them to others. 'We declare…so that' - everything which the Father and Son share with us is for the purpose of drawing others into fellowship with the Godhead. When people taste of the life-giving revelation which we share, they become hungry for more of God and we have the opportunity to lead them closer or introduce them to Christ.

Prayer: Father, thank you that You are continually revealing Yourself to those who are hungry. Cause me to see and hear in the spirit; take me deeper, higher, further. I long to share the love of God with others, amen.

January 22nd

Psa 36:7 How precious is Your loving-kindness, O God! And the sons of men take refuge under the shadow of Your wing. They feast on the abundance of Your house….

When we make God our refuge and dwelling place, there is provision for the deepest hunger and most desperate thirst. We are free to feast and as soon as we have devoured a portion of revelation and understanding, the Holy Spirit is waiting with a fresh plate heaped with more which He wishes to show us in Christ. There is abundance in God's house! All of the treasures of wisdom are found in Christ. The amount of understanding and wisdom we receive depends upon the level of our hunger and perseverance in pressing in.

The seven-fold Spirit of God not only has the fear of the Lord and knowledge to impart, but also revelation, wisdom, counsel and might. Let us not leave the table straight after eating the Hors d'oeuvres, but rather ask the Holy Spirit to feed our spirits with the whole menu. We can only possess the full revelation of Christ if we receive impartation from all seven of the flaming torches before the Throne!

Prayer: Lord, open my eyes to see wonderful things in Your Word. Precious Holy Spirit, please minister spiritual understanding and wisdom to me. I want to receive the counsel You have reserved for me and operate in the spirit of might as I work with You extending the kingdom, amen.

January 23rd

*Psa 36:7 How precious is Your loving-kindness, O God! And the sons of men take refuge under the shadow of Your wing. They feast on the abundance of Your house; **and You shall make them drink of the river of Your pleasures.***

Not only is our hunger satisfied dwelling under God's wing. We are also made to drink of the stream of His pleasures! This word translated 'pleasures' is the Hebrew word 'eden'. This river we can drink from is the same kind of river which watered the garden when Adam walked with God! Is that not a picture of restoration to our original position! There is a river whose streams make glad the city of God (psalm 46:4). This river only flows as we abide in His presence for here there is fullness of joy and pleasures forevermore.

Prayer: Father, cause me to drink of this stream of Your pleasures. Quench the thirst within with Your living water. You said those who are weary can come to You and be refreshed. As I drink freely of this water of the living Word, may rivers flow from my innermost being for others to be refreshed also, in Jesus Name. Amen.

January 24ᵗʰ

Psa 36:9 For with You is the fountain of life; in Your light we shall see light

The fountain, the source of life is Christ. He said, "I am the way, the truth and the life". It is as we partake of the life which is in Christ that we too live forever. There is no source of life outside of Christ.

Jesus rebuked the Pharisees because they searched the written scriptures, thinking them to be the source of eternal life "and still you will not come to Me that you might have life" (John 5:40). We must not make the same mistake. Endlessly reading the Word of God is not going to infuse us with life. We MUST come to the fountain of Life, Jesus and spend time in His life-giving presence. It is only as we are exposed to His light, that we receive light or revelation of Truth. In the presence of the sun, there is no need to light matches in order to see. Our surroundings are clearly in view. As we dwell in the light of His presence, we suddenly understand spiritual concepts that were vague before – in His light we see light!

Prayer: Lord, I no longer want to read Your Word by candle-light. Send forth Your light and truth. Wherever there is darkness in my understanding, let the true Light enter. The entrance of Your Word brings light. Let Your Word find entrance in me, amen.

January 25th

*Joh 6:63 It is the Spirit that makes alive, the flesh profits nothing. The words that I **speak** to you are spirit and are life.*

The word 'speak' means 'to utter' – in other words, it is the Spirit-quickened spoken words of Jesus that impart life to us. We need to hear what the Spirit is saying both to us personally and the Church. The Holy Spirit is with us in order to take of that which is Christ's and open it up to us. Just as Jesus broke bread with those disciples on the road to Emmaus and their eyes were opened to 'see' Him; so too we need the Holy Spirit to break the bread of the written Word with us so that we see (receive revelation of) Jesus.

We must always spend time in the Word with alert ears for the voice of the Spirit otherwise we will fall into the same ditch as the Pharisees who interpreted everything by the letter of the Law. We are to be ministers not of the letter but of the **Spirit** because the letter kills but the Spirit gives life (2 Cor 3:6)

Prayer: Father, forgive me for the many times I have tried to minister to people by the letter instead of the Spirit. I want to be a carrier of life, not death. Holy Spirit, would You come and break bread with me. Fellowship with me over a meal of the Word and give me something life-giving to chew on all day. Lead me into all Truth, in Jesus' Name, amen.

January 26th

Rom 1:20 For from the creation of the world His invisible attributes are plainly seen, being understood by the things made, both His eternal power and divinity, so that they are without excuse.

The Spirit of God not only speaks through the Word of God but through creation and everything that He has made declares His glory. When an artist creates a painting, he is making visible something which is within his mind or imagination. Often artists express their emotions through paintings. God, the Original Creative One, also expressed Himself in everything that was brought forth.

Just as we gaze at a painting and try to hear what the artist was saying through this particular work, so too we can allow our ears to become attuned to the messages hidden within every part of creation. Let us today take a minute vacation and become still enough for the ears of our hearts to catch what the Spirit is whispering right in our own gardens!

Prayer: Lord, the whole earth IS filled with Your glory – right now - I just need to begin to see it and to hear the expression of Your heart in creation! Speak to me in a way I haven't experienced before; I want to break out of the boxes of my past understanding and discover You somewhere I haven't seen You before! Surprise me, Lord, in Jesus wonderful Name, amen.

January 27ᵗʰ

Joh 6:57 As the living Father has sent Me, and I live through the Father, so he who partakes of Me, even he shall live by Me.

The source of Jesus' life was the Father – and the source of our life is Jesus. The same River of Life that flows from the throne of the Father has been ministering life to every saint through the ages – yet it never runs dry! When we partake of this life-giving water, we are partaking of Christ because He is the way, the truth and the LIFE. Because the Godhead is self-existent and has no beginning or end, this river will never stop flowing. It flows freely to us and through us to others.

Do we experience a continual supply of this living water or are there blockages? If there is an intermittent supply, the hindrance lies within us – strongholds of wrong understanding, fears, idols and spiritual pride act as stones and weeds choking up the supply pipes. It's high time we remove all barriers between us and the river of life!

Prayer: Holy Spirit, You come to lead me into all truth. Show me anything in my heart that is reducing the flow of this life-giving river to a trickle. Search me and examine my thoughts and help me to pull out everything that is blocking the way to life more abundantly, amen.

January 28ᵗʰ

1Jo 1:7 But if we walk in the light, as He is in the light, we have fellowship with one another, and the blood of Jesus Christ His Son cleanses us from all sin.

God is light and there is no shadow of turning in Him. When we try to walk in his presence with darkness in our hearts, there can be no intimacy because light can have no fellowship with darkness.

The above verse has so often been used to describe our fellowship with other believers but in actual fact, when read in context, we discover that John was describing the recipe for fellowship with the Father and the Son (1 John 1:3). Spiritual pride will cause us to deny that there is anything wrong in our lives. We are prone to seeing the faults in others but are often blind to our own. John writes that if we say we have no sin, we deceive ourselves.

Part of walking in the light involves acknowledging the sin in our own hearts. Once we do this, the blood of Jesus cleanses us and we can enjoy rich fellowship with God. Check out Colossians 3:8,9 and Galatians 5:19-21 to see if anything rings a bell.
Prayer: Lord, so often I think there are 'big' sins and 'small' sins. Yet, any sin has an effect on my intimacy with you. Deliver me from self-deception and self-righteousness first of all. I need your grace as much as anyone else, amen.

January 29th

Joh 15:4 Abide in Me, and I in you. As the branch cannot bear fruit of itself unless it remains in the vine, so neither can you unless you abide in Me.

Any gardener knows that if a vine branch does not remain in connection with the main stem, it will progressively wither and die. This process may take a day or two and those walking past may not initially discern that it has been severed from the vine.

However, ultimately it is inevitable that its real state will be discovered.

For there to be lasting fruit in our lives, we must receive the life-giving flow of sap from Jesus, the Vine, every day. Abiding in the vine is a parallel to abiding in the light. When we harbor undealt-with sin in our hearts, others may not detect it for a season but sooner or later, the absence of fruit and our withered appearance will indicate that we are not in fellowship with the Father and the Son.

Prayer: Father, I desire an uninhibited vital connection with You. Forgive me for putting off things Your Spirit convicts me of, thinking I will attend to them later. They only damage my relationship with you and I begin to deceive myself that everything is alright between us. Shine Your light in the deepest cupboards of my heart. I want to bear much fruit, amen.

January 30th

Joh 15:5 I am the Vine, you are the branches. He who abides in Me, and I in him, the same brings forth much fruit; for without Me you can do nothing.

Jesus clearly states that without Him we can do nothing. Yet, if we are honest, both the Church and we as individuals have started many things in the Name of God which have actually been the good ideas of man. Sooner or later they either have petered out and ground to a halt OR we have to labor and sweat in our own strength in order to keep them running. Either way, peace and joy are conspicuously absent.

A branch bearing fruit does so effortlessly as long as it remains attached to the vine. All the life-giving nutrients and water it needs are supplied through this vital connection. In the same way, if what you are involved in originates in Christ, everything you need - both in terms of wisdom to carry out the task and the necessary strength to bring it to fruition – will be supplied through your vibrant relationship with the Vine. Perhaps you are involved in something which seems good, yet you are in a state of striving and stress continually. The absence of rest within your heart may be an indication that you are doing it without the Vine; that it was a good idea, not a God-idea for you.

Prayer: Father, help me to disentangle myself from projects You never assigned me to. Help me leave the rat-race and return to a place of rest, only doing that which You desire and require. Amen.

January 31st

Joh 5:19 Then Jesus answered and said to them, Truly, truly, I say to you, The Son can do nothing of Himself but what He sees the Father do. For whatever things He does, these also the Son does likewise..

Jesus Himself did nothing of His own initiative. He took His cue from the Father, saw or understood the Father's desire and intention and then acted accordingly. It is imperative that we stop leaning on our own understanding and acting from that faulty foundation. We must enter the kingdom as a little child and walk in **simple obedience** if we really desire to see God move.

Theology and the doctrines of man have robbed the Church of the light yoke which Jesus requires us to wear. If we begin saying what we hear the Father saying and doing what we see Him doing, we will begin to have the same results which Jesus had, because the rivers of living water are flowing through us.

Prayer: Father, I don't want to be heavy-laden with the doctrines of men. Help me to return to a simple child-like walk hand in hand with You. Reveal Your heart to me as we meet different people so I can share living water with them, in Jesus' name, amen.

February 1ˢᵗ

Joh 5:30 I can do nothing of My own self. As I hear, I judge, and My judgment is just, because I do not seek My own will, but the will of the Father who has sent Me

The first key is to stop seeking our own will and to begin to desire the will of the Father with all our hearts. This is not as easy as it sounds. We can start the day surrendering all to the Lord, but a little later find ourselves demanding our rights, justifying our behavior or defending ourselves hotly when falsely accused. Sometimes we talk so much we cannot hear the gentle whisper of the Holy Spirit! No wonder the Word urges us to be **slow** to speak and quick to listen.

Prayer: Father, forgive me for making idols out of my own opinions and for acting as if what I want is more important than what You want. If I am honest, I really don't have a clue about making the right choices unless You guide me. I don't want to be double-minded anymore. I want to live my life accessing the mind of Christ, amen.

February 2ⁿᵈ

Joh 5:30 I can do nothing of My own self...

Do we really believe this? Or do we go through most of our days self-sufficient in our own evaluation and understanding of people and events? If Jesus Himself, Who came from the bosom of the Father and existed before the world began, understood that He was **completely** dependent upon the Father, surely we should be more so!

Yet all too often we rush ahead, assuming that our extensive experience and spiritual knowledge are a sure foundation from which to make judgments –both in the Church and our personal lives. In the final analysis, all this is the Pride of Life – a subtle pathway leading to the worship of the creature rather than the Creator! We are raised in a society that applauds self-sufficiency and independence but God's ways are not our ways. We must realise that without Him, we can do nothing of eternal value!

Prayer: Father, today I want to acknowledge that every breath I take is with Your permission. Forgive me for so often leaning on my own understanding and not acknowledging You. No wonder my paths take precarious turns! I am starting to understand why my life doesn't overflow with fruit. Cleanse me of pride, Lord, in Jesus Name. Amen.

February 3rd

Joh 7:18 He who speaks of himself seeks his own glory, but he who seeks the glory of Him who sent Him is true, and no unrighteousness is in Him.

Most of us talk too much and say too little! How often does the little word 'I' come up in our conversations? I think, I feel, I want…evidence of the fact that we are largely self-conscious and seldom God or others conscious.

Out of the abundance of the heart, the mouth speaks. One who continuously steers conversation around topics to do with themselves or their interests has Self sitting firmly upon the throne of their heart. This is idolatry - and idolatry is sin, whether it is seen in the largest Christian ministry or the most sheltered life. Do we honestly seek the glory of the Father? Our conversation is a good measuring stick! And what about our thought-life? Do we constantly focus on ourselves and our needs and desires?

Prayer: Oh Lord, in Your searchlight I see that my life is still largely about me – my wellbeing, my giftings, my ministry. Try as I might to hide my own self-absorption, my mouth gives me away every time. Wash me with Your blood. I want to turn away from this stench of idolatry and really seek Your glory from now on. Help me, Holy Spirit, amen.

February 4th

Pro 16:2 All the ways of a man are clean in his own eyes, but the Lord weighs the hearts

So often we assume that because we are pleasing to man, we are also pleasing to God. This is never more evident than in the Church. Because the Church has been infiltrated with so much self-serving humanistic teaching disguised as real food, many believers cannot even discern between what truly originates from the Spirit of God and what is earthly and sensual. Consequently the praise of men is not a good thermometer to use when measuring your spiritual progress. Men look on the outward appearance of spirituality but the Lord looks on the heart.

He tenderly rebukes those He loves, because He knows the hindrances to our growth and fruit-bearing potential are in our own hearts. He prunes the branches in order to bring forth more fruit in the next season. Faithful are the wounds of our Friend Jesus.

Prayer: Father, it is Your assessment of me that I trust because You can see clearly right to the bottom of my heart. I welcome Your conviction of sin and rebuke because I am secure in the fact that You love me regardless of how I am doing spiritually. Shine Your light. See if there is any wicked way in me and remove it. Amen

February 5th

Son 1:13 A bundle of myrrh between my breasts is my Beloved to me. Son 1:14 My Beloved is to me like a cluster of henna in the vineyards of Engedi.

It is important we don't become more sin-conscious but rather more Christ-conscious. Myrrh was used to deal with infection and has strong antibacterial and deodorizing properties. As we embrace Christ as a bundle of myrrh between our breasts, He deals with all sources of impurity in us. Myrrh kills every foreign invader; every corrupting influence that seeks to harm the body. Your Beloved works in this way within your heart as you embrace Him ever more closely.

Myrrh was also used to embalm dead bodies. It speaks of death to self, death to our own will and absolute surrender to our Beloved.

The word for 'henna' is also translated 'ransom' or 'atonement'. As the myrrh reveals the impurities within, Christ, our 'cluster of henna' has also provided the atonement and paid the price for their removal.

Prayer: Lord Jesus, within You is found all we need for redemption and cleansing daily. As I behold You, I am changed from glory to glory. I surrender to You afresh. amen.

February 6th

*Joh 16:13 However, when He, the Spirit of Truth, has come, He will guide you into all truth. For He shall not speak of Himself, but **whatever He hears, He shall speak**. And He will announce to you things to come. Joh 16:14 He will glorify Me, for He will receive of Mine and will announce it to you.*

Even the Holy Spirit does not speak of His own account. He also hears and then speaks. The whole Godhead works in awareness and dependence upon one another. When we begin to walk in a life of oneness with the Lord, we become a link in this chain of life-giving flow. As the Holy Spirit takes something of Christ's and reveals it to us, we are then able to share it with others, so that praise and glory arise to the Father and Jesus.

The Holy Spirit also speaks to us in advance about things that are going to happen, things God is wanting to do. In this way, our hearts are prepared so that we can co-labor with Him and step out in obedience at the right time.

Prayer: Holy Spirit, thank you for leading me into all truth and revealing Jesus in me. Give me boldness to step out in action once You have shown me what the Father wants to do. Make my spiritual hearing completely clear so I can report accurately what You are saying and help me not to be afraid of the opinions of man, in Jesus Name, amen.

February 7th

Mal 3:1 ...and the Lord, whom you seek, shall suddenly come to his temple, even the messenger of the covenant, whom you delight in: behold, he shall come, says the LORD of hosts. Mal 3:2 But who may abide the day of his coming? and who shall stand when he appears? for he is like a refiner's fire, and like fullers' soap

We are the Lord's temple and as we seek Him, He comes to work in us in a deeper way. However, sometimes His presence causes more discomfort than peace initially because He comes as a refiner's fire and fuller's soap. The refiner's fire causes all the dross to float to the surface of the silver so that it can be skimmed off. If you are becoming aware of many ugly things popping up to the surface in your heart during the trial you are undergoing, don't despair. This is for the purpose of removing all dross from the crevices of your heart. If you can see them, it means they are on their way out!

Prayer; Lord, thank you that You do a relentless thorough work of cleansing this temple. How grateful I am for the power of Your Blood in cleansing me of sin! Amen.

February 8th

Jeremiah 15:19 Therefore thus says the LORD: "If you return, then I will bring you back; you shall stand before Me; If you take out the precious from the vile, you shall be as My mouth..."

Do we want to be the Lord's mouthpiece, speaking in the power and authority of the Throne of Heaven? If so, then we must submit to the refining work of the Holy Spirit's fire. It is disconcerting to be faced with the things which surface in us during times of pressure and trial but always remember that the refining has a purpose – it is to prepare you to be the Lord's mouthpiece in a broken and confused world. If something has surfaced, it is with the purpose of you laying hold of it, calling it what it is and asking the Lord to remove it far from your heart.

Before we can speak and divide light from darkness, bringing deliverance and healing, the separation process must first take place within our own hearts. We must be holy and set-apart for His purposes for out of the abundance of the heart, the mouth speaks.

Prayer: Father, I long to be Your mouthpiece in the earth. Help me to separate the precious from the vile. Give me understanding and discernment so that I may sift out that which is worthless in my heart and cast it from me, in Jesus Name, amen.

February 9th

Isa 50:4 The Lord GOD has given me the tongue of the discipled, that I should know how to speak a word in season to him that is weary: he wakens me morning by morning, he wakens my ear to hear as instructed.

God wants to instruct us every morning so that we can be bearers of a word 'in season' – that means a word spoken at exactly the right time, one which meets the need of the person. This is what it means to be God's mouthpiece – we say what He instructs us to say. So we are like the postman delivering a message from God to those He loves.

The question is, are we willing to make ourselves available to receive the messages He wants to send? This means a rearranging of priorities and an adjusting of schedules – making time to be quiet before Him - but what a small price to pay to be a bearer of words of Life! Are we willing to be wakened morning by morning to hear His counsel or do we prefer our pillows? In these dark days, the Spirit is speaking much in the early hours of the morning watch to equip His saints for what that particular day holds. Don't miss His vital input!

Prayer: Holy Spirit, please help me to rearrange my activities and get rid of worthless pursuits so that I may set aside time to sit and receive the instruction of the Father, in Jesus Name, amen.

February 10th

Job 12:13 With him is wisdom and strength, he hath counsel and understanding.

God is the source of all true wisdom and counsel. The Church has for too long borrowed the wisdom of the world in dealing with issues. We 'Christianize' psychology teachings and vainly hope they will be successful in bringing forth the life of Christ within the Body. What a waste of time this is for the Word declares that man's wisdom is foolishness in God's eyes. No wonder the church is largely weak and without power. We are depending upon the arm of flesh and are largely devoid of the Spirit.

Part of separating the precious from the vile is weeding out the wisdom of man from our belief systems. It is so interwoven in our thinking that only the Holy Spirit is able to show us what is really truth and what is actually worthless fanciful nonsense!

Prayer: Father, the entrance of Your Word brings light. Send light into my heart and make plain that which is worthless in my understanding. I don't want to lean on the shaky wisdom of man but upon Your eternal Truth. Holy Spirit, lead me into all Truth, amen.

February 11th

Isa 31:1 Woe to those who go down to Egypt for help, and lean on horses and trust in chariots, because it is great; and in horsemen, because they are so very strong, but they do not look to the Holy One of Israel, nor do they seek the Lord!

Egypt represents the world. The Church has for too long gone to the world for help. We borrow their self-improvement courses and apply their business principles in order to make our congregations grow. We look at huge corporations and are impressed by their size and strength and influence in the marketplace. We try to use the strength of the human intellect to bring a worldly measure of success in our fellowships. Yet God says, "*Woe to those who go down to Egypt for help*".

The methods which have their source in the lust of the flesh and the pride of life will never bring life to the Church of Jesus Christ. The world says 'be your best self'. Christ says 'die to self'. We borrow the help of Egypt in vain for the flesh is diametrically opposed to the Spirit. We are to look to the Holy One of Israel and seek the Lord.

Prayer: Lord, I am so easily drawn in by the persuasive words of men's wisdom. I have wasted so much time trying to improve that which You place no value in. Straighten my compass needle so that my journey can be towards true North again. I am looking for a city whose maker and Builder is God, in Jesus Name, amen.

February 12th

Job 28:28 And unto man he said, Behold, the fear of the Lord, that is wisdom; and to depart from evil is understanding.

There is a starting place in acquiring the wisdom of God – it begins with the fear of the Lord. Until we acknowledge that all our wisdom is foolishness and that only God truly is wise, we will not begin the journey into wisdom. The fear of the Lord means that we respect His opinion more than our own; that we believe what He says rather than trusting in our own imaginations. If God declares something to be evil, we do not have the luxury of our own opinion on the matter.

Eve made this tragic mistake – God declared it was not good for them to eat of the tree of Knowledge of Good and Evil. Yet Eve 'saw that the tree was good for food, and that it was pleasant to the eyes, and a tree to be desired to make one wise' and went with her own judgment rather than trusting God's superior wisdom. The rest is history. How many others have followed in her footsteps, dabbling in things the Father has declared evil and then wondering why death begins to envelop their inner sanctuary.

Prayer: Father, forgive me for the times I have willfully gone against Your choices for me. I have been wise in my own eyes so many times. Today I acknowledge that all my human wisdom is foolishness – because your Word says so. Help me take the first steps on Wisdom's path in the fear of the Lord, amen.

February 13th

Psa 25:12 What man is he that fears the LORD? him shall He teach in the way that he shall choose. His soul shall dwell at ease; and his seed shall inherit the earth. The secret counsel of the LORD is with them that fear him; and he will show them his covenant.

When the Spirit of the Fear of the Lord fills our heart, the Lord comes alongside to instruct and teach us in making right choices. We begin to receive the secret counsel of God from the Spirit of Counsel (Isaiah 11) and He also shows or reveals to us the contents of His covenant. In other words, we begin to understand all that He has prepared for us personally because we are His covenant sons and daughters.

The key to opening this intimate relationship is the Fear of the Lord. Do we seek direction and counsel for our lives? Then we must begin to walk in a deeper measure of the Fear of the Lord, hating what He hates and loving what He loves. We must ask for a visitation of the Spirit of the Fear of the Lord because it is the beginning of true wisdom.

Prayer: Father, please show me where I have not been walking in the fear of the Lord, so that I may repent. I desire your secret counsel to be my portion, amen.

February 14th

Psa 86:11 Teach me thy way, O LORD; I will walk in thy truth: unite my heart to fear thy name.

Sometimes we fear the Lord in certain areas, yet in others we continue blindly (or stubbornly) living in a way that is displeasing to Him. The word 'unite' above means 'to become one, to join'. We must fear the Lord with our whole heart, not live in a fragmented double-minded way. The psalmist here asks God to join the different areas of his heart so that he wholeheartedly fears the Lord and can walk in the Truth.

Prayer: Father, I desire my heart to come into unity so that I may fear You in a greater measure. I will run in the path of Your commandments when You give me a heart that is willing (psalm 119:32). Let the Spirit of the fear of the Lord be my portion, in Jesus name, amen.

February 15th

Isa 33:5 The LORD is exalted; for he dwells on high: He has filled Zion with judgment and righteousness.   And wisdom and knowledge shall be the stability of your times, and strength of salvation: the fear of the LORD is His treasury

The fear of the Lord is His treasury – this means to the measure that we walk in the fear of the Lord, we create a treasury or storehouse within where God can deposit His treasure and weaponry. Do we desire to be full of spiritual knowledge, wisdom, revelation, counsel and might? Then we must walk in the fear of the Lord in deeper measure. Our spiritual storehouse is only as large as our decision to turn from human wisdom and counsel and fully embrace God's Word as the only Truth.

How big is your treasury? If you desire wisdom, you must carve out a place for it to be poured into by actively seeking to increase the fear of the Lord in your life.

To fear the Lord is to hate evil. To what measure do we call 'a proud look, a lying tongue and he who sows discord amongst brothers (Prov 6:16)' evil? We may call it evil, yet we often walk in those very things.

Prayer: Father, I am always pulling logs out of others' eyes. Yet I am often unaware of the splinter in my own. I think myself better than others – that's a proud look. Forgive me Father. Search my thoughts and cleanse me of the things You hate. Enlarge the treasury of the Fear of the Lord in me, in Jesus Name, amen.

February 16th

Pro 1:28 Then shall they call upon me (Wisdom), but I will not answer; **they shall seek me early, but they shall not find me:** *Pro 1:29 For that they hated knowledge, and did not* **choose** *the fear of the LORD: Pro 1:30 They would none of my counsel: they despised all my reproof. Pro 1:31 Therefore shall they eat of the fruit of their own way, and be filled with their own devices.*

The fear of the Lord is not something that comes upon us from above. Rather, it is something we must **CHOOSE**! This scripture is very sobering because it shows us that if we do not consciously daily choose the fear of the Lord, then when we seek the wisdom found in Christ, it will elude us.

Practically, choosing the fear of the Lord means receiving His counsel and accepting and responding to His reproof. In other words, we must maintain tender hearts which allow His Spirit-quickened Word to gain entrance and bring change. When the first prick of the Sword of the Word comes, we so often push it away because it is painful. It is easier to keep doing what we are doing than to allow conviction to really penetrate our hearts.

Prayer: Father, so often I push away the point of Your sword and harden my heart. I don't really like knowing the areas I need to change. Forgive me for despising Your reproof and going my own way. I want to choose the fear of the Lord every day. Help me, Holy Spirit, amen.

February 17th

*Isa 66:1 Thus says the LORD, The heaven is my throne, and the earth is my footstool: where is the house that you build for me? and where is the place of my rest? Isa 66:2 For all those things has my hand made, and all those things have been, says the LORD: but to this man will I look, even to him that is poor and of a contrite spirit, and **trembles at my word**.*

God does not inhabit buildings built with human hands. He will only fill the temple He has built in the image of God and that is US. However, there are conditions to this habitation. God is looking for people who will 'TREMBLE AT MY WORD', people who realize their own poverty of spirit without Him and have repentant hearts.

This word 'Word' refers to a spoken word, conversation, command or warning. Do we tremble when the Spirit-quickened word comes to us? Are we quick to obey, knowing we have heard the voice of the God of heaven and earth? Or do we treat these whispered words in our hearts with disrespect, shelving them for later or arguing and elevating our own opinions above what God has said to us?

Prayer: Father, I want to be one who trembles at Your word. Forgive me for the times I have brushed aside Your whispers and disregarded Your warnings. I want to answer when You call and hear and obey quickly when You speak, amen.

February 18th

Pro 3:11 My son, despise not the chastening of the LORD; neither be weary of his correction: Pro 3:12 For whom the LORD loves he corrects; even as a father the son in whom he delights. Pro 3:13 Happy is the man that finds wisdom, and the man that gets understanding.

It is evidence of the Father's love for us when He takes the time to correct us. He cares about the path we take and knows the consequences of our foolishness. The Spirit is quick to nudge us back onto the right path but we must heed the nudges. We must not behave like stubborn mules who insist on continuing on their own chosen paths or we will live to regret it, eating the fruit of our own ways.

Wisdom and understanding come as a result of embracing the Lord's chastening and correction. It is simply pride which prevents us from receiving correction. Let us allow God to make course corrections because He knows what tomorrow holds. Humility and the ability to receive correction are marks of Christian maturity. Unfortunately, they are not qualities applauded by today's fleshly church circles.

Prayer: Lord, I don't want to walk by the light of my own understanding any longer. It is Your kindness which prompts You to correct my path. Thank-you for delighting in me and taking such detailed interest in every detail of my existence. Amen.

February 19th

Pro 7:4 Say to wisdom, You are my sister; and call understanding your kinsman,
*Pro 7:5 so that they may keep you from the strange woman, from the stranger who **flatters** with her words.*

The strange woman is not just a girl in a short skirt, plying her trade on the street corner. She is also a spirit that offers counterfeit wisdom, which is earthly, unspiritual and demonic (see James 3:15). She will flatter you and stroke your flesh and lure you straight into the Babylonian religious system with her wiles.

Only the Spirit of Wisdom that is before the throne of God can protect you from falling prey to this seductress. Don't lean on your own understanding but embrace Wisdom closely. Seek out her counsel daily and you will walk in safety.

Prayer: Lord, I don't want to fall prey to the deceitful charms of the cohorts working for the religious spirit. Grant unto me wisdom and understanding, that I may walk with them daily and get to know them well, in Jesus Name, amen.

February 20th

*Pro 7:13 And she caught him and kissed him, and with a hard face she said to him,Pro 7:14 I have peace offerings with me; today I have paid my vows. so I came out to meet you, earnestly to seek your face, and **I have found you**. I have decked my bed with coverings, with striped cloths of **Egyptian** linen. I have perfumed my bed with myrrh, aloes, and cinnamon.*

43

Here we see the modus operandi of the seductive spirit. She pursues you because she sees your potential in God and your gifts. She wants to ensnare you and form an intimate relationship with you. She seeks you out, making a big fuss of you, telling you that you are God's gift to mankind. She appeals to your spiritual pride but her intention is to enslave you and use your strength to fortify the kingdom of the Great Harlot in Revelation 17:5. Do not let yourself be led to her bed. It is covered with the linen of Egypt, representing worldly works instead of righteous deeds. Her perfumes embody the fragrance of mixture – myrrh and aloes are spices which speak of death and are used in embalming but cinnamon is a spice associated with romance and being raised up. This is not the bed of death to self that Christ bids us rest upon.

Prayer: Father, grant me sharper discernment that I may recognize the fragrance of mixture and flattery and flee from it. Help me to tell the difference between sincere encouragement and flattery with underlying motives. Open my spiritual eyes and ears, in Jesus Name, amen.

February 21st

Pro 5:3 For the lips of a strange woman drip honey, and her palate is smoother than oil; Pro 5:4 but afterward she is as bitter as wormwood, sharp as a two-edged sword.

Honey represents revelation. The seductive spirit has revelation to offer but its source is not the throne of God. It will be appealing and appear to be spiritual wisdom but it flows from the Tree of the Knowledge of Good and Evil. The words will seem to be coated in oil or anointed.

Remember this, that Christ Jesus is made unto us wisdom from God. Any wisdom that is offered you that does not bring you closer to Jesus and glorify Him is probably falling from the lips of the strange woman. Any wisdom that elevates self so that you feel you are just like God is from the same apple Eve bit into.

Wormwood was used as a test for adultery in the Old Testament. No wonder the seductive spirit's honey turns bitter in your stomach! Do not be found in bed with the strange woman. Return to the God who made you.

Prayer: Lord, I don't even know how much of the strange woman's honey I have swallowed. Please search out any and every small piece hiding in my heart and show me the Truth so that I may cast all counterfeit wisdom far from me, amen.

February 22nd

*Pro 9:1 Wisdom has built her house; she has carved out her seven pillars; Pro 9:2 she has killed her beasts; she has mixed her wine; she has also set her table. Pro 9:3 She has sent out her young women; she cries upon the highest places of the city, Pro 9:4 The simple one, let him turn in here. To one lacking heart, she says to him, Pro 9:5 Come, eat of my **bread** and drink of the **wine** I have mixed. Pro 9:6 Forsake the foolish and live; and go in the way of understanding.*

Wisdom has a house held up by the seven pillars of the seven Spirits of God. She sends out an invitation to anyone who lacks wisdom to come in and feast. Contained in the invitation is the menu she offers – BREAD and WINE. This is how we know that the real Spirit of Wisdom has prepared the meal laid out – we are called to eat of Christ, to share communion with Him.

Any message that has Jesus as the centerpiece is coming from Wisdom's table. Only the Spirit of God can take that which is Christ's and share it with us. You really don't want to eat at any other restaurant!

Prayer: Father, I hear Your invitation and I want to come and feast on the abundance of Your house. Spirit of Wisdom, come and reveal the unsearchable riches of Christ to me, amen.

February 23rd

Pro 9:13 A foolish woman is noisy; she is simple and knows nothing. For she sits at the door of her house, in a seat in the high places of the city, to call those who pass by, who are going straight on their ways; The simple one, let him turn in here. And to one lacking heart, she says to him, Stolen waters are sweet, and bread eaten in secret is pleasant

There is another restaurant in the high places of the city. Do not think that the higher you go in your spiritual walk, the safer you will be from deception! This foolish strange woman calls the simple and pretends she has something that will benefit them. A companion of wise men becomes wise, a companion of fools suffers harm. If you spend time with her, you will learn nothing of value yet she will tell you that you possess great spiritual knowledge.

She also has a menu of the day – stolen waters and bread. The great Babylonian Harlot has no source of living water in herself – she must steal from the world, from business principles, from psychology. The bread she offers must be eaten in secret, behind closed doors. God is a God of light – any spiritual knowledge you are being offered which is secret does not have its source in the

Bread of Life. God's Bread is available to all who seek it – there is no selective spiritual elite with God.

Prayer: Father, I resolve to eat only at tables which offer BREAD and WINE. If Jesus is not the main meal of the day, I want no part in it. Sharpen my spiritual sight when reading menus, Lord, amen.

February 24th

*Psa 81:16 And He would have fed them also with the finest of the wheat; and with **honey out of the rock** I would have satisfied you.*

The Father wants to feed us with honey from the Rock, not the supermarket! Honey represents revelation and the supermarket sells mass-produced so-called honey of many different brands. Some bottles have extra sugar added to appeal to your fleshly palate.

Let's not risk tasting honey which may have come from the strange woman's lips (Proverbs 5:3) even if we have seen it advertised on TV. God offers an endless supply of honey from the Rock of Ages. It is part of the inheritance purchased for you by the Blood of Calvary. It's time to open your mouth wide so He can fill it!

Prayer: Lord, no more worldly wisdom for me. I am coming straight to the Source of True Wisdom and Revelation. Fill me with insight into Your Word, in Jesus Name, amen.

February 25th

*Son 4:11 Your lips, My spouse, drop like the honeycomb; **honey and milk** are under your tongue; and the smell of your garments is like the smell of Lebanon.*

The Bride of Christ does not only have the milk of the Word under her tongue. She also has HONEY – revelation which allows her to minister in a Spirit of Wisdom into situations. Her lips drip honey too but in contrast to the lips of the strange woman, the lips of the Bride bring words of life and restoration.

The proof of intimate union of the Bride with her husband is the fruit of her lips which brings praise to God in the lives of all who are touched. Honey must be extracted from the comb in order to be enjoyed. Don't expect to be spoon-fed. Study to show yourself approved - and expect honey from the comb to be your portion in the process. As honey falls from the lips of the Bride, the eyes of others are enlightened for she IS the Light of the World, a city set on a hill. All of the words from God's mouth essentially say 'let there be light'!

Prayer: Father, it is so exciting to think I can co-labor with You in spreading Light and Truth. I am tired of a milk- only diet. Move me on to maturity, Lord. Feed me with honey so that I, in turn, may dispense it to others, amen.

February 26th

Pro 10:20 The tongue of the just is as choice silver; the heart of the wicked is worth little. Pro 10:21 The lips of the righteous feed many; but fools die for lack of wisdom.

The Bride of Christ rules in righteousness and justice because she does not judge by herself. As she hears, she speaks. As honey pours into her heart, she speaks a pure word like choice silver, with all the dross of soulish interpretation removed. This word is anointed and will break the yoke in those who hear and receive it.

Her lips feed many with real meat because she has been feeding on Christ in private. What is the quality of the words which come from your lips? Are your words full of the dross or do they give people something solid to sink their teeth into – something nourishing to them spiritually which will help bring them to maturity? It's time to stop handing out cups of milk because people are dying all around us for lack of wisdom.

Prayer: Holy Spirit, it is You who takes that which is Christ's and imparts it to us. I desperately need wisdom and He is the Source. Please give me honey to share with those I meet today. Feed me with the meat of the Word so that I may chew it, digest it and nourish others with nuggets of Truth, in Jesus Name, amen.

February 27th

Pro 24:13 My son, eat honey, because it is good; and the honeycomb is sweet to your palate; Pro 24:14 **so shall the knowledge of wisdom be to your soul;** *when you have found it, then there shall be a reward, and your hope shall not be cut off.*

Receiving God's wisdom will nourish your soul and bring health and strength to you. Real honey is a powerful killer of bacteria and heals wounds; it calms nerves and brings sleep. It releases endorphins which are natural painkillers.

In the same way, honey from the Rock will neutralize the attack of the enemy in your life; it will heal the wounds of your heart; it will give you peace and bring you to a place of rest from all striving; it will bring joy and deliver you from pain.

Prayer: Lord, revelation from You addresses every area of need I have. When my heart is overwhelmed, lead me to the Rock that is higher than anything I face, amen.

February 28th

Rev 19:11 And I saw heaven opened, and behold a white horse; and he that sat upon him was called Faithful and True, and in righteousness he doth judge and make war.
Rev 19:12 His eyes were as a flame of fire, and on his head were many crowns; and he had a name written, that no man knew, but he himself. Rev 19:13 And he was clothed with a vesture dipped in blood: and his name is called The Word of God.

The Living Word rides forth from heavenly places, rightly judging and warring. This is the place from which our battles must be fought. We must not war in prayer according to our earthly understandings nor the knowledge and teachings of man. Only as we war with the Word which is faithful and true and unchanging, will we achieve victory. Without the victory of the cross of Calvary, we would have only a written Word on a page. The life is in the blood and it is the Life-Blood of the Lamb clothing this Word that gives authority in the spiritual realm. We are also told elsewhere in Scripture that it is the Spirit that gives life – so it is the Spirit-quickened understanding which we receive when studying the Word that equips us to wage war with it.

Prayer; Holy Spirit, open my eyes to see wonderful things in the Word so that I may judge righteously and wage war that brings change wherever I am, in Jesus Name, amen.

February 29th

Rev 19:14 And the armies in Heaven followed Him on white horses, clothed in fine linen, white and clean.

We know these armies represent the Bride because we are told in verse 8 that because she had prepared herself, she was granted to be clothed in white linen. The Bride is an army of saints which dwell in heavenly places, seated with Christ, have ceased their own works of the flesh.

The Bride rides with the Living Word. Where He goes, she follows. She has laid down her own opinions and will and is yielded to the Word. She has accepted His supreme authority in her life and is wedded to Him.

Am I wedded to the Word in the fear of God? When the Spirit quickens a scripture to me, do I become one with it, living it out and speaking it or do I store it on the shelf as an interesting concept?

Prayer: Jesus, Living Word, I want to ride with you and the armies of heaven. Where You go, I will go, amen.

March 1st

Isa 11:1 And there shall come forth a rod out of the stem of Jesse, and a Branch shall grow out of his roots: Isa 11:2 And the spirit of the LORD shall rest upon him, the spirit of wisdom and understanding, the spirit of counsel and might, the spirit of knowledge and of the fear of the LORD

The Word that rides the white horse in Revelation is also the Rod or Branch that springs from the stem of Jesse in Isaiah. Christ, the Living Word is adorned with the seven Spirits of God.

If we, as the Bride, wish to follow the Word wherever He goes, we must receive light from these seven torches before the throne of God. We must be led by the Spirit so that we do not operate according to the wisdom of men.

The wisdom of man complicates things. The wisdom of God brings light and makes things clear and profoundly simple. By this very wisdom Jesus confounded the Pharisees of His day by giving answers that cut through all their rhetoric – how desperately we need the ministry of the seven Spirits of God to cut through to the essence of every situation we face.

Prayer: Father, Your Word says I have the mind of Christ. The same sevenfold light that He walked by is available to me. I don't want to assess any situation by the feeble light-bulb of man's wisdom. Holy Spirit, send forth Your light and truth to me, amen.

March 2nd

Isa 11:3 And shall make him of quick understanding in the fear of the LORD: and he shall not judge after the sight of his eyes, neither reprove after the hearing of his ears

The fear of the Lord is the beginning of wisdom and as the above scripture indicates, when we walk in the fear of the Lord, He enables us to receive understanding quickly. How exciting it is when a scripture we have read countless times, is suddenly opened up to us and we can understand what the Spirit of God is saying! It makes us realize that our natural eyes and ears cannot grasp the things of the Spirit – therefore we cannot rely upon them in assessing situations.

Have you ever met a person and immediately sensed something about them that you have not been told by man? Jesus operated like this all the time because He lived His life guided by the seven Spirits of God and not His natural senses. It's time to come up higher, Bride of Christ.

Prayer; Father, make me of quick understanding so that I am not tempted to rely on my natural senses. Teach me to flow in the things of the Spirit and open the eyes of my heart, so that I may behold wonderful things in your Word, amen.

March 3rd

Isa 11:4 AMP But with righteousness He shall judge the poor, and shall decide with justice for the downtrodden of the earth. And He shall strike the earth and the oppressor with the rod of His mouth, and with the breath of His lips He shall slay the wicked.

Part of judging with righteousness and justice is discerning when to use our mouths as a rod and when to minister grace and kindness. The earth represents the flesh – Jesus used a rod when dealing with fleshly behavior and the enemy; yet spoke words of healing and restoration to those who had been under the same enemy's grasp.

When we operate by our own understanding, we are tempted to restore Judas and hang Peter. Jesus however could see past the surface. It is imperative we are led by the Spirit in every situation we are called to respond. Too many people have been mutilated by the mouths of misdirected believers, unable to wield the two sides of the two-edged sword in the appropriate manner.

Prayer: Father, I need to clearly see the whole truth before I can apply Your Word in a situation. Forgive me for striking bruised reeds with the rod of my mouth when You wanted me to bind them up and strike the one who bruised them. Teach me to operate in righteousness and justice, in Jesus Name, amen.

March 4th

Eph 1:3 Blessed be the God and Father of our Lord Jesus Christ, who blessed us with every spiritual blessing in the heavenlies in Christ;

When we read the above verse, we must take note of the fact that it is written in the past tense! God has ALREADY blessed us with EVERY spiritual blessing. Why then do we keep asking Him to do something He has already done? When we pray like this, we are in unbelief – we believe something that is contrary to the

Word of God. No wonder we wait year after year without any seeming answer!

So, if every possible blessing is already ours, where on earth are they then? Well, this is the key – they are not on earth! They are found and enjoyed in heavenly places in Christ. Until we ascend in our understanding and renew our minds; LINING UP OUR BELIEFS WITH THE WORD, we cannot ever access or begin to experience these spiritual blessings, even though they are waiting, wrapped up and preserved unchanged for us.

Prayer: Father, I never realized I was so divided within. I want to repent of walking in unbelief for so long. Help me, Holy Spirit, to line up my every thought with the Truth. I want to experience every blessing You intended for me. Amen.

March 5th

2Co 10:5 pulling down imaginations and every high thing that exalts itself against the knowledge of God, and bringing into captivity every thought into the obedience of Christ;

Within our minds and hearts are a veritable milling mass of unruly thoughts which rebel against lining up with the plumbline of the Truth expressed in the Word of God. We make the mistake of allowing our own thoughts and understanding to dictate how we should pray, instead of beginning with the Word and praying the Truth.

If we begin to pray truth over ourselves, we will find that our carnal understandings of how things work, begin to be brought into line with Truth, because the Holy Spirit shines His spotlight on every rebellious little belief causing disorder within. Once exposed, we must then bring that troublesome opinion into captivity, binding it to the Rod of Truth and making it bow its knee before the Word. It is much like disciplining a child. Every childish thought is brought into submission to the parental authority of the Word. By doing this, we grow to maturity within, conforming our inner man to the standard of Christ.

Begin to pray the apostolic prayers that Paul prayed for the Church over yourself, asking for revelation as you pray. Suddenly lights will be switched on within you!

March 6th

Jam 1:6 But let him ask in faith, doubting nothing. For he who doubts is like a wave of the sea, driven by the wind and tossed. For do not let that man think that he shall receive anything from the Lord; Jam 1:8 he is a double-minded man, unstable in all his ways.

We are told in the Word that we have the mind of Christ. This means we have been made aware of His thoughts and intentions toward us through the Word. If we then continue to cling to our own opinions in some areas, we are double-minded.

To pray in faith, we must be single-minded and conform our beliefs to the mind of Christ - otherwise we receive nothing from the Lord. For example, if we believe that the anointing of God must come upon us, we are double-minded because the Word declares in 1 John 2:27 that the anointing abides within us! We are yoked to an Old Testament religious mindset when we wait for a horn of oil to be poured on our heads. The truth is that it is continuously poured out within as we abide IN CHRIST in heavenly places. We must renew our minds and ask the Lord to give us undivided hearts. Take captive every thought to the obedience of Christ and harness your vain imaginations. The Spirit has wonderful things to show you.

It is said that a person can be so heavenly minded that he is no earthly good. However, God says that only if you **are** heavenly minded, will you be **any** earthly good!

Prayer: Oh Lord, how much precious time I have wasted being double-minded. Help me, Holy Spirit, to loose myself from the religious yoke around my neck, in Jesus Name, amen.

March 7th

2Co 3:14 (But their thoughts were blinded; for until the present the same veil remains on the reading of the old covenant, not taken away.) But this veil has been done away in Christ. 2Co 3:15 But until this day, when Moses is read, the veil is on their heart. 2Co 3:16 But whenever it turns to the Lord, the veil shall be taken away.

The veil over the hearts of the Pharisees was unbelief. They looked at Jesus but only saw Him dimly because they did not believe His words. The only thing that removes the veil is repentance, the turning of the heart back to the Lord.

Unfortunately the Church of today is also veiled by unbelief even though she claims with her mouth that she can see. The veil is done away with in Christ. Let us as the Bride, repent of all our unbelief. Our Father **has** positioned us in our appointed place alongside our Bridegroom and we are already in heavenly places – we just cannot SEE that we are. Only as we repent, will the Father lift the veil and we will behold our Beloved face to face.

Prayer: Father, I am becoming more and more aware of the thickness of this veil of unbelief. I want to cry out like the father of that epileptic boy, "Lord, I believe. help my unbelief!". Lift it, Father. Let me really see, amen.

March 8th

Eph 1:13 in whom also you, hearing the Word of Truth, the gospel of our salvation, in whom also believing, you were sealed with the Holy Spirit of promise, Eph 1:14 who is the earnest of our inheritance, to the redemption of the purchased possession, to the praise of His glory.

The earnest of our inheritance is the down-payment, the guarantee that we will receive the whole inheritance. The possession which was purchased in the above verse is our inheritance, which was paid for in Blood. Now our inheritance is not a plot in heaven when we die. An inheritance is enjoyed by the person who inherits while he or she is ALIVE. This is vitally important to understand in order to dismantle unbelief concerning our right to lay hold of ALL which was purchased at the cross NOW!

Our inheritance is the Promised Land but this does not mean Israel or our ministry or fancy houses and cars. Paul strove to know Him ever more deeply and clearly. Once we belong to Christ, we must press on to seize and lay hold of Him – He is our inheritance. We must walk in an ever-unfolding revelation of the riches in Christ – this is the possessing of our inheritance. We have to stop thinking in earthly terms and become heavenly minded.

Can we truly say, "I am my Beloved's and He is mine'? Have we laid hold of Christ and all that we inherit IN Him? Do we really believe we possess what the Word says is ours in Christ?

March 9th

Eph 1:17 that the God of our Lord Jesus Christ, the Father of glory, may give to you the spirit of wisdom and revelation in the knowledge of Him, Eph 1:18 the eyes of your understanding being enlightened, that you may know what is the hope of His calling, and what is the riches of the glory of His inheritance in the saints,

The spirit of wisdom and revelation is not just to give us wares to stock our spiritual resume. It is to increase our knowledge of HIM! To 'enlighten' means to 'bring light, provide revelation, give understanding'. The reason Paul prays this request for the Ephesian saints is so that they may know and understand the parameters of the rich inheritance they possess because Christ is in them. This is where our inheritance is already located – inside us. It is like a parcel all wrapped up, which we need to unwrap and discover its contents. This is a mystery because the Word also tells us that these spiritual blessings are in heavenly places in Christ. How can they be in heavenly places and in us at the same time? Simply because Christ is in us – so our inheritance is within Him in us!

Prayer; Father, sometimes these spiritual principles bewilder my mind but I want to believe by faith that as Your Word says, You have already given me everything I need for life and godliness through the knowledge of Christ. So, like Paul, I want to know Him and be found in Him. Send your light so I can see my inheritance and unwrap it, Father, amen.

March 10th

Eph 1:19 and what is the surpassing greatness of His power available to us as believers, according to the working of His mighty strength Eph 1:20 which He worked in Christ in raising Him from the dead, and He seated Him at His right hand in the heavenlies,
Eph 1:21 far above all principality and authority and power and dominion, and every name being named, not only in this world, but also in the coming age.

The same power that raised Christ from the dead is AVAILABLE to us as believers now, not one day when we die. We have been taught such a lot of religious hogwash over the decades that it has incapacitated and weighed us down. The simple faith of a child gives us entry to the Kingdom of God and resurrection power is part of our inheritance in Christ.

Every time disease is present, death is in operation at a cellular or limb level. The same Spirit that raised Christ from the dead quickens mortal bodies by releasing Life and banishing death at every level it is found. When we begin to operate from a place of comprehension of where we **actually** are seated (far above principalities and powers), it will revolutionize the way we pray and much of what is termed 'spiritual warfare' will fall away.

Prayer: Lord, so much of what I've been taught is based on unbelief. The only war that still needs fighting is in my own mind – You took care of the rest! Thank you that I get to share in the spoils of the battle You fought and won, amen.

March 11ᵗʰ

Rev 5:6 And I looked, and lo, in the midst of the throne and of the four living creatures, amidst the elders, a Lamb stood, as if it had been slain, having seven horns and seven eyes, which are the seven Spirits of God sent forth into all the earth.

Christ, the Lamb that was slain is our inheritance. This Lamb with seven eyes and seven horns is the One we are pressing in to know more deeply and clearly. He is the One who is worthy to open the seven seals on the book. The seven Spirits of God are the ones that enlighten us concerning the discovery of the Word. They open the seals on the book which is the Word of God and give us understanding and revelation, unveiling the glorious riches within Christ, the Living Word.

How can we wield the Word in righteousness and justice if the seven seals have not been removed and we understand the spirit of what is said! Religion has beaten people on the head with a sealed book for generations. The letter kills but the Spirit gives life!

Prayer: Jesus, Lamb of God, open the seals as I read this Book. Thank you for paying the price and being found worthy to open them for me! Let your seven-fold Spirit take that which is Yours and give it to me, in Your wonderful Name, amen.

March 12ᵗʰ

Joh 1:17 For the Law came through Moses, but grace and truth came through Jesus Christ.

From the time Jesus came as a Man, grace and Truth have been available to us as His disciples. I believe that as we hunger and thirst for the water that comes from the river of Life, fresh understanding of grace and truth will be released to the Bride in this season – grace which is multifaceted and helps in every time of need and truth which dismantles every stronghold of wrong belief within our hearts.

The Spirit of Grace is able to open our eyes to all the treasures of wisdom hidden in Christ that we may walk in an ever-increasing experiential measure of grace and truth. It is one thing to see truth but another to lay hold of it and make it your own. Paul pressed on to lay hold of that for which he was laid hold of by Christ. Let us do the same.

Prayer; Father, I don't want to just glimpse truth as it rushes past me – I want to possess and receive the full benefits of the Truth that is revealed to me by Your Spirit. I want to walk in grace and truth so that I may minister them to others, in Jesus Name, amen.

March 13th

Matt 9:29 According to your faith be it unto you...

What a far-reaching and profound statement Jesus made to people when He said this! Faith is a currency which purchases us entry into all that God has stored up for us. However, it is **not** faith in faith itself as has been preached by many in past years. Only believing that Jesus is who He said He is, the Living Word, will cause us to wholeheartedly throw the whole weight of our lives upon His statements.

When Jesus said, "it is finished", we either choose to embrace this truth and live our lives accordingly OR we continue to work our way towards God, performing religious deeds and staggering up the steep hill of self-righteousness. How sad it is for people to choose the impossible way when there is a ready-made vehicle called 'the righteousness of God in Christ' which immediately transports us into His presence! It depends on what we believe as to what we receive and experience.

Prayer: Father, I want to put my faith in the Truth so that I may experience the benefits outworking in my life. Please show me which building blocks in my beliefs are actually stumbling blocks in my quest to know You and be found in You, amen.

March 14th

Mat 13:58 And he did not many mighty works there because of their unbelief.

Are we seeing many mighty works in our midst? If not, then we must face the possibility that it is because of our unbelief! What is unbelief? When the above instance was recorded in Jesus' home town, we discover that it was familiarity which caused the people to have unbelief. They said, "oh, we know Him, we know his whole family, we've known them for years". The Word made flesh was right in front of their eyes and they acknowledged His wisdom but their own experience over the years put a stumbling block before them and the Word could perform few mighty works because their head knowledge got in the way.

Sometimes we become so familiar with the Word, especially when we have known it for many years, that we think we have it all wrapped up! We recognize the wisdom it contains but are unable

63

to access the power wrapped up inside it because familiarity has bred unbelief!

Prayer: Father, forgive me for becoming so familiar with Your Word that I hardly see what is right in front of me! I repent of my unbelief. Take the scales off my eyes and help me to discover the real power contained within verses I thought I knew backwards, in Jesus Name, amen.

March 15th

Heb 3:18 And to whom did He swear that they should not enter into His rest, but to those who did not believe? Heb 3:19 So we see that they could not enter in because of unbelief.

No matter how much we strive to enter the Sabbath rest of God, if we harbor unbelief in our hearts, we will never experience it. That is how serious the effect of unbelief is – it causes us to wander year after year in the wilderness instead of entering in and experiencing all that is promised us as citizens of the Kingdom.

We are so self-righteous without realizing it because we really can't see that unbelief lurks in our hearts. Yet sadly, much of what we profess has not moved beyond being a mental acknowledgment of Truth. Believing and faith happen at a heart level and this is where unbelief often rules from the wings.

Have you ever said, "I can't really hear God's voice"? Well, the Word says, 'My sheep hear My voice and they follow Me'. God says you hear Him, you say you don't – this is simply saying, "I don't believe You, God". UNBELIEF.

Prayer; Father, I am beginning to see that at a heart level my convictions don't always line up with the Truth You have declared. Please forgive me and uncover any other areas where unbelief is holding sway. Amen.

March 16th

Mar 16:14 Afterward He appeared to the Eleven as they reclined. And He reproached their unbelief and hardness of heart, because they did not believe those who had seen Him after He had risen.

Hardness of heart is also linked with unbelief. These disciples had just witnessed the crucifixion and burial of Jesus. Their whole belief system was severely rattled by what they had gone through. Trauma and the resulting confusion it brings concerning long-held beliefs causes our hearts to harden – it is a self-protection mechanism to avoid further shock and pain penetrating. The problem is that it also prevents good news from penetrating.

Even Truth cannot penetrate a hardened heart. Someone who has had fellowship with the resurrected Christ can bring their powerful testimony but our hardened heart and unbelief prevent us experiencing anything for ourselves. Only repentance will bring a softening.

Prayer: Lord, I acknowledge that hard things I have been through have caused me to harden my heart towards You and begin to distrust You. Please forgive me for my unbelief. Let the oil of Your Holy Spirit come and soften my heart today. Lord, I believe, help my unbelief, amen.

March 17th

Heb 4:12 For the word of God is quick, and powerful, and sharper than any two-edged sword, piercing even to the dividing asunder of soul and spirit, and of the joints and marrow, and is a **discerner of the thoughts and intents of the heart.**

This verse follows straight on from the one urging us to labor to enter into God's rest. The Word of God is like a mirror into which we gaze. Do we look like the description in the Word. Do we go away from that place walking in what we have seen?

The Word discerns the thoughts and intents of our hearts. The road to hell is paved with good intentions. Unless we align our thoughts to the Truth expressed in the Word, taking captive every thought to the obedience of Christ, good intentions walk hand in hand with unbelief and produce a life devoid of the power of God. True believing produces action – seeing and obeying.

Prayer; Father, for too long I have meditated and hesitated. Even the Pharisees meditated on the Word and yet they were a hopeless bunch. I want to live a life of simple active faith, just hearing and obeying. Help me, Holy Spirit, in Jesus Name, amen.

March 18th

1Co 2:3 And I was with you in weakness and in fear, and in much trembling.1Co 2:4 And my speech and my preaching was not with enticing words of man's wisdom, but in demonstration of the Spirit and of power,

We have sadly seen very little of the demonstration of the Spirit and of power in recent times in church circles. Perhaps the reason is that there has been too much preaching with enticing words of men's wisdom.

The soul and intellect of man can come up with doctrines which sound so logical and even 'spiritual' but the results speak for themselves. Multitudes of believers struggle with mental, emotional and physical issues and the wisdom of man has been unable to produce lasting results. How desperately the Church needs a demonstration of the Spirit and of power for we do not seem to <u>experience</u> the good news which we preach at the world.

Prayer: Father, I want my life to demonstrate Your authenticity. I am tired of the wisdom of man which has no ability to impart life. I repent of leaning my weight on soulish wisdom, in Jesus Name

March 19th

1Co 2:4 And my speech and my preaching was not with enticing words of man's wisdom, but in demonstration of the Spirit and of power,1Co 2:5 so that your faith should not stand in the wisdom of men, but in the power of God.

For too long the Church has placed their faith in the wisdom of men and as a result have not experienced a demonstration of the power of God. We have become a self-help bureau offering tips on living your best life or scaling the ladder of success – we are like the prodigal son eating pig-swill when the solution is to return to the Father and His wisdom.

In His house we receive authority once again to operate in the Spirit of might. However, first we must turn our backs on the pig-sty and the slops it offers and recognize we have been swallowing earthly wisdom, off-cuts and peelings from the world's table.

Prayer: Father, I am sickened by the diet I have been gobbling up for years. My spiritual taste-buds need detoxing. I want to return to the only source of true Wisdom and drink from a clean fountain, amen.

March 20th

1Co 4:20 For the kingdom of God is not in word, but in power.

The kingdom of God is meant to be demonstrated, not only talked about. This is what sets the gospel of the kingdom apart from every course in psychology or philosophy – visible proof of the presence of the Kingdom dispels any doubt as to its authenticity! Jesus sent out His disciples, instructing them to heal the sick and cleanse the lepers because this was evidence of the coming of the Kingdom of God.

Unfortunately the Church has largely presented the gospel, particularly in the West, as something to be talked about in great detail; yet there is seldom demonstration to prove beyond a shadow of doubt that Jesus Christ is alive in our midst. Jesus came preaching the gospel of the Kingdom and when the atmosphere of heaven invades earth then demons cry out as they leave and the sick are healed.

We are called to preach this very <u>same</u> gospel; not the gospel of salvation alone but the gospel of the Kingdom IN POWER! Ephesians 1 speaks of the incomparably great power available to us as Believers. We must begin to tap into that reservoir.

PRAYER: Father, let my witness be one of power and not just words. You came to set the captives free. Do this through me I pray, amen.

March 21st

Mar 16:15 And He said to them, Go into all the world, proclaim the gospel to all the creation. Mar 16:16 He who believes and is baptized will be saved, but he who does not believe will be condemned .Mar 16:17 And miraculous signs will follow those believing these things...

Jesus said to His disciples, "Go into all the world, proclaim the gospel to all the creation." Then He described the visible signs which would follow this action.

The word 'go' comes before the manifestation of power and miracles. Until we are obedient to His commandment to go, we will not begin to see the signs following. Perhaps the reason for the lack of power in the Church of today is because we do not 'go'; we 'come' to meetings and talk about going. The glory of God will be poured out to a needy world as we rise from the pews and go into all the world – be that the house next door or other continents! Let us not talk more than we walk out what we believe! Let it be said of us, "and they went..."

Prayer: Father, simple obedience to the words of Jesus will cause You to work with me, confirming Your Word with signs following. Show me where You want me to go and who You want me to speak to. I am willing to obey Your still small voice, leaving the results of my obedience in Your hands, amen.

March 22nd

Mar 16:20 And going out, they proclaimed everywhere, the Lord working with them and confirming the Word by miraculous signs following. Amen.

We are co-laborers with the Lord. If we will be obedient to the Spirit's leading and go out 'proclaiming everywhere' that He sends us to, then He works with us, providing the proof that what we share is the Truth. We need never worry that He will not show up. If we boldly share the power contained in the death and resurrection of Jesus to reconcile the world to Himself, then He demonstrates the power of this Kingdom of Light by healing and delivering those who come to Him.

Let us lay aside unbelief and the fear of man and begin to be bold ambassadors of the Kingdom of God. We have good news to share! Ask the Spirit for a word of encouragement or a word of wisdom for someone you meet along the way today and watch a life being touched by Heaven as you share it!

Once you begin to step out in faith, aware that the Lord is working with you, your life will never be the same!

Prayer: Father, thank you that You go with me and work with me proving the presence of Your Kingdom. I am excited to be a fellow-laborer in Your vineyard! Amen.

March 23rd

Act 1:3 to whom He also presented Himself living after His suffering by many infallible proofs, being seen by them through forty days, and speaking of the things pertaining to the kingdom of God.

After His resurrection, Jesus spent forty days with the disciples and the Word tells us he spoke of things pertaining to the KINGDOM OF GOD! These were His last days on earth with them and He did not discuss doctrine or church structure or any other subject which the Church of today finds so pertinent. In His parting days with these men who would take the good news into all the world, Jesus spent all His time explaining the Kingdom to them.

During these discussions He spoke of the baptism in the Holy Spirit which would give them power to be witnesses of the Kingdom. Without the power of the Holy Spirit, the Kingdom of God will never be extended for it is through His power that healing, deliverance and even resurrection occur. Let us seek Him for fresh infilling and empowering for the task ahead of us. Spreading the gospel of the Kingdom and being filled with the Spirit go hand in hand!

Prayer: Precious Lord, fill me afresh with Your Holy Spirit and fire that I may be aglow and burning with the Spirit as I serve You. Thank you that the same power that raised Christ from the dead is available to me as a believer, amen.

March 24th

1Co 2:1 And I, brethren, when I came to you, came not with excellency of speech or of wisdom, declaring unto you the testimony of God. 1Co 2:2 For I determined not to know anything among you, save Jesus Christ, and him crucified.

When Paul spoke concerning the Kingdom of God, he began and ended with Jesus and the crucifixion. This powerful event was the center of all that he shared. Why is this? Jesus Himself said, "I am the Door" and "I am the Way". There is no other entry point for the Kingdom of God other than the cross of Jesus Christ. We cannot enter it through a course in The Purpose-driven Life or any other method. This is why water baptism is so crucial. When we demonstrate through a prophetic action that we identify with the death and resurrection of Jesus, we declare to the Kingdom of Darkness that we are no longer citizens of that country – we have crossed the border using the passport of Jesus Christ, the Spotless Lamb, and have entered once and for all into another Kingdom; of which we immediately become citizens! The cross is really a crossroads where mankind chooses which country they want to be permanent residents of – the kingdom of Self or the Kingdom of God.

Prayer: Father, sometimes I go through that border-post again, back to the darkness of being led by my flesh. Strengthen me with power in my inner man to resist that pull and to rather be led by Your Spirit into a deeper experience of the Kingdom of Light, amen.

March 25th

Jam 3:15 This wisdom does not come down from above, but is earthly, sensual, demonic..

There is an earthly wisdom and there is a heavenly wisdom. Before we are born-again, the only wisdom we are able to operate in is the one described above. However, once we cross over into the Kingdom of the Son, we have access to the mind of Christ and can ask for heavenly wisdom.

Unfortunately much of what is today presented in church circles has its roots in earthly sensual wisdom for it appeals to the flesh and puts the spotlight on Self. When we declare that in Christ we too have died to the world, then our flesh should no longer be the focus. On the other side of the cross, the only thing which Paul encourages us to do to the flesh is to put any fleshly impulses to death!

Let us no longer waste time restoring, stroking or in any way propping up the flesh. We are citizens of a Kingdom which does not operate on demonic wisdom. Sensual wisdom does all it can to keep the flesh alive and kicking. Until we are conformed to Christ's death we cannot access resurrection power. The prophetic action of baptism must be <u>daily</u> lived out.

Prayer: Father, help me to put off the old man with its lusts and to put on Christ and all the wisdom He has for me, amen.

March 26th

Jam 3:17AMP But the wisdom that is from above is first pure, then peace-loving, courteous, considerate, gentle, willing to yield to reason, full of compassion and good fruits, wholehearted, straightforward, impartial and unfeigned, free from doubts, wavering and insincerity.

The wisdom found in Christ has a character – His character – because Christ Jesus is made unto us wisdom from God. When we ask for wisdom, we actually receive an impartation of His nature.

When trying to discern the source of wisdom presented, it is helpful to consider what the opposite of heavenly wisdom looks like according to this verse. If the counsel you are receiving is in any way impure, argumentative, rude, inconsiderate, harsh, stubborn, judgmental or hypocritical, then you can be sure it is earthly or soulish wisdom.

Sometimes it is helpful to hold a mirror up and scrutinize the counsel we offer to others. Are we ourselves operating in soulish wisdom or that which is found in Christ?

Father, forgive me for so often pouring out counsel that does not pass the litmus test described in James 3. I want to permeate the air with the fragrance of Christ, not the rotting stench of my own soulish opinions - help me, Father, amen.

March 27th

Joh 14:6 Jesus said to him, I am the Way, the Truth, and the Life

The cross is the entry point to the Kingdom of God but we do not pass through Jesus and out the other side into another place – we enter through Him for He is the Way; we enter into Him who is Light and Truth and we dwell in Him who is Eternal Life.   The Kingdom of God is only found IN Christ. He is not just a ticket to some better place – He is the place in which all that was purchased for us is found.

We do not move on from salvation at the cross to more advanced teachings – there is a simplicity to be found in Christ. We need Him, nothing more, nothing less! As Paul says in Hebrews 1, he upholds ALL things by His mighty word of power. Christ is both the Door and the destination. Let us stop looking to the horizon for something more and realize that all that we ever need is to be found in Christ!

Prayer: Father, forgive me for thinking that Christ is not enough. I realize I have not even begun to discover the depth of the riches that is to be found in Him. My determined purpose is to know Him ever more deeply, amen.

March 28th

Joh 14:9 Jesus said to him, Have I been with you such a long time and yet you have not known Me, Philip? He who has seen Me has seen the Father. And how do you say, Show us the Father? Joh 14:10 Do you not believe that I am in the Father and the Father in Me? The Words that I speak to you I do not speak of Myself, but the Father who dwells in Me, He does the works.

These verses explain why the new Age teachings which say that many roads lead to God are so wrong. God the Father and Jesus are inseparable. Jesus came as the sole representation of the glory of God. The movements of the Father and Jesus are so interlinked and in harmony as to be inseparable. If, as Jesus stated here, the Father dwells in Him, then Jesus can be the ONLY way to reach the Father, for He cannot be found outside of Jesus Christ!

The gospel of the Kingdom that Jesus came preaching is the gospel of the Kingdom of the Father. In the Lord's prayer, we pray for the Kingdom of the Father to come and this kingdom is only experienced IN CHRIST.

Prayer: Lord Jesus, You are my destination, my home. I look no further and strive no longer except to be found IN You, amen.

March 29th

Phi 3:8 But no, rather, I also count all things to be loss for the excellency of the knowledge of Christ Jesus my Lord, for whose sake I have suffered the loss of all things, and count them to be dung, so that I may win Christ

What was Paul counting as loss in order to gain Christ? It included all his religious upbringing, all his theological knowledge, all his previous experience as part of the established religious system of the day; his so-called spiritual bloodline and the fact that he was born into a known religious family who had produced a long line of spiritual elite (Pharisees). Paul turned his back on everything the religious establishment of the day considered to be an advantage and turned toward the knowledge of Christ. He considered the gaining of Christ to be a greater prize than any accolade the religious society of his day had to offer. He turned his back on position and the praises of men and considered them to be worthless in comparison to the treasure of Christ.

The question is – are we prepared to do the same? – do we consider the knowledge of Christ to be of such value that everything else is worthless in comparison? May God give us such a fresh revelation of the beauty of Christ that everything else that has previously crowded our lives will pale into insignificance in the dazzling light of His face. Then we shall be free of the fear of man and hunger no more for the praises of men. Then we will be free to follow the Lamb wherever He goes!

Prayer: Lord, bring me to the place where it is true of me that I count ALL things loss compared to knowing You! Amen.

March 30th

Phi 3:9 and be found in Him; not having my own righteousness, which is of the Law, but through the faith of Christ, the righteousness of God by faith,

Paul was determined to be found in Christ. Where are we to be found? If God comes looking for us, will He discover our permanent address to be 'In Christ' or will He find us hiding behind the fig leaves of our religious efforts? Our attempts at righteous behavior and spiritual works are filthy rags in God's sight and if we are honest with ourselves, our motivation for doing these things stems from a feeling of nakedness and inadequacy before God. We feel we have nothing worthwhile on our resumes, we are naked in His sight and so we think up programs and performances and countless other things which seem good in our sight. We always feel we must DO something worthwhile to be acceptable to God. Yet, none of these things bring intimacy with God. If anything we bury ourselves underneath mountains of designer-fig leaves and God is hidden from our sight. Determine to be found in Christ, hidden within the folds of His robe of Righteousness for here you will find intimacy with the Father and the Son.

Prayer: Father, You nailed the requirements of the Law to the cross and now I choose to leave it there and to dwell within the place prepared for me in Christ, not having my own righteousness but possessing the pure righteousness of God by faith, amen.

March 31st

Phi 3:10AMP that I may know Him and the power of His resurrection and the fellowship of His sufferings, being made conformable to His death, if by any means I might attain to the resurrection of the dead, while still in the body.

The death of Jesus was first and foremost a death of his own will and preferences. When He wrestled in the garden of Gethsemane, before the crucifixion, He had to come to a place where He surrendered and said, "not my will but Yours be done." This was part of His suffering where He sweated drops of blood. For all of us, there awaits this appointment where we wrestle with our own desires while knowing the will of the Father. Only surrender will conform us to the death of Jesus. Only the laying down of all our instincts of self-preservation and protection will open the door for us to access the resurrection power of Christ. Jesus said, "he who loses his life for My sake, will find it". It is the releasing of all that we hold dear, including our own life, into the hands of God. To surrender control of the whole of one's life to another is a sign of complete trust. When we accomplish this (and it is a daily dying), whatever comes our way, we can endure because we have peace in the knowledge that the Father works all things for our good and His glory.

Prayer: Father, help me to die daily that Your wonderful resurrection life may been seen at work in the earth. Help me not to defend and protect myself but rather to die to my own reputation in the eyes of men and live for Your pleasure, amen.

April 1st

2Co 4:10 Always bearing about in the body the dying of the Lord Jesus, that the life also of Jesus might be made manifest in our body. 2Co 4:11 For we which live are always delivered unto death for Jesus' sake, that the life also of Jesus <u>might be made manifest</u> in our mortal flesh. 2Co 4:12 So then death works in us, but life in you.

If we remember that our dying to self and all its demands will cause resurrection life to be manifested within us, it makes the choice so much easier. This is the joy set before us as we face death to self – that the same resurrection life which raised Jesus after death is our portion. However, it is important to remember that the reason for which this overflowing life manifests through us is the needs of others. Death works in us so that the zoe life of God can flow from our earthen vessels to heal and deliver and restore others.

It is not to make us look good to others or to elevate our positions in the local Church. If we truly desire to see the lame walk and the blind see, then we must take up our cross daily.

Prayer: Father, Jesus thought of me when He walked with His cross. He thought of the joy of seeing Your life work in me. I want to see You pour out Life on others and so I gladly choose to lose my life and be found hidden in You. There is so much need and so few who surrender fully. May I be counted as one of them, Father, amen.

April 2nd

Phi 3:12 Not as though I had already attained, either were already perfect, but I am pressing on, if I may lay hold of that for which I also was taken hold of by Christ Jesus.

Jesus took hold of us for a purpose – He was the first-born of many brethren –that's us! He was also the first-born from among the dead and WE are supposed to be the many brethren from among the dead. In other words, as we partake of His death, the same power which raised Him from the dead is also our portion! How glorious!

We must press on to take hold of this wonderful Truth and see it manifested within us. We may not have experienced much of it yet – even Paul said he had yet to have it fully manifested within him - but we must be single-minded in our pursuit of the fullness of what Christ obtained for us. The Greek word for 'lay hold of' in this verse means 'to seize violently and possess'!

Prayer: Father, I want to violently seize and possess this Kingdom of resurrection power You have for me! I don't want to know about it – I want to personally experience the very same life that Jesus does at this moment. I press on by faith to apprehend it, in Jesus Name, amen.

April 3rd

Phi 3:13 My brothers, I do not count myself to have taken possession, but one thing I do, forgetting the things behind and reaching forward to the things before, Phi 3:14 I press toward the mark for the prize of the high calling of God in Christ Jesus.

Paul says that one thing is imperative in this quest to possess the full knowledge and experience of Christ – we must forget what lies behind. For Paul, this meant his theological training and the doctrines he had studied for so many years, not to mention his good standing in the synagogue and the best seats at meetings! He turned his back on all of it because he had a glimpse of the treasure that was in Christ and he wanted more. The prize that he pressed forward to lay hold of was the high calling of God IN Christ Jesus. Paul said that any calling or position he had previous held was absolutely inferior to being in Christ. **THIS** was the prize – being found in Christ. He did not need the prizes and the awards of men any longer for He knew that Christ was the greatest prize any man could wish for and he wanted to immerse himself in the depths of the riches and beauty found there.

Prayer: Father, all my previous goals in life, even the spiritual ones, seem so paltry comparing to the achievement of knowing Christ and being found in Him. I lay them down at the foot of the cross and run unimpeded into the experience of the prize You have for me. Thank you for this lavish gift, this incomparable inheritance which is Christ, amen.

April 4th

Phi 3:15 Let us therefore, as many as are perfect, be of this mind. And if in anything you are otherwise minded, God shall reveal even this to you.

The word 'perfect' above actually comes from the Greek word meaning 'complete, of full age, a man'. It therefore refers to maturity. Elsewhere, in 1 Corinthians 13:11, Paul says that when he became a man he put away childish ways of thinking and doing.

A child wants instant gratification and is only concerned with 'playing church'. Proverbs tells us that foolishness is bound up in the heart of a child. One of the hallmarks of spiritual maturity is a move away from the doctrines of man which tickle the ears and stroke the flesh and progressing on to the knowledge and discovery of Christ Himself. It is only as we do this that we can be fully joined to the Head of the Body and receive all the instruction and nourishment we need to walk in abundant life. To move on to maturity in Christ, we have to first recognize that the high calling IN Christ is the only prize worth pressing toward. Then we must put away childish things and focus fully on the wisdom to be found in Him, who is our inheritance.

Prayer: Father, I want to put away childish ways of speaking, understanding and thinking. Please show me where I am not moving toward maturity, so that I may fully comprehend that Christ is my inheritance, amen.

April 5th

1Co 2:12 Now we have received, not the spirit of the world, but the spirit which is of God; that we might know the things that are freely given to us of God.1Co 2:13 Which things also we speak, not in the words which man's wisdom teaches, but which the Holy Ghost teaches; comparing spiritual things with spiritual.

Once we embrace the fact that Christ is our inheritance, the Holy Spirit begins to reveal to us the things which are freely ours in Christ. Then we can share these things with heavenly wisdom, using the words the Holy Spirit gives us. He compares spiritual things with spiritual, not natural things with spiritual – because this is earthly wisdom.

We never have to prepare long speeches before the time because the Holy Spirit will give us the right words to say at the moment we need them – this is the essence of being led by the Spirit.

Prayer: Holy Spirit, thank you for revealing the riches of Christ to me and for giving me the words I need to communicate these spiritual truths at the right moment, amen.

April 6th

1Co 2:14 But the natural man receives not the things of the Spirit of God: for they are foolishness unto him: neither can he know them, because they are spiritually discerned

In this verse the reason for the renewing of our minds is explained. The way of thinking that comes naturally to us is not helpful when receiving from the Spirit of God. We do not need more mental discernment but stronger spiritual discernment.

God's order of working is that we receive revelation in our spirits from the Spirit of God first (when reading the Word or spending time in His presence worshipping) and then we use this revelation as a standard and conform our thoughts to it. The natural man leans on his own understanding and therefore the things of the Spirit make no sense to him.

Until we are led by the Spirit instead of the flesh we will never progress in our spiritual understanding. God's ways are so high above ways and His thoughts so different to the thoughts of man.

83

Prayer: Father, I see now that my own understanding is a huge obstacle in my spiritual progress. Please send Your light and Truth to my spirit man so that my mind can be renewed, amen.

April 7th

Rom 8:6 For to be carnally minded is death, but to be spiritually minded is life and peace Rom 8:7 because the carnal mind is enmity against God, for it is not subject to the Law of God, neither indeed can it be.

When we lean on our own understanding and operate according to earthly wisdom, our flesh will rule us. However, if we set our minds on things above, we experience life and peace. We can only set our minds on these things if we are receiving revelation from the Spirit of God. Then we can renew our minds according to what He shows us. To be carnally minded is to place ourselves as enemies of God because the soulish ways of the flesh are opposed to the way of the Spirit. Fluctuating emotions and cravings to satisfy self will continually drive us and torment us.

All of the treasures of wisdom and insight into spiritual things are hidden in Christ and the precious Holy Spirit is faithful to reveal them to us as we seek to know Christ better. Do we realize what a wonderful gift the Holy Spirit is to us? He causes us to experience life and peace.

Prayer: Thank-you, Jesus for sending us the counselor, the Holy Spirit. He will lead me into all truth as I learn to know His still small voice. I am predestined to be conformed into Your image – Hallelujah! I yield to the Spirit's guidance afresh, amen.

April 8th

Ps 32:8 I will instruct you and teach you in the way which you should go; I will counsel you with My eye upon you.

Jesus called the Holy Spirit 'the Comforter', which also means 'counselor, advocate, friend' and informed His disciples, "He shall teach you all things and bring all things to your remembrance, whatever I have said to you".

The Holy Spirit within us reveals to us all we need to know concerning the Word and God's will for our lives. We should not longer seek so much outward guidance and begin to train our inner ear for the voice guiding us inwardly. When we have problems, do we run to man or seek to get alone with God and hear the Spirit's counsel?

Prayer: Precious Lord, I have relied too heavily on the counsel of men and have often chosen the wrong path as a result. Please forgive me for disregarding the Comforter and His advice. Train my inner ear to clearly hear His voice, amen.

April 9th

Eze 44:15 But the priests, the Levites, the sons of Zadok, who kept the charge of My sanctuary when the sons of Israel went astray from Me, they shall come near Me to minister to Me, and they shall stand before Me to offer to Me the fat and the blood, says the Lord God Eze 44:16 They shall enter into my sanctuary, and they shall come near to my table, to minister unto me, and they shall keep my charge.

The Zadok priesthood are a type of the priestly role we assume as priests after the order of Melchizedek(Heb 5:10). Jesus was the forerunner, being faithful to the mission His Father appointed Him. In the same way, because of their faithfulness to God when others went astray, the sons of Zadok were allowed to come _near_ to minister to the Lord. We minister to Him by worshiping not only with our mouths but with our lives. Faithfulness and walking in the fear of the Lord is an inward thing, as we daily make choices to conform our lives to the Word and the conviction of the Spirit. Oh, what a great honor to be appointed the place NEAR to the throne, ministering to the Lord! There were other priests that ministered only to the people but the Zadok priests could draw near, right into the holy presence of the throne of the universe.

Prayer: Father, I desire to be one who draws near You and ministers to You. May the sweet fragrance of my laid-down life satisfy Your hunger and bring You pleasure, amen.

April 10th

Eze 44:17 And it shall come to pass, that when they enter in at the gates of the inner court, they shall be clothed with linen garments; and no wool shall come upon them, whiles they minister in the gates of the inner court, and within

Linen garments signify that these Zadok priests are clothed in the robe of righteousness purchased for them by the Blood of the Lamb. They do not enter based on their own spiritual exploits or self-righteousness. They are found in Christ, possessing a righteousness by faith, not by works. They are not clothed in the garments of pride woven from the praises of men.

Just as the saints riding behind the Word on white horses (wearing linen garments) are alert to the slightest change in direction from the One who rides ahead of them; so too, these faithful priests are not self-conscious but Word-conscious, their eyes and ears trained on the One whom they minister to, ready to meet His smallest request.

Prayer: Father, deliver me from self-consciousness and make me more aware of You than I am of myself, that I my minister effectively to Your needs, amen.

April 11th

. Eze 44:18 They shall have linen bonnets upon their heads, and shall have linen breeches upon their loins; they shall not gird themselves with anything that causes sweat.

Linen is also applied to their heads (thought life) and their loins (fruitfulness). No wool was allowed on their bodies because it caused them to sweat while carrying out their duties. Sweat on the brow was part of the sentence given to Adam when banished from Eden. By his own hard labor he would cause the earth to bring forth. However, in Christ the curse has been broken and the Zadok priests depict God's people functioning from a place of Sabbath rest, having ceased their own fleshly works.

How important it is for us to only wear the spiritual linen garments provided for us and to refuse to put on any garment or spiritual identity in the Church which causes us to sweat. If we are using great fleshly effort to get things done, then it is unlikely that we are fulfilling a role ordained by the Father.

Prayer: Father, thank-you that true fruitfulness flows out of intimacy and no striving is necessary to bring it to pass. Show me any woolen garments that I still have in my spiritual cupboard so I can remove them, amen.

April 12th

Eze 44:19 And when they go forth into the utter court, even into the utter court to the people, they shall put off their garments wherein they ministered, and lay them in the holy chambers, and they shall put on other garments; and they shall not sanctify the people with their garments.

When you are ministering to the Lord in the inner holy chambers, this is a private matter between you and God. He sees your linen garments, the garments of consecration, holiness and righteousness. You do not parade them before men when you minister. You are to put on ordinary garments and not elevate yourselves above others by openly displaying that you have been with Jesus in intimacy. In much the same way, a wife does not appear outside her bedroom in the garments she wears especially for her husband in times of intimacy. The Lord will share things with you in this place and not everything is for the ears of men. We must learn to rein in our tongues and avoid the temptation to prove to others how spiritual we are by indiscriminately sharing the things occurring in the holy chambers. Only as the Spirit leads, are we released to minister using the wisdom gleaned in that holy place.

Prayer; Father, I have so often tried to impress men with my spiritual knowledge and expertise. Forgive me for sharing the secrets You have shared in my ear without Your permission. Set a guard at my mouth, Lord, in Jesus Name, amen.

April 13th

Eze 44:23 And they shall teach my people the difference between the holy and profane, and cause them to discern between the unclean and the clean.

Here we see that the Zadok priests are given wisdom in order to teach God's people and equip them with the necessary knowledge to discern what is really of God and what isn't. This is important in an age where so much fleshly teaching has infiltrated the Church. Evil parades itself as good and messengers of satan present themselves as ministers of righteousness.

Jesus Himself looked past the self-righteous robes of the Pharisees and called them white-washed tombs. Although outwardly they wore the right religious robes in order to appear spiritually mature, inwardly there was no life present. Before we can teach others, we need to be taught ourselves by the Holy Spirit, Who reveals the hidden things. Then we can detect the wolves in sheep's clothing.

Prayer: Father, I need sharper discernment in order to accurately ascertain the true nature of things. Please teach me, amen.

April 14th

Eze 44:24 And in controversy they shall stand in judgment; and they shall judge it according to my judgments...

When we have learnt to listen to the Father's voice and not to immediately judge situations by our natural senses, then we are able to help others who have issues against one another. We see this principle in operation as King Solomon presided over the case where two women were arguing over one child. The wisdom with which he ruled in the case, caused what was hidden to be revealed and the true mother received her child back.

This wisdom came from above, from a God who can see the depths of men's hearts. We can only declare God's judgments when we have laid down our own understanding and wait to receive His counsel. He always speaks a word that divides between soul and spirit. The application of His wisdom brings swift solution to problems. Why rely on our own limited knowledge and understanding. Rather let us pause, ask God what He thinks and then use that information to judge the situation!

Prayer: Lord, Your counsel is far superior to my limited assessment of situations. Your wisdom is infinite and always just. May Your Spirit of Counsel be my portion that I may judge wisely, amen.

April 15th

Eze 44:28 And it shall be unto them for an inheritance: I am their inheritance: and ye shall give them no possession in Israel: I am their possession.

Christ is our inheritance. If you are being taught that the gospel wins you houses and cars and lands, you are receiving another Jesus. He is the prize for which we run the race.

The spirit of mammon has so infiltrated the teachings of the contemporary church that we consider success to be measured by the size of our buildings and our offerings. Yet Jesus and the disciples turned the world upside-down without building a multi-storey sanctuary or storing up a bank-balance. Those who have learnt God's value-system understand the inestimable value of the inheritance assigned us as co-heirs and waste no time setting up earthly kingdoms.

Prayer: Father, the knowledge of Christ is of far more value than rubies or pearls. Thank you for the incredible inheritance bequeathed to us, your children, amen.

April 16th

Mat 25:32 And all nations shall be gathered before Him. And He shall separate them from one another, as a shepherd divides the sheep from the goats.

Some people preach that in this scene depicted above, the Lord separates whole sheep nations from the goat nations as a result of their treatment of Israel. They say this based on the fact that Jesus divided the groups according to the way they had treated His 'brothers', assuming that Jesus referred to the Jews as His brothers.

Herein is a case of not rightly dividing the Word of God. In another instance, related in Mark 3:31, His brothers and mother came to call Him and Jesus responded like this: 'And He looked around on those who sat about Him, and said, Behold My mother and My brothers! For whoever does the will of God, the same is My brother and My sister and My mother'.

God's favor and protection are on those who sit at His feet and hear His Word and afterwards gladly obey Him. Just as Daniel walked in the Lord's protection and blessing in the midst of an ungodly nation, so too will we, if we walk in the fear of the Lord, regardless of what is happening to those around us. The eye of the Lord is upon those who fear Him, to deliver their soul from death and keep them alive in famine (ps 33:18)

Prayer: Lord, I want to study to show myself approved, rightly dividing the Word. Thank you that Your Holy Spirit teaches and guides me as I discover Truth and remove error from my belief-system, amen

April 17th

Mat 25:33 And he shall set the sheep on his right hand, but the goats on the left.

The appointed seat at the right hand belongs to the son of the right hand, which is Jesus. He is seated at the right hand of the Father. It is at the right hand of the Father that there are pleasures evermore (ps 16). It is His strong right hand that helps us possess the land (ps 44) it is God's right hand that holds the sword and got the victory (ps 98:1). The seat at the right hand is the place of power, protection, provision and victory! What a wonderful place to be appointed.

There are pleasures at God's right hand because it is here we are positioned in Christ and the pleasures are the glorious riches of our inheritance in Christ. We do not have enough days here on earth to discover the length and breadth and depth of all that is ours in Christ!

Prayer: Father, thank you that You place me, as a sheep of Your pasture, on Your right hand. Reveal to me by Your Spirit all that You have stored up for me in this place, in Jesus Name, amen.

April 18th

Mat 25:34 Then the King shall say to those on His right hand, Come, blessed of My Father, inherit the kingdom prepared for you from the foundation of the world.

We do not inherit something assigned to us when we die! The inheritance is left by the person who has died, in this case Jesus Christ. There comes a point when Christ on the throne of His glory does a separating work between those who are really His sheep and those who are not. Then He releases His blessed sheep into an experience of the Kingdom of God that will cause them to taste and see that He is good!

The angels which come with Jesus are those who minister to and help the heirs of salvation. There is a release of angels on assignment in this day causing his sheep who have been tested and approved to experience the full benefits of the glorious inheritance spoken of in Ephesians 1.

Prayer: Father, I do desire to fully inherit and experience the kingdom prepared for me as one of Your sheep. Help me to be found amongst those You set firmly on Your right hand, amen.

April 19th

Mat 25:35 For I was hungry, and you gave me food; I was thirsty, and you gave Me drink; I was a stranger, and you took Me in; Mat 25:36 I was naked, and you clothed Me; I was sick, and you visited Me; I was in prison, and you came to Me.

The measuring rod Christ uses to determine a sheep from a goat is their treatment of Him. What does this mean? Don't we worship Him and love Him and serve Him? He explains that however we treat the members of the Body of Christ, it is measured as treatment of Christ. So this is the judgment that begins in God's house, His Church. Before God judges the world, He must apply the same measuring rod to the Church. He is just and so cannot have different measuring rods.

The measuring rod is the character of Christ. How much is displayed in us? We know we are born of an incorruptible Seed, Christ, but has it borne fruit in our lives?

Prayer: Father, the possibility that You might discern some goat in me is disturbing. Apply Your ruler to my heart and life and show me the areas of blindness in my own perception of my Christian walk. Show me if the character of the Shepherd is in me, amen.

April 20th

Mat 25:40 And the King shall answer and say to them, Truly I say to you, Inasmuch as you did it to one of the least of these My brothers, you have done it to Me.

So He comes to measure how we have treated the Body of Christ, by looking at our treatment of the least important member (in our estimation). Paul says the eye cannot say to another member of the Body, I have no need of you.

The fact that we tend to consider some members of the Body less important than others is arrogant, but that we would even consider discarding a limb is shortsighted at best! We would not consider chopping off our own foot as we know the discomfort it would cause us. Yet, in the depths of our hearts, we evaluate the Body of Christ in order of importance and consider the ones we really can't relate to must be unnecessary to us because we have nothing in common with them. The foot is so different to the eye in shape and function. Both are indispensable yet the one looks at the other and considers itself more important – what arrogance, what ignorance!

Prayer: Father, forgive me for using my own ruler to measure Your Body. Bring to mind the ones I have considered the least and give me salve for my eyes so I can see them the way You see them. Forgive me for my pride, amen.

April 21st

Mat 25:35 For I was hungry, and you gave me food; I was thirsty, and you gave Me drink; I was a stranger, and you took Me in; Mat 25:36 I was naked, and you clothed Me; I was sick, and you visited Me; I was in prison, and you came to Me..........Mat 25:40 And the King shall answer and say to them, Truly I say to you, Inasmuch as you did it to one of the least of these My brothers, you have done it to Me.

Jesus does His separating work using the measuring stick of how we have treated those we consider the least of the brethren in the Body Of Christ. So often, we as the Church are so concerned with feeding and clothing the poor outside the Body. Yet here we find that Jesus begins with how we treat the poor and the naked WITHIN The Body. Mother Theresa said that the hunger for love was the worst kind of hunger that existed. Within the Body there are people that we greet but do not even really see, because we consider them 'the least' and we are in too much of a

hurry to find the ones we consider worthy of our attention to even hear the reply they give to our casual, "how are you?"
The deafness and blindness of the Body of Christ to one another must be healed before we can think of exporting an authentic gospel to the world.

Prayer: Father, forgive me for showing partiality. So often I look but do not really see the person You love , standing in front of me. Open my eyes and ears, in Jesus Name, amen.

April 22nd

Jam 2:15 If a brother or sister is naked and destitute of daily food, Jam 2:16 and if one of you says to them, Go in peace, be warmed and filled, but you do not give them those things which are needful to the body, what good is it?

When Jesus separates the sheep from the goats, it is because the goats speak a blessing with their mouths – 'be warmed and filled' – but their hearts are so hardened that they do nothing to help that blessing to manifest, even though they have the power to do so.

Is this not the same as honoring the Lord with our lips but our hearts remaining far from Him? Jesus was so moved at the thought of the multitude being hungry that He multiplied a little boy's lunch to feed them. Yet so often we know that our brothers and sisters are in need but harden our hearts toward them; all the while maintaining an outward appearance of spirituality and generosity.

Prayer: Father, forgive me for misrepresenting You to the members of Your family. They are also my family, even the ones I consider to be the least important. Make my mouth and my actions match, in Jesus Name, amen.

April 23rd

Luk 3:8 Bring forth therefore fruits worthy of repentance, and begin not to say within yourselves, We have Abraham to our father: for I say unto you, That God is able of these stones to raise up children unto Abraham.

John the Baptist prepared the way for Christ to be seen in the earth. He warned the Pharisees that a sign of true repentance was accompanying action or fruit. It was not enough to claim to be descendants of Abraham. In the same way, it is not enough to declare we are sons of Abraham by faith – our faith must bring forth fruit of the character of God.

When we realize we have not walked the talk, we must accompany our repentance with the appropriate action. And not just any form of fruit must be shown – it must be worthy of repentance – real evidence of changed hearts! If we say we love God, this must be demonstrated in our actions of love toward our brethren in the Body, especially 'the least of these'. Paul says that 'those members of the body, which seem to be more feeble, are necessary' (1 Cor 12:22). This is because they give the rest of the Body the opportunity to be an expression of the love of Christ, surrounding and honoring them.

Prayer: Father, may my repentance prepare the way for Christ to be seen in my earthen vessel. May Your love be expressed in deeds which confirm the words I profess, amen.

April 24th

Luk 3:11 He answered and said to them, He who has two coats, let him give to him who has none. And he who has food, let him do likewise.

John was preparing the way for Christ to be unveiled in the earth and part of this preparation was to confront people about the kind of fruit their lives were producing. His anointed words brought deep conviction and they were desperate to put things right. Part of the solution that John gave them was to check out the abundance they had in their closets and grocery cupboards and freely give to those who had nothing.

A hallmark of the church in the early days of the book of Acts was that 'there were none needy among them'. In the midst of the Body today are the modern-day widows and the orphans; single mothers and children growing up without fathers. Have we taken the time to get to know them and find out if they are in need? Do we think of them when we purchase yet another outfit to add to the abundant array in our closet? Do we notice that these children are still wearing last year's worn-out school shoes while our own have numerous pairs lined up at home?

Prayer: Father, forgive me for self-indulgence when members of my own church family are silently going without. Show me how I can put this right, in Jesus' name, amen.

April 25h

Jam 5:1 Come now, rich ones, weep and howl for your hardships coming on. Jam 5:2 Your riches have rotted, and your clothes have become moth-eaten. Jam 5:3 Your gold and silver have corroded, and their poison will be a witness against you, and will eat your flesh as fire. You heaped treasure in the last days.

Precious saints, in these last days all that we have heaped up for ourselves will stand as a witness against us. The affluent parts of the Body have been blessed in order that they may be generous and take care of other members in the Body who are in need. What is the point of having closets full of clothing, much of which we never wear? How can the love of God be in us if we are able to come into contact with someone in the family of God who is hungry and yet be unmoved?

The disease which is destroying many parts of the church in the western world is Self-indulgence. Wealthy local congregations redecorate their buildings annually while just down the road poor congregations are meeting in buildings without a roof or chairs. Do we not understand that we are part of the same family?

Prayer: Father, I am ashamed of my overflowing wardrobe when I see it the way You see it. Forgive me for my hardness of heart. When I neglect 'the least of these', I have neglected You, amen.

April 26th

1Co 12:25 that there not be division in the body, but that the members should have the same care for one another. 1Co 12:26 And if one member suffers, all the members suffer with it; if one member is glorified, all the members rejoice with it.

If one part of our natural body is in pain, it affects the rest of our system. When a limb is wounded, a whole rescue mission is mobilized in the form of blood-clotting agents delivered to the site, pain-reducing substances released into the area and until the wound is healed, the surrounding muscles and ligaments take the weight of the affected part.

In the same way, God intends for us to weep with those who weep; He wants us to have compassion on one another and do whatever we can to meet the need of our brother or sister, be it practically in supplying food and clothing or emotionally in encouraging and supporting them and spiritually by praying with and for them.

It is time to look past the comfort-zones of our own little cliques in the Body and begin to really see the wounded and struggling right under our noses!

Prayer: Father, I always gravitate towards those who I get on with in the Body. Open my eyes to really notice the widows and orphans right in front of me, or down the road from me, worshiping in bare feet, amen.

April 27th

Rev 3:17 Because you say, I am rich and increased with goods and have need of nothing, and do not know that you are wretched and miserable and poor and blind and naked,

When Jesus looks at His Body, He sees the whole Body. He sees those clothed in their finery, sitting in air-conditioned buildings and He sees those in rags, huddled around a single torn-out page of the Bible. The former group praise Him for the prosperity they live in, not realizing that Jesus sees the latter group as part of the same Body and is saddened at the way 'the least of these' are ignored.

Do we not realize that the Body is only as healthy as its weakest member? When we are cold, we do not get warmly dressed in multiple layers but leave our feet naked and blue with cold. As long as another part of the Body of Christ is without the daily necessities of life and we have knowledge of it, to say we are rich and have need of nothing is blindness at best - and at the worst, a tragic hardness of heart and complete lack of recognition that there is ONE Body and we are all part of one another.

Prayer: Father, burn this truth deep into my heart – there is One Body. If my brother is in need, it does impact me whether I spiritually alive enough to realize it or not. Give me salve for my eyes and soften my heart. Amen.

April 28th

1Jo 3:16 By this we have known the love of God, because He laid down His life for us. And we ought to lay down our lives for the brothers.

Love is demonstrated in the laying down of our lives and the denial of ourselves so that others may benefit. Jesus said that the world would know that we are His disciples by our sincere love for one another. Love is something that is seen in a person's actions. Jesus washed the disciples' feet as an object lesson.

He intended more than a small ritual with a basin and towel. In those days, the lesser always washed the feet of one greater. Yet here was Jesus, the King of the universe, demonstrating and more than that, modeling, the lives His disciples were to live. Love moves one to minister to our brothers and sisters in whatever way is necessary to remove the dust and debris of the journey of life from their weary feet.

Prayer: Father, give me a fresh revelation of Your love. Holy Spirit, shed this love abroad in my heart afresh, amen.

April 29th

1Jo 3:18 My children, let us not love in word or in speech, but in deed and in truth.

There are those who would say that these things we discuss are basic issues, learnt in spiritual infancy and that they would prefer meat or some rich revelation. However, the Holy Spirit desires to heal the wounds in the Body of Christ so we may present an authentic demonstration of Truth to the world. It is on account of bypassing or forgetting these foundational gems of Truth that the Body is in the sorry state it is today.

The Lord is moving in His Body as a Refiner's Fire, putting His finger on these very issues. It is love that holds the Body of Christ together as one. It is time for the Body to begin to mend the broken bridges and the dislocated limbs by demonstrating love in DEED and TRUTH. To refuse to allow God's love to flow through you to another member of the Body is to participate in the severing of life-flow to that member – and if carried out by many towards the same target will result in a diseased and weakened limb.... And eventually death will set in. We must not let this happen! LET EVERY JOINT BEGIN TO SUPPLY NOW IN JESUS NAME.

Prayer: Father, make me a channel of Your love, in every way and on every level. I want to be a bridge-builder and a joint-healer, in Jesus precious Name, amen.

April 30th

1Jo 3:14 We know that we have passed from death to life, because we love the brothers. He who does not love his brother abides in death.

This verse is so foundational to knowing we are really in the Truth – yet it is seldom preached on. Beloved, an outward sign that we really do have resurrection life within us is sincere love for the brethren! THIS is the confirmation to ourselves that our names are written in the Lamb's Book of Life – if we experience the powerful action-producing love of God deep within, moving us to express His heart to the rest of the Body.

If we are experiencing an ever-increasing river of God's love and compassion towards others, it is because the very river of Love is within our hearts. If we do not experience this, it is time to get alone with God and ask Him to reveal to us the stones and debris which have blocked this life-flow towards our brothers and sisters.

Prayer: Father, show me any stumbling block to the free-flow of Your love within my heart - however big or small, I want it removed, amen.

May 1st

*1Jo 3:23 And this is His commandment, that we should believe on the name of His Son Jesus Christ, **and love one another**, as He gave us commandment. 1Jo 3:24 And he who keeps His commandment dwells in Him, and He in him. And by this we know that He abides in us, by the Spirit which He gave to us.*

It is easy to feel a gushing theoretical love for the church across the sea in some other nation. What is difficult is to practically love the living stones right on our doorsteps that sometimes feel more like pebbles in our shoes! Only the supernatural power of the Love of God can accomplish this feat. Human love soon falls at the wayside, gasping for air, when the road gets steep.

Paul said he would glory in his weaknesses that the power of Christ may rest upon him. When we come to the end of our natural fleshly love stores and finally admit to God that we are poor in spirit and need His love to do it in us; a mighty gusher of the Kingdom will be unleashed! As John says in the above verse, the Spirit is the key person of the Godhead, accomplishing the outpouring of Love in our hearts.

Prayer Father, I admit that there are some people in the Body I really struggle to love. I am poor in spirit in this area. I need the supernatural love of God to work a miracle in my heart. Come Holy Spirit and do what You do best, amen.

May 2nd

Mat 14:14 And Jesus went out and saw a great crowd, and He was moved with compassion toward them. And He healed their sick.

Jesus was moved with compassion for people and out of this, healing power flowed to those in need. Paul says in 1 Corinthians 13 that we can give all we have to the poor but if we are doing it out of religious obligation and not from a foundation of love, we have achieved nothing. Compassion is the key which unlocks the flow of God's powerful river of healing to minister at every level, be it in the realm of spiritual bondage, emotional woundedness or physical infirmity.

Compassion moves us. Jesus felt with the feelings of these people's infirmities. The question is, what do we feel when we see someone in spiritual bondage or emotional brokenness or physical suffering? Are our hearts hard and cynical or moved by the feeling of other's infirmities, Like Jesus was?

Prayer; Father, so often I behave like a Pharisee when I see people in need, quickly summing up their situation according to my limited wisdom and passing judgment upon them for their state. Please forgive me. Do a work in my heart that unlocks the well of Your compassion within me. Deliver me from the bitter root that produces a cynical attitude, amen.

May 3rd

Mar 6:34 And going out Jesus saw a large crowd. And He was moved with compassion toward them, because they were like sheep without a shepherd. And He began to teach them many things.

When Jesus looked on people, He saw that they were struggling to know the right direction to go because no-one was leading them towards Life. Out of the compassion which moved His heart, came the teaching He gave.

When we encounter people who have lost their way and are going round and round the same mountain because they know of no other path, what is our heart reaction? Do we feel the Father's compassion for them or do we judge them according to our concept of their spiritual state? If compassion does not well up within our hearts towards the fellow-sheep caught in the thicket, then the advice which comes forth from our mouth is unlikely to be water flowing from the river under God's throne.

Prayer: Father, I so desire to speak words which bring life. I think of Your river which brings life wherever it goes. Cause that river to burst forth in me even if You have to break my hard heart to accomplish it, amen.

May 4th

Pro 15:4 AMP A gentle tongue with its healing power is a tree of life: but a perverse tongue breaks the spirit.

The word 'perverse' means 'vicious' and comes from a root meaning 'to wrench or ruin'. The word 'break' can also be translated 'to fracture, crush or shatter, to maim or cripple'. When the compassion of God moves us to speak, it will bring healing and life to the person.

The power of life and death is in the tongue. Tragically, many times we have used our tongues to crush and maim members of the family of God. The Body of Christ is wounded and bleeding, carrying the wounds which we ourselves have inflicted. Words spoken in anger or in the heat of disagreement leave lingering effects. Even words spoken out of the hearing of the person concerned have the ability to either heal or fracture.

Let us ask the Holy Spirit to set a guard before our mouths and stop us before we speak words that wound. Let us use our tongues to build up, set free and heal.

Prayer; Father, forgive me for using the weapon You have given me to use against the enemy to inflict wounds on this very Body of which I am a part. Help me to be a bridge-builder and not a demolition expert, amen.

May 5th

Rev 12:15 And the serpent cast out of his mouth water as a flood after the woman, that he might cause her to be carried away of the flood.

There are only two spiritual rivers in the earth at present; the river of the water of Life and the river which satan is releasing to destroy the Church. Which river is flowing from our mouths towards the Body of Christ? Is it the voice of the Pharisee which points fingers at Jesus in others and continually finds fault according to the letter of the Law? Or is it the voice of the faithful High Priest who forever stands as a bridge between us and the Father?

James speaks of the problem of the tongue and says a fountain cannot bring forth both bitter and sweet water from the same source. Therefore, it is imperative that we use the Holy Spirit's searchlight to ascertain which fountain we are allowing our hearts to promote. The mouth of the bitter fountain must be shut once and for all, in order to create space for the fountain of Life to gush forth. Only repentance gives God access and only His power can forever cut off any unclean river.

Prayer: My Jesus, I want to be Your spokesman. I want to be a reporter for Heaven's radio station. Please come and shut down any flow of bitter water from my heart. Forgive me for being an undercover-agent for the enemy -wash my heart first with the river that brings Life, amen.

May 6th

Rev 12:10 And I heard a loud voice saying in heaven, Now is come salvation, and strength, and the kingdom of our God, and the power of his Christ: for the accuser of our brethren is cast down, which accused them before our God day and night.

When the accuser of the brethren is cast down, the kingdom of God comes on the scene in power. This verse tells us that satan accuses the brethren day and night before the throne. The only way he is able to do that is by finding someone in the Body who is willing to voice his accusation.

It is time for the unmasking of the accuser of the brethren in the midst of the Body of Christ. He is not wearing horns and a forked tail. He is dressed in the most respectable religious garment and is often heard at prayer meetings saying "thank you Lord that I am not like other men…" He is always praying 'them versus us' kind of prayers, pointing fingers at sectors of the Body that are in some way spiritually inferior. Are you willing to cast him down?

Prayer: Father, give me true discernment to unmask the Pharisee lurking in the wings of my own heart, in Jesus Name, amen.

May 7th

Rev 12:11 And they overcame him by the blood of the Lamb, and by the word of their testimony; and they loved not their lives unto the death.

To cast down the accuser of the brethren, we must have a revelation of the message the Blood of Jesus is shouting. His blood speaks a better word than the blood of Abel. Abel's blood calls for justice but the blood of Christ calls for mercy. Satan will always try to point out the weaknesses and flaws in the rest of the Body of Christ. He loves to find fault and produce evidence to back up his accusations before the throne.

So as we stand before the throne, what is the word of our testimony? We can either be witnesses for the prosecution or witnesses for the defense. It is our choice. If we choose to join our voice with that of the faithful High Priest, Jesus, the sound of the Blood issues forth from us. If we are to not love our lives and are willing to say, "Father, forgive them, they don't know what they are doing", then the enemy is cast down and the Kingdom of God can manifest in power.

Prayer: Father, sometimes this is easier said than done, especially when I or my loved ones are the ones who have been wounded. Work in me what is pleasing in Your sight. Cause the sound of the Blood to be my life-song, amen.

May 8th

Act 3:19 Therefore, repent and turn back to God in order for your sins to be blotted out, in order that times of refreshing shall come from the presence of the Lord

Following repentance, the Lord sends seasons of refreshing in His presence. He knows we are dust and even as the potter allows his vessels time out of the fiery kiln in-between firings, so too the Master Potter knows that we desperately need times of refreshing and restoration during the application of the refiner's fire.

If He did not do this, many of us would break under these purifying dealings. This is not His purpose – His desire is to form us, not break us. Jesus was broken for us and so the refiner's fire is applied in order to destroy only the chaff and hay and stubble. The result is that the gold and silver and precious stones in our lives become clearly visible, no longer obscured by the layers which hid them before.

Prayer: Father, I am so grateful for the rest periods in this fiery process. Refresh me in Your presence today. Let Your living water flow, in Jesus Name, amen.

May 9th

Isa 42:3 A bruised reed will he not break, and a dimly burning wick will he not quench: he will bring forth justice in truth.

Sometimes, the force of our circumstances causes us to buckle at the knees. We wonder at times if we will make it out the other side. It is important at these times to remember the Father's heart towards us. Whatever He has allowed to touch our lives is not intended to destroy us but to cause Christ to be seen in our earthen vessels. It is the enemy who comes to steal, kill and destroy but Jesus came in order to give us life. Let us not confuse the motivations of these two opponents.

So on days when we feel our wick is burning very dimly, it is quite in order to lie at the feet of Jesus and just rest in His compassionate presence, knowing He does not condemn our frailty nor expect more of us than we are able to give in the fury of the storm. Receive grace to help in time of need. Before long we shall find ourselves strengthened from within and able to stand and watch Him bring forth justice in truth.

Prayer: Jesus, I so want to become all You plan for my life – but today, Lord, please send me an angel to feed and strengthen me in preparation for the next leg of our journey, amen.

May 10th

Isa 66:9 Shall I bring to the birth, and not cause to bring forth? says the LORD: shall I cause to bring forth, and shut the womb? says thy God.

The most dangerous time for the child is during the journey from the womb to independence in the outside world. On this torturous journey there is disorientation, extreme pressure and exhaustion. It is a relatively short distance but can often take hours and both the mother and child are pushed to the limits of their endurance.

In the same way, when we come to the kairos time for the bringing forth of God's promised fulfillment, there is the overwhelming urge to give up and the danger of injury to both the child and mother. This season of travail is the time to move forward step by step by faith alone, clinging to the unswerving and unfailing Word which the Spirit has given us. He will not shut the womb once the labor process has started – this is His promise in the above verse. So let us not be swayed by exhaustion or the fears that assail us in this stretching time. He will bring to pass His purposes and surely complete them.

Prayer: Father, You are an unchanging God in a changing World. I hide in You, Rock of Ages. Show me when to push and when to just breathe in preparation for the next advance towards fulfillment and the joy that is waiting, amen.

May 11th

Est 2:12 And when the turn of each young woman had come to go in to King Ahasuerus, after she had been purified twelve months, according to the law of the women (for so the days of their anointing were done, six months with oil of myrrh, and six months with sweet odors, and with the perfumes of the women).

Myrrh was used to draw out impurities, deal with infection and to heal wounds. It was also used to embalm dead bodies and is associated with suffering. In the preparation of women for the king, there was a measured season for the application of myrrh. It was the first anointing that was ministered to these women. In the same way, the Holy Spirit helps in the preparation of the Bride. There is a season for drawing out impurities; a time for bringing dross to the surface – but there is also an end to that season. The Father desires to bring to death some areas in our lives in order to bring forth the new. This is an intense season; a season of deep workings of the Spirit within our hearts; a season of the valley of the shadow of death and of the tomb – but also a measured season, with a beginning and an end. As surely as there is a dusk and a night season, there will also come a dawn and a new day.

Prayer: Father, thank you that You have placed a visual demonstration in the earth of the eternal truth that every night season is followed by a dawn. I greet my dawn by faith today, Father. Amen.

May 12th

Est 2:12 And when the turn of each young woman had come to go in to King Ahasuerus, after she had been purified twelve months, according to the law of the women (for so the days of their anointing were done, six months with oil of myrrh, and six months with sweet odors, and with the perfumes of the women).

When Esther went through this process of preparation, she was not only being prepared for intimacy with the king – she was being prepared for an appointed place of authority as the wife of the king. The season of myrrh is so necessary as it deals with and removes every area of infection and wounding.

It is imperative that we rule and administer decrees from a place of wholeness and not out of woundedness. The application of the Holy Spirit's myrrh deals with the logs in our eyes, roots of bitterness and every foothold of darkness.

At times it is extremely uncomfortable to be made aware of infection that has been lurking below the surface in our hearts.

113

It offends our spiritual pride to be confronted with the presence of unspiritual attitudes hiding in the wings of our very own inner chambers. However, this spiritual spring-cleaning must take place.

Prayer: Precious Holy Spirit, thank you for your faithful application of myrrh. I have not enjoyed this season but today I am thankful . I want to minister out of the fountain of life within and not the brackish water of old wounds. Complete the work You have begun in me, amen.

May 13th

Hos 6:1 Come, and let us return unto the LORD: for he has torn, and he will heal us; he has smitten, and he will bind us up.

The application of myrrh, the season of fire and the fuller's soap – all these dealings are in order that we may <u>return</u> from every place we have wandered away from our Father. His intended purpose is to tear down **in order to** bring healing; to break down faulty construction in our lives in order to bind up and rebuild in strength and truth. We are often unable to discern areas of weakness woven into the structure of our spiritual understandings. In order for us to withstand the intense shakings that are coming on the earth, the Lord in His kindness comes privately, beforehand, to shake what can be shaken within– to prepare us for what is ahead. Then we become aware of faulty beliefs or mindsets we have been clinging to and they can be cast aside.

As He dismantles the old in order to establish the new, there is a process of transition. We are neither what we used to be nor **where** we used to be – but we are still not who we will be; nor have we yet reached the new place appointed for us to stand.

This transition time is a time to hold onto faith that His plans for us are for GOOD, to give us a HOPE and a FUTURE!

Prayer; Father, I am in Your hand. You are busy working out Your purposes in me. Some things are going and new things are being deposited. I trust You and Your wisdom. Have Your way in me, amen.

May 14th

Isa 54:2 Enlarge the place of your tent, and let them stretch forth the curtains of your habitations: spare not, lengthen your cords, and strengthen your stakes;

In order to enlarge a tent, to make space for what God is going to bring, one has to first take down the old tent poles. Then a larger tent must be constructed. It is no good just joining new fabric onto the edge of the old tent – it will just tear along the join. The preparation for enlargement first involves a dismantling of the old in order to make way for the new.

For us, this involves the dismantling of the structure and limited boundaries of our beliefs concerning both ourselves and God. The container of our old mindsets does not have space enough to hold the new thing that God wants to pour out in our lives. However, we as human beings are creatures of comfort.

We like the security of knowing the boundaries of the circumstances we are used to. Change is an uncomfortable thing, especially when one has to dismantle the old without a clear picture of what the new will entail. WE, like our father Abraham, are called to leave the old and prepare to set out in the direction of the new – even though we have no clear idea of what it will look like!

Prayer: Father, enlargement sounds like a great idea but dismantling the old to make way for the new is nerve-wracking! Help me. Don't let fear imprison me in my old small tent, amen.

May 15th

21/07/25

*Isa 54:2 Enlarge the place of thy tent, and let them stretch forth the curtains of thine habitations: **spare not**, lengthen thy cords, and strengthen thy stakes;*

The direction of the Father in this enlarging process is that we are to 'spare not'! This means 'do not hold back, hinder, refrain or reserve'. It speaks of not letting our own narrow understanding get in the way of the BIG thing that God wants to do in and through us. It also warns us not to try and keep anything back 'incase' we want to return to our old tent! Reckless abandon to the God's mysterious GOOD purpose is in order. Our BIG God wants us to throw out our SMALL mindsets about what He is able to do in our lives. A poverty mentality goes far beyond the subject of finance.

It is time to dismantle and bury once and for all any marrow concepts of God's ability in and through us. We must ENLARGE our expectation of the moving of His hand towards us and on our behalf!

Prayer: Father, I am throwing out this old tent I have lived in and all my limited theories of the size of what You want to do in my life! You want to do abundantly above what I could think or imagine. Hallelujah!

May 16th

Isa 54:2 ...spare not, lengthen thy cords, and strengthen thy stakes; Isa 54:3 for you shall break out on the right hand and on the left.

There is a lengthening and a strengthening required in order to prepare for what is coming. Lengthening speaks of the extent and outer reaches of what God wants to do – There will be wider influence. The process of lengthening involves stretching on our part – uncomfortable but very necessary for what lies ahead!

Strengthening of the stakes is in order to be able to withstand any stormy wind that may assail you in this new place. When God increases the extent of gifting and influence in your life, the enemy is not happy. Any extension of God's kingdom means a corresponding decrease in the influence of his dark kingdom. God wants to plant you surely in this new appointed position, so follow His instructions, even though at present you are unable to see the full extent of what He is planning to do. He already is aware of the stormy wind that is gathering on the horizon. God does a sure work of preparation for this expansion and we must employ the wisdom from above as we obediently follow His directions. He wants to make us storm-proof.

Prayer: Father, You see the end from the beginning. I yield to Your superior wisdom as You prepare me for the good things ahead, amen.

May 17th

*Isa 54:3 for you shall **break out** on the right hand and on the left.*

The Hebrew word for 'break out' means 'to break through or down or over, to break or burst out (from womb or enclosure)'. Beloved Bride of Christ, breakthrough is at the door. Just as a baby violently emerges from the womb of preparation, so too God's precious saints who have been prepared in the darkness of the secret place, are about to emerge into a new chapter.

The bursting forth is not only in one direction but on every side. This is why the restriction of our old 'tent', our mindsets, must be enlarged. What is about to burst forth is far beyond what we could think or imagine. Every place where there has been an invisible wall blocking your progress, God says you are about to break through that barrier. Every place where there has been a ceiling pressing down upon your head, preventing your rising and increase, God says you are going to burst through that limitation. Begin to see it by faith, cast aside the old limited mindsets about who you are in God and what He can accomplish through you! God says, "You shall break out of this enclosure!"

Prayer: Father, if You say it, who am I to argue with You. I believe it and begin to embrace it by faith even now, amen.

May 18th

Isa 32:1 Behold, a king shall reign in righteousness, and rulers shall rule in justice. Isa 32:2 And a man shall be as a hiding place from the wind, and a shelter from the tempest, like streams of water in a dry place, like the shadow of a great rock in a weary land.

The reason God wants to make us storm-proof is this – He wants us to become a place of shelter for others. The earth is entering a time of intense shaking. People's hearts will fail them for fear.

The darker it gets, the more the Church of Jesus Christ will shine like a beacon, guiding the storm-lashed and weary to the safe harbor of Christ. He wants to make us a shelter from the tempest, a place where the shadow of the Almighty can be experienced.

The world and its systems are running out of answers in these trying times. The wisdom of man is failing. Only the wisdom found in Christ will stand unshaken in these shaking times. Will you allow God to make you a large tent where people can find refuge and see Jesus?

Prayer: Jesus, make me a strong tower for others as I embrace a deeper revelation of You as my own strong tower, amen.

May 19th

*Psa 18:19   He brought me forth also into **a large place**; he delivered me, because he delighted in me.*

God is moving you from the place of preparation into a LARGE place. The womb is quite big enough for the baby to grow in during the nine months before the birth. During this time God is adding muscle and bone; every small detail required to make this child perfect is put in place. All the child does is take in nutrition and practice small movements in order to become familiar with its limbs.

However, the real testing and use of the limbs comes after the birth. The child is brought into a large place, a place without limits or boundaries of space. This is so different from the confined area of the womb. The baby has had no experience of a place without edges or limits before. In the same way, the place

God is steadily moving you towards is so different from the place you have been prepared in. The concept 'without limitation' means nothing until you begin to experience the largeness of this appointed place God has prepared for you to stand, and more than that – to walk in!

Prayer: Father, I throw off the shackles of my old expectations of what You are able to do. Surprise me, Father with a demonstration of Your greatness, amen.

May 20th → 6/7/23

Psa 18:19 **He brought me forth** *also into a large place;* **he delivered me***, because he delighted in me.*

I receive this word

It is God who is bringing us forth into this prepared place. He has not assigned an angel to do it. He himself is the gynaecologist or birth-coach watching over the whole process of our breakthrough. He is the One who delivers us – and the first thing we set eyes on as we emerge out of this time of travail is His face!

Job went through a time of intense travail but as he emerged out the other side, he said, " I have heard of You by the hearing of the ear; but now my eye has seen You." (Job 42:5) The process of birth pangs, the tumultuous travail period, ends with a revelation of the face of our Father – we see Him as never before and with that comes the deep understanding that in all we have undergone to bring us to this place, the loving hand of our Abba Father has been evident. He brings us into a new place because He delights in us.

Prayer: Father, I have heard that all things work together for good for those who love You and are called according to Your purpose. Thank-you that I shall soon come to the place not only of hearing this, but also seeing and understanding it, amen.

May 21st →6/7/23
I receive this word today

Psa 16:5 The Lord is the portion of my inheritance, and of my cup; You shall maintain my portion. Psa 16:6 The lines have fallen to me in pleasant places; yea, I have a beautiful inheritance.

This large place we are being brought into is the revelation and manifestation of Christ within us, our inheritance.

In the womb a baby can hear the voice of its father and even leap for joy on hearing it. However, once the birth is complete, the child's experience of its father is greatly enhanced. No longer is it hearing father's voice muffled and distorted by layers of flesh and amniotic fluid. Hearing has become acutely clear and added to this is the wonder of seeing his face, smelling his fragrance and feeling his embrace.

Beloved, the exhausting journey of trail, the extreme pressure and disorientation of the appointed course, will be more than compensated by the experience of our Father God as never before. We move from a place of hearing only to the awakening of every other spiritual sense within us. It is time to TASTE and SEE that the Lord is good!!

Prayer: Father, such hope and excitement awakes in me as I look forward to experiencing my beautiful inheritance – Your presence and Your touch and fragrance tangibly with me in a way I have not yet known. Hallelujah – bring me to fullness, to the end of this journey You initiated in my life. I press towards You, Lord, amen.

May 22nd

Act 7:59 And they stoned Stephen, calling upon God, and saying, Lord Jesus, receive my spirit. Act 7:60 And he kneeled down, and cried with a loud voice, Lord, lay not this sin to their charge.

Stephen means 'crown'. He represents the Bride of Christ in the end-time ministry, who lays down her life for the extension of the Kingdom. Stephen echoed the words of Jesus on the cross, effectively saying, "Father, forgive them. They know not what they do'. He depicts the Bride who has the character of Christ so strongly manifested in her that she responds as He would in any situation. The Word has become flesh in her. She is bold, not compromising Truth as she proclaims whatever the Spirit lays upon her heart. Her words cut men's hearts.

The Bride of Christ will suffer persecution for her stand, just as Stephen did. However His death triggered the next phase of the harvest. A grain of wheat was willing to fall to the ground and die for the cause of the gospel and it yielded a rich harvest! Also, this Bride will, like Stephen, see Christ more clearly than all the religious men surrounding her with stones in their hands and hate in their hearts! And because she sees His face, she is able to respond as He did before His murderers.

Act 7:55 But being full of the Holy Spirit, looking up intently into Heaven, he saw the glory of God, and Jesus standing at the right hand of God. Act 7:56 And he said, Behold, I see Heaven opened and the Son of Man standing on the right hand of God.

May 23rd

Act 8:1 And Saul was consenting unto his death. And at that time there was a great persecution against the church which was at Jerusalem; and they were all scattered abroad throughout the regions of Judea and Samaria, except the apostles.

From the outward appearance, it seems that this great persecution that broke out against the Church was the work of the enemy. However, note the areas to which the disciples were scattered - Judea and Samaria! They were mentioned by the Lord in His promise concerning the coming of the Spirit:

Act 1:8 But you shall receive power, the Holy Spirit coming upon you. And you shall be witnesses to Me both in Jerusalem and in all Judea, and in Samaria, and to the end of the earth.

Prior to the persecution breaking out, the believers had only fulfilled the very first part of the promise. They had been His witnesses in Jerusalem, but the other areas had not been ventured into. They were meeting from house to house and enjoying the apostles teaching and fellowship and didn't move towards being a part of the complete fulfillment of this great promise. God used the persecution that broke out as a tool to thrust the equipped disciples into the greater harvest field! Today, as persecution increases and spreads in the western nations, it will effectively thrust the true Church out of their holy huddles and into the next phase of the harvest.

Prayer: Lord, help me to look past the outer appearance of what is occurring, to see Your hand in all things that touch my life, amen.

May 24th

Act 8:3 As for Saul, he made havoc of the church, entering into every house, and hauling men and women off, committed them to prison. Act 8:4 **Therefore they that were scattered abroad went everywhere preaching the word.** *Act 8:5 Then Philip went down to the city of Samaria, and preached Christ unto them.*

Like seed in the hand of the Sower, believers shall again be scattered everywhere and go forth preaching the Word. To the untrained eye it may look like a chaotic dispersion, but to the eye of God, every seed falls exactly where the wind of His Spirit blows it. Philip was blown by the wind of the Spirit to Samaria and found open ears and hungry hearts. God was also working with him, confirming the Word he preached with signs and wonders.

Joh 3:8 MSG You know well enough how the wind blows this way and that. You hear it rustling through the trees, but you have no idea where it comes from or where it's headed next. That's the way it is with everyone 'born from above' by the wind of God, the Spirit of God."

Jerusalem and the upper room in particular had been the womb where the disciples were prepared and equipped for the great task ahead. The violent birth pangs of persecution propelled those born of the Spirit into the harvest field and the Kingdom manifested. As it was then, so shall it be again, for there is nothing new under the sun!

May 25th

Act 8:26 And the angel of the Lord spoke unto Philip, saying, Arise, and go toward the south unto the way that goes down from Jerusalem unto Gaza, which is desert. Act 8:27 And he arose and went

Notice first, the Lord spoke – and immediately he got up and obeyed. This handful of seed that the Lord will scatter in this day will be those who offer themselves willingly in the day of His power (Psalm 110). They will take up their cross daily, dying to self and all its demands, and obeying the voice of the Spirit. They will not lean on their natural understanding but wait for each clear instruction from the Head, which is Christ.

Act 8:29 Then the Spirit said unto Philip, Go near, and join thyself to this chariot.

For those who are afraid at the thought of being sent into the harvest field, take comfort in this – all one needs is the ability to hear the voice of the Holy Spirit and the willingness to obey even when you don't see the bigger picture! The whole purpose of the mission was not explained to Philip in the beginning. He was just told to be at a certain roadway. There he then received his next instruction. For those who like to be in control of everything around them, this life of step-by-step adventure is torture! If we like to direct operations and have all our ducks in a row, we will find ourselves opposing and resisting the urgings of the Spirit in favor of the known, the understood and the predictable.

May 26th

Anyone who does horse-riding knows that the horse must be trained to follow the slightest nudge or direction from the rider. There is a bridal company that has been trained away from the eyes of man to respond to the slightest nudge of the Holy Spirit or the faintest direction from the Living Word. Hear Solomon as he describes his beloved, " I have compared you, O my love, to a mare in Pharaoh's chariots' (Songs 1:9). This pure bridal company clothed in white garments move forward as one body under the orders of the King of Kings. The unspoken communication and working together between this horse and Rider are like a symphony to behold. They are fearless, as His mighty horse in battle, ears trained for the inner voice of the Master, or even the slightest nudge to change direction.

Zec 10:3 ... for the Lord of Hosts has visited His flock the house of Judah, and has made them as His beautiful horse in battle.

This beautiful white horse, ridden and controlled by the Word of God, goes forth with Him, waging war in righteousness and justice! Rev 19:11 says, 'And I saw Heaven opened. And behold, a white horse! And He sitting on him was called Faithful and True. And in righteousness He judges and makes war'.

This warrior-bride, depicted by the white horse carrying His presence are the vehicle through which His righteous judgments are executed in the earth.

May 27th

Isa 42:13 The LORD shall go forth as a mighty man, he shall stir up jealousy like a man of war: he shall cry, yea, roar; he shall prevail against his enemies. Isa 42:14 I have for a long time held my peace; I have been still, and refrained myself: now will I cry like a travailing woman; I will destroy and devour at once.

The Lord is riding forth on His white horse as a mighty man or a warrior. He is crying aloud and roaring even now in the heavenlies. Can you hear it? What is He crying? It is the cry of travail, as He brings to birth His purposes in the earth. For a long time He has been silent and His people have wondered if He can hear their prayers for deliverance and justice and recompense. They have waited in the path of His judgments and clung to the promises given by the Spirit. It has seemed an interminably long wait. Yet, at the appointed time the Lord declares, " NOW will I cry, now will I arise!"

Psa 12:5 For the oppression of the poor, for the sighing of the needy, now will I arise, says the LORD; I will set him in the safety for which he pants.

Lift up your head and be expectant!

May 28th

Isa 26:20 Come, my people, enter into your chambers, and shut your doors behind you: hide yourself as it were for a little moment, until the indignation is past. Isa 26:21 For, behold, the LORD comes out of his place to punish the inhabitants of the earth for their iniquity: the earth also shall disclose her blood, and shall no more cover her slain.

Have you noticed how the Lord is globally lifting the covers off deeds of darkness that have been hiding, undetected, for many years. Every day there are new disclosures of mismanagement and fraud, even mass graves of political opponents discovered in every corner of the globe. All that has been previously hidden, is now being brought into the light so that it may be judged by the light. This is part of shaking until what cannot be shaken remains. All that is built on deceit, unrighteousness and ungodliness is now being disclosed in order to make a clear distinction between those who are of God and those who are not! The day of disclosure is also the day of recompense. Remember Haman who functioned undetected by the king in the second most powerful position of the land. He used his position as a platform to launch the evil plans in his heart. For a while it seemed he would be successful but the day of disclosure arrived and he was promptly removed. Beloved, all that has been secretly working against you is about to exposed, that you may have full understanding of the face of your enemy. Until this unfolds, hide in the secret place. Go into your chamber that you may not be affected by the Lord's dealings in this regard.

May 29th

Psa 91:7 A thousand shall fall at your side, and ten thousand at your right hand; it shall not come near you. Psa 91:8 Only with your eyes you shall look and see the reward of the wicked.

In the secret place of the Most High there is safety. When there is terror and destruction coming upon the wicked, those who have fled to the Lord for refuge are at rest in the knowledge that their lives are in His hand. He is a God of justice and wages war in righteousness.

Isa 34:8 For it is the day of the LORD'S vengeance, and the year of recompense for the cause of Zion.

Recompense for the cause of Zion; payback and restoration time for those whose names are registered in Heaven as members of the Church of the First-Born. The Lord hates robbery and will give you your recompense faithfully. All flesh shall know that the Lord, the Mighty One of Jacob is your Savior and redeemer. Remember that God hardened Pharaoh's heart in order to display His glory. Even if it seems that things are getting worse instead of better in your situation, look with the eye of faith and see God setting the stage for Him alone to receive all the glory for what is about to unfold on your behalf! Just as the Israelites saw with their eyes the reward of the wicked but it did not come near them, so too will you witness the mighty delivering hand of God working for you and against your enemies!

May 30th

Gen 9:14 And it shall come to pass, when I bring a cloud over the earth, that the bow shall be seen in the cloud

Jesus is coming in the clouds – He is coming <u>in</u> His people before He comes <u>for</u> His people. When this happens, it will be the day of the latter rain. Rain comes from clouds which are saturated with water. His cloud of witnesses are being saturated even now with the water of the Word.

Way back in Genesis there is a prophetic hint of this day in God's promise to Noah. He declares in the day when He brings a cloud over the earth; when His cloud of witnesses are brought into position in the day of latter rain, then a rainbow shall be seen in the cloud. The rainbow is a prophetic picture of the seven-fold Spirit of God operating in His prepared witnesses, who are seated in heavenly places in Christ.

This company, a cohesive heavenly Body, which has been prepared for Christ to be manifested through, is moved by the wind of the Spirit and will pour out the blessings of the latter rain upon the earth. Through these vessels operating in the sevenfold ministrations of the seven torches before the Throne will pour out a blessing that cannot be contained. They have become the windows of Heaven and as God opens these windows and releases them in this end-time ministry, a time of great fruitfulness and restoration will take place amongst God's people.

May 31st

Eze 1:28 <u>*As the appearance of the bow that is in the cloud in the day of rain,*</u> *so was the appearance of the brightness round about. This was the appearance of the likeness of the glory of the LORD. And when I saw it, I fell upon my face, and I heard a voice of one that spoke.*

Ezekiel saw the throne of God and it was surrounded by what he calls 'brightness'. Then he clarifies the appearance of this brightness – it looked like a rainbow which appears in the cloud in the day of rain! Then he goes on to say that it was a representation of the glory of the Lord! The glory of the Lord looks like the seven colors of light, which represent the seven spirits of God in their different and unique manifestations. We already established yesterday that in the day of latter rain, these seven spirits shall be seen in the cloud of witnesses. The glory of the Lord comes as light upon you, the sevenfold light of the Spirit which is before the throne. God says that darkness shall cover the earth, and gross darkness the people: but He shall arise upon His people.

In a time when the world around us looks very dark, in fact when 'gross darkness' is blanketing the people of the earth – then God chooses to send His sevenfold light upon His people! The Hebrew word for 'darkness' figuratively means 'misery, destruction, death, ignorance, sorrow, wickedness'. When these conditions abound all over the earth, our Father chooses to display His jewels, radiating the glory of the Lord!

June 1st

Isa 54:2 ...spare not, lengthen thy cords, and strengthen thy stakes

The word translated 'strengthen' is also translated 'to encourage (self), be established, to fasten'. The stakes are the things which anchor our 'tent' to the Rock of Ages. They represent our beliefs about who God is. Firmly rooted beliefs in the character and nature of our God hold us steady in the midst of any storm. God says that the process of preparing for enlargement requires us to strengthen our beliefs in just Who we are founded upon. David was well-known for doing this. When outward circumstances looked dark, he encouraged himself in the Lord. He addressed his soul and presented it with a magnificent array of God's record of faithfulness and power.

Beloved, we must daily encourage ourselves by remembering how powerful our Rock is and how eager He is to show Himself strong on behalf of those who earnestly wait for Him! Anchor yourself ever more deeply upon unfailing Truth! As we journey through the birth canal towards manifestation, let us close our eyes to the natural surroundings and begin to rehearse the awesome track-record of this mighty God we belong to.

Prayer: Mighty God of Jacob, I remind myself just Who it is that I have surrendered my life to. You have not lost power or desire to move on behalf of those you love since day one. I worship You, Rock of Ages. I lift up Your Name, unchanging God! Amen.

June 2nd

Rom 4:20 He staggered not at the promise of God through unbelief; but grew strong as he gave praise and glory to God; fully persuaded that, what God had promised, he was able also to perform.

Abraham grew strong AS he gave praise and glory to God. Here is the key to drawing strength from the treasury of God's glory – strength flows from our praise. But praise about what? Abraham praised God for the manifestation of the promise! However we can only do this IF we are FULLY persuaded as to God's ability to perform what He has promised. Unbelief in God's power or desire to fulfill His promise will rob us of the ability to praise God for the assured answer.

The result of this will be that we are weak and easily toppled during the waiting period. The question is this – is God who He says He is? If so, then the next question is – does God ever lie? The answer to that is an emphatic 'NO' . God is Truth and whatever He speaks is a portion of Truth uttered into the atmosphere. It MUST accomplish the task to which it has been sent! So let us continue to praise God with expectation because the full manifestation is on its way – and closer than we realize!

Prayer: Father – unchanging God in a changing world – I give You glory for the creative power of the Words You have already released over me! You call things that are not in existence as though they were – and they manifest. WOW, I worship You, amen.

June 3rd

*Psa 77:10 And I said, This is my infirmity: **but I will remember** the years of the right hand of the most High. Psa 77:11 **I will remember the works of the LORD**: surely I will remember thy wonders of old. Psa 77:12 I will meditate also of all thy work, and talk of thy doings.*
Psa 77:14 Thou art the God that does wonders: thou hast declared thy strength among the people.

David was famous for encouraging himself in the Lord. When he was surrounded by trouble or wrestling with storms within, he would remind himself what kind of God he served and he recalled the amazing works of God that he had heard about. He told his problem about his God and as a result he drew a fresh supply of strength from God's treasury.

So often the problem lies in our ability to endure while we await the manifestation of the promise. There is no doubt that God will perfect and perform His Word but as frail earthen vessels, there are times when we feel we are about to disintegrate from the length and strength of the battle. This is why we must tap into the secret reservoir of strength that is available to us through praise. Why drag ourselves to the finish-line when it is possible to run with head held high and arms upraised, fortified from within by divine power?

Prayer; Father, I want to keep my eyes fixed upon You, your wonder and magnificence. As I wait upon You and meditate on Your power and ability, I will renew my strength. Thank you, amen.

June 4th

2Co 4:17 For our light affliction, which is but for a moment, works for us a far more exceeding and eternal weight of glory; 2Co 4:18 While we look not at the things which are seen, but at the things which are not seen: for the things which are seen are temporal; but the things which are not seen are eternal.

Another key to standing in these days is to fix our eyes on the unseen. Paul says that the affliction (i.e. trouble, persecution and pressure) we are going through only lasts a moment in the light of eternity. If we allow our attention to be captured by that which is going on around us as things grow darker, we will find ourselves overcome. We must fix our eyes on Jesus, the Author and Finisher of our faith, who for the joy set before Him, endured the cross. What he saw with the eye of faith gave Him the strength to complete His earthly assignment.

We must train the eyes of our hearts to see as Stephen saw when he was being stoned. He saw the glory of God and Jesus standing at God's right hand - and it gave him the strength to endure his suffering and also to release forgiveness. When unkind words and vicious accusations are thrown at us, do we see Jesus and His glory or are we focused on the hate-filled faces of our enemies?

Prayer: Father, help me to keep looking on the things that are unseen. Let my whole attention be upon Jesus and the glory of God so that I may keep an eternal perspective when persecution comes my way, amen.

June 5th

Heb 10:32 But remember your former days, in which having been enlightened you endured a great conflict of sufferings [or, a great struggle with sufferings], Heb 10:33 partly on the one hand by being publicly exposed both to insults and to afflictions, partly on the other hand by having become sharers of the ones being treated in this way. Heb 10:34 For indeed you sympathized with me in my chains, and you accepted the seizure of your property with joy, knowing to be having for yourselves a better and lasting possession in the heavens.

The saints of Paul's day were not as affected by materialism as we are today. They 'accepted the seizure of their property with joy' -why? Simply because their focus was on that which was unseen. They considered the loss of earthly goods as light affliction in comparison with the great value of what was stored up for them in heaven. Paul said elsewhere, 'if you have food and clothing, with these you should be content'.

The western church has become so materialistic that we do not realize how the strong grip of the tentacles of mammon hold us down. It is time to cast aside every weight including the weight of unnecessary and surplus material possessions. We must prepare ourselves to respond quickly when the Spirit bids us follow Him.

Prayer: Father, help me to sort out what is really necessary and what is actually a hindrance and a weight in the many things I possess. I need to de-clutter both internally and externally, amen.

June 6th

1Ti 6:9 But they who will be rich fall into temptation and a snare, and into many foolish and hurtful lusts which plunge men into destruction and perdition. 1Ti 6:10 For the love of money is a root of all evils, of which some having lusted after, <u>they were seduced from the faith</u> and pierced themselves through with many sorrows.

Doctrines of demons subtly introduced from the pulpit seduce people away from the true faith and cause them to focus upon something other than Christ. One of these doctrines perverts God's idea of prosperity and encourages believers to harness their faith in order to feather their own nests. The true gospel calls us to die to self while the gospel of mammon calls us to adorn self with material possessions. Even the current teaching that there is a huge wealth transfer coming to the church (because the wealth of the wicked is stored up for the righteous) is luring many into looking for their proverbial ship to come in, instead of looking for the extension of the Kingdom of God.

Contrary to what many proclaim, the church does **not** need more money in order to advance the gospel of the Kingdom. What we need are more believers who are willing to be conformed to the death of Christ, that they may operate in resurrection power!

Prayer: Father, I can see how easily I am tossed about by every wind of doctrine. Help me to leave behind the self-seeking behavior of teenage Christianity. Bring me to a place of godly contentment with my lot, amen.

June 7th

1Ti 6:10 For the love of money is a root of all evils, of which some having lusted after, they were seduced from the faith and pierced themselves through with many sorrows. 1Ti 6:11 But you, O man of God, flee these things and follow after righteousness, godliness, faith, love, patience, and meekness.

The word used for 'flee' in the above verses is in the present continuous tense – in other words, it is an action that is done continually. Paul is warning Timothy that this will not be a one-time battle but a continuous war that he will have to fight in order to get victory. We live in the world but we are not of the world. This means we are bombarded on a continual basis by worldly values. Paul gives Timothy wise advice because he gives him some things to flee towards. It is not enough to run away from covetousness.

We must have a goal to reach towards. Without a vision people dwell carelessly and are soon overcome by the lust of the eyes and the flesh. However, if we are making every effort to increase our faith, godliness, love etc then our gaze is captured and we are not so easily seduced away from the narrow path that leads to life.

Pro 4:25 MSG Keep your eyes straight ahead; ignore all sideshow distractions. Pro 4:26 Watch your step, and the road will stretch out smooth before you. Pro 4:27 Look neither right nor left; leave evil in the dust.

Prayer: Father, deliver me of self-indulgence and self-gratification disguised as spirituality, amen.

June 8th

Act 2:44 And all who believed were together and had all things in common. Act 2:45 And they sold their possessions and goods and distributed them to all, according as anyone had need.

One of the hallmarks of the early church is that they got rid of unnecessary belongings in order to be able to give to other believers in need. What the church needs is not more wealth but the redistribution of wealth within its own walls. John points out to the Church, " But whoever has the goods of the world and continuously sees his brother having needs and refuses to show him compassion, how does the love of God abide in Him?" (1Jo 3:17)

All of us have knowledge personally of believers who are living in need and lack daily necessities. All of us have surplus goods piled up in our homes which we have not had need of for some time. Why is there a disconnection between parts of the Body? Isn't every joint supposed to supply so that the Body can edify itself in love? These are searching questions and we would prefer to wriggle out of the spotlight...

Prayer: Father, help me cut the strings that tie me to earthly goods so that I can rightly use the wealth right under my own nose for the benefit of my brethren, amen.

June 9th

Act 4:32 And the multitude of them that believed were of one heart and of one soul: neither said any of them that ought of the things which he possessed was his own; but they had all things *common. Act 4:33 <u>And with great power gave the apostles witness of the resurrection of the Lord Jesus: and great grace was upon them all.</u> Act 4:34 Neither was there any among them that lacked: for as many as were possessors of lands or houses sold them, and brought the prices of the things that were sold, Act 4:35 And laid them down at the apostles' feet: and distribution was made unto every man according as he had need.*

Oh, how we long for great power to be manifest in our midst. How we pray for an outpouring of great grace upon us. However, we neglect to notice that this verse is sandwiched in-between two others which deal directly with our attitude to our possessions and wealth. Could it be that the breaking of the stronghold of mammon upon the minds and hearts of believers is a key to releasing the power of God in our midst? Selfishness and greed are the exact opposites of the love of God. God so loved that He gave. When will we as believers love one another more than we love our earthly possessions? How we need to cry out for forgiveness because what we preach and what we live send two different messages. If we really desire to walk in great grace and witness with power, then we need to make some adjustments in our value systems and household inventories!

June 10th

Pro 30:7 Two things have I required of You; deny me them not before I die: Pro 30:8 Remove far from me vanity and lies: give me neither poverty nor riches; feed me with food appointed for me: Pro 30:9 Lest I be full, and deny You, and say, Who is the LORD? or lest I be poor, and steal, and take the name of my God in vain.

Both poverty and riches cause men to sin in different ways. Poverty makes men covet the possessions of others and they are driven to steal. Riches make men self-sufficient and proud, placing self on the throne of their lives. Being satisfied with one's earthly lot and practicing gratefulness to God for a daily supply of necessities without comparing ourselves with our neighbor's circumstances is a key to avoiding the snare of covetousness or pride. Our lives belong to God and just like Paul, we may have times of hardship and times of plenty. There are lessons to be learnt in both seasons.

Phi 4:11 Not that I speak in respect to need, for I learned to be content in whatever state I am. ... Phi 4:13 I am capable of doing all things through Christ, the One strengthening me.

It is Christ within Who gives us the ability to dwell in contentment! Too bad this particular verse has been quoted out of context for so long in the Church in order to apply it to our own self-appointed spiritual endeavors! Paul spoke of the strength of Christ being supplied in order to dwell contented, no matter one's circumstances!

1ᵗʰ June

Psa 15:1 A Psalm of David. Lord, who shall dwell in Your tabernacle? Who shall dwell on Your holy hill?

Our desire must be to abide in the tabernacle of the Lord – not to visit there on occasion, but to dwell there continually. To be one of those appointed permanent camping space on Mount Zion, we have to fulfill certain requirements. Salvation is a free gift but it is meant to be a doorway to a lifestyle marked by the presence and power of God. However, God is holy and Mount Zion is also referred to as His holy hill. The high priest in the Old Testament wore a plate on his forehead which said 'holiness to the Lord'. Only those who are holy; wholly set apart for the Lord, are able to DWELL in His tabernacle.

The plate was on the forehead, signifying a mindset in God's royal priests. We must have the same mind as Paul who said, "it no longer I who live but Christ who lives in me!" He was wholly set-apart for God. Self had been put to death at the cross and what remained was the life of Christ flowing from him. Are we living our lives as consecrated vessels, aware that we are not our own but have been bought with a price? We must be separated unto the Lord as he has a work for us to do.

Act 13:2 As they ministered to the Lord and fasted, the Holy Spirit said, So, then, separate Barnabas and Saul to Me for the work to which I have called them.

12ᵗʰ June

Psa 15:2 He who walks uprightly, and works righteousness, and speaks the truth in his heart; Psa 15:3 he does not backbite with his tongue, nor does evil to his neighbor, nor takes up a reproach against his neighbor; Psa 15:4 in whose eyes the reprobate is despised, but he honors those who fear the Lord; he has sworn to his hurt, and does not change it; Psa 15:5 he has not put out his money at interest, nor has he taken a bribe against the innocent. He who does these things shall not be moved forever.

Here David describes the lifestyle of one who dwells on the Lord's holy hill. It can be summed up in a word – INTEGRITY. How desperately the world needs to encounter believers who truly live with integrity. When one enters a smoke-filled room, one's clothing soon smells of that smoke. In the same way many believers have begun to have an odor of compromise because they live in a world of compromise. Truth and light have one thing in common – they are consistent no matter how far you investigate below the surface. They are without mixture. It is time for us as believers to live lives without mixture and double standards. Then we can DWELL in His tabernacle.

Prayer: Father, forgive me for glossing over grey areas in my behavior. I want to be full of light and single-minded. Convict me every time I am tempted, for the sake of comfort or convenience, to let a little darkness cloud my focus, amen.

13th June

Psa 43:3 Oh send out Your light and Your truth; let them lead me; let them bring me to Your holy hill, and to Your tabernacles.

We need God's light and truth to find the way to His holy hill. Jesus said, "I am the Light of the world" and "I am the way, the truth and the life; no man comes to the Father but by Me". So we see that it is not just any light or statement of truth we need, but the light of the revelation of Christ. He is the way to God's holy hill. Any practice of Christianity that does not keep Christ and Him crucified at the center of its focus has degenerated in a religious exercise.

How many sermons are preached on a Sunday without even the mention of the name of Christ? We have been fed on self- help and self-improvement sermons which are no help at all in finding our way to the hill of the Lord. They only lead us further into the swamp of the kingdom of Self. This journey of ascending the holy hill is really the working out of our salvation which we are to do with fear and trembling. Jesus lived His time on earth with a single eye, totally focused on the Father's pleasure. He provided us with a practical example of what holiness looks like. This why we need revelation of the Truth and Light He embodies in order to walk in His footsteps. We are a HOLY priesthood and a HOLY nation.

1Pe 1:15 but according to the Holy One who has called you, you also become holy in all conduct, 1Pe 1:16 because it is written, "Be holy, for I am holy."

14ᵗʰ June

Isa 55:2 Why do you spend money for what is not bread? and your labor for what never satisfies? Listen carefully to Me, and eat what is good, and let your soul delight itself in fatness.

In today's Christian world we have become so used to spending money in order to acquire books, tapes and DVDs that we hope will strengthen us spiritually. Yet at the end of the age, God tells us there will be a famine of the Word. So often we have spent our money for that which is not bread. Its title may have alluded to the freshest loaf from heaven's bakery but after finishing it, we are no more spiritually nourished or strengthened.

Isa 55:1 Ho, everyone who thirsts, come to the waters; and he who has no money, come, buy and eat. Yea, come, buy wine and milk without money and without price.

God Himself offers a free banquet. The only price attached is the sacrifice of our time! "Listen carefully to Me and eat what is good" He says. Listening takes time and attention. It is easier to buy a book and read it than to personally sit and listen for the voice of the Spirit. In the days ahead, when the unscrupulous money-changers book tables have been overturned by the jealous Bridegroom cleansing His temple, then those who have heeded the call to 'come...listen...and eat' will freely share that which they have received without cost – that others may also let their souls delight in fatness!

15th June

Isa 49:20 ... The place is too narrow for me; make space for me so that I may dwell.

For those of us who have been long in the place of preparation, frustration arises because we feel confined and restricted. All we long for is breakthrough so that we may live in peace and ease of movement. However, God does not bring us to the point of birth and bring about safe delivery just to move us to a more spacious place. The birth or breakthrough marks the beginning of a new season – a season where we walk out the good works He has prepared for us.

The word 'narrow' in the above verse also means 'anguish, distress, tribulation'. The place of preparation involves many of these things and because of our discomfort in the forming process, there is the danger of becoming focused ONLY on breakthrough; of spending our time thinking only of being released from this confined space. We must begin to seek the Lord for revelation of what awaits us AFTER the birth process. We must begin to lay hold of His purposes for us BEYOND the travail and transition season.

Prayer: Father, I see that I have become focused to some extent on my own release from the furnace of preparation. Enlighten the eyes of my heart that I may begin to behold not only my breakthrough but that which lies beyond, in Jesus Name, amen.

16ᵗʰ June

*Rev 4:1 After these things I saw, and look, a door having been opened in heaven, and the first voice which I heard was like a trumpet-blast speaking with me, saying, **"Come up here, and I will show to you what must occur after these things"***

The Father wants us to come up higher so that we may get a new perspective and see things from His vantage point. Those who have been shaped in the darkness of the secret place need to lift their vision and allow the Spirit to show us what will happen <u>after</u> 'these things'.

In order to be shown what is to occur in the future, it is necessary to 'come up here' and enter through the door in heaven. This door is none other than Jesus Christ Himself. Only as we abide in Christ can we arise to a higher place of understanding and revelation of the plans of God. The enemy would love to have us so focused upon the travail and birthing process that we see nothing of lies ahead of us. An earthly perspective weighs us down. It is understanding of what God has prepared for us that gives us the determination and stamina to keep pressing through to this new place.

Prayer; Father, thank you that through Jesus I can enter heavenly realms and begin to see what is going to happen in Your future plans for me. I desire to know the hope to which I am called, amen.

17th June

Rev 4:2 And immediately I was in the spirit. And behold, a throne was set in Heaven, and One sat upon the throne.

The first thing John saw from this higher place was the throne of God. Before we can even begin to see and understand the things which God has prepared for us, we must have a fresh revelation of the throne and Him Who is enthroned! Until the knowledge that our God is King over all of heaven and earth has really laid a hold of our hearts, we will be unprepared to grasp what He wants to do through us personally.

We must lose sight of ourselves and the smallness of our abilities and strength and become filled with the revelation of the greatness of our God and the power of His throne. Then we will not be inclined to argue with His plans for our lives for we will understand that it does not depend upon our ability or inability but upon His power and authority.

Prayer: Father, open the eyes of my heart to see You upon the throne. Give me a fresh revelation of Your majesty and power that I may lose sight of myself and see only Your greatness, amen.

18th June

*1Co 2:9 But as it is written, "Eye has not seen, nor ear heard," nor has it entered into the heart of man, "the things which God has prepared for those who love Him." 1Co 2:10 But God has revealed them to us **by His Spirit**; for the Spirit searches all things, yea, the deep things of God.*

Before John could see the throne, he had to be in the spirit. Only by revelation of the Spirit of God can we receive understanding, firstly of His greatness, and secondly of the things He has prepared for those who love Him. Reading the Word by itself will not give us that understanding. Trying to guess where our talents will lead us will not give us this revelation either. Asking other people's opinions will only confuse us - only the Holy Spirit has access to the deep things of God.

What blueprints for your life are hidden deep in the recesses of God's heart? The natural eye cannot see them, nor can the natural ear hear His whispers. We must ask the Spirit to reveal them to us! Joseph had only a dream with types and shadows in it – it was but a dim portrayal of what was about to play out upon his release from prison! But God knew every detail!

Prayer: Precious Holy Spirit, You Who know the secrets of the Father's heart, please begin to show me what the Father has prepared for me in the coming season, in Jesus Name, amen.

June 19th

Eph 3:20 Now unto him that is able to do exceeding abundantly above all that we ask or think, according to the power that works in us,

Remember we spoke a few days ago of enlarging the place of our tent, stretching the narrow parameters of our concepts of God – in order to make space for what he wants to do? Well, the above verse explains why we need to do this – God wants to do EXCEEDINGLY ABUNDANTLY above and beyond the capacity of our minds to even dream up! So stretching is the first step of the process.

The second important thing to remember is that this exceeding abundance of creative manifestation is linked to God's power working IN us! So old mindsets are dismantled to clear out and make room for His power to operate more freely in and through us! We don't realize we are cramping God's style with our narrow beliefs of His abilities!

Prayer: Father, I apologize for hemming You in with my small beliefs. Open my eyes to see how big You really are and how much You want to do in and through me, in Jesus' Name, amen.

June 20th

*Heb 12:2 Looking unto Jesus the author and finisher of our faith; who for the joy that was set before him **endured** the cross,*

Jesus had knowledge of what was before Him. He knew what awaited Him on the other side of the cross and this knowledge gave Him the power to ENDURE the suffering of the cross. Beloved, for us, the same principle holds true.

When we have revelation of what God has prepared for us AFTER the time of travail, it will forge within us strength and endurance to patiently experience the difficult season of travail – because we know the glorious afterward!

We must begin to press in and receive the spirit of wisdom and revelation to discover the parameters of the good works God has prepared for us to walk in. There is Joy set before us. May our eyes be opened to catch sight of it. For this will infuse us with endurance to run the race with patience. The valley of preparation may be dark but if you will lift your eyes and see by faith the joy set before you in the next chapter, it will give you strength to press through.

Prayer: Precious Holy Spirit, all the good works prepared for me are in Christ, that wonderful Open Door in the heavenlies. Grant me the spirit of wisdom and revelation that I might understand the purposes of the Father, in Jesus Name, amen.

June 21st

*Rom 5:3 But not only [this], _but_ we also boast [or, take pride] in afflictions, knowing that affliction produces **patient endurance**, and patient endurance produces proven character, and proven character hope [or, confident expectation], and hope [or, confident expectation] does not disappoint us, because the love of God has been poured out in our hearts by the Holy Spirit,*

We read here that affliction or tribulation also produces endurance. Psalms tells us that even though a righteous man falls seven times, he will rise again because the Lord upholds him with His hand. Beloved, the wrestlings, the unexpected blows that wind us, the attacks without and within all serve to build endurance in us so that we are equipped to finish the course appointed us. God never leaves us but is right there holding out a hand and helping us to our feet again.

From the endurance that develops, our character is formed. We become vessels who can be entrusted with the secrets of Heaven. The refining process has done its work and we have become arrows sharpened in the shadow of His hand and He can send us where He wills.

Prayer: Father, the time in the shadows is not pleasant. The sharpening process is painful but I understand You are preparing me deep within to withstand any stormy wind that would try to blow me off-course. I trust Your wisdom, amen.

June 22nd

Isa 6:5 Then said I, Woe is me! For I am undone; because I am a man of unclean lips, and I dwell in the midst of a people of unclean lips: for mine eyes have seen the King, the LORD of hosts

The first thing John saw in Heaven was One seated on the throne. When Isaiah saw this same scene, he was undone. He realized just how holy and powerful God was – and he also realized how unclean he was in comparison. He suddenly understood that the words of his mouth were unclean and that the things he had spoken fell far short of what was expected of him. Great conviction came upon him. Our eyes need to be opened to SEE Him afresh.

The first thing that follows a fresh vision of the King of Kings is a season of repentance and re-consecration. This is to prepare us as vessels to receive the plans He wants to share with us.

Prayer: Father, the words of my mouth and the meditations of my heart must be pleasing in your sight. As I gaze upon Your majesty, I realize how small and unclean I am compared to You. How grateful I am for the Blood of the Lamb, which cleanses me, amen.

June 23rd

Isa 6:6 Then one of the seraphs flew to me, having a live coal in his hand, snatched with tongs from the altar. Isa 6:7 And he laid it on my mouth and said, Lo, this has touched your lips; and your iniquity is taken away, and your sin purged. Isa 6:8 And I heard the voice of the Lord, saying, Whom shall I send, and who will go for us? Then I said, Here am I; send me!

Once Isaiah has been through a cleansing process, the Lord asks a question. It seems the Godhead is just asking amongst themselves, wondering what the best plan is – then Isaiah puts up his hand and volunteers. He does not even know what the assignment is yet but the cleansing and re-consecration has worked in him a willing heart. He has seen a vision of the God whom he serves and is willing to go anywhere and do anything He asks.

Beloved, we need first a fresh vision of the One upon the throne. If we cannot see Him clearly, how can we become like Him? It is as we behold Him that we are changed from glory to glory. The earth needs to see His face in us.

Secondly we need an encounter with a fiery coal from the altar to cleanse us and bring us to the place of willingness to volunteer as a messenger of the Lord. Isaiah didn't even know what message he would be carrying before he signed up for the task. Would we be as willing to put our name forward? The volunteering came before the unfolding of the blueprint in Isaiah's case. Willing bondservants are what the Lord needs in this hour.

Prayer: Father, please forgive me for not trusting You enough. I always want to know what I am in for before I will step up to the plate. Work in me a willing heart, one which just hears Your desire and runs to meet it, in Jesus Name, amen.

June 24th

Psa 110:3 Your people shall offer themselves willingly in the day of Your power, in holy array from the womb of the morning spring forth Your young men who are as the dew.

From the womb of the morning will come forth young warriors that have emerged from a season of travail. They will volunteer willingly; there will be no manipulation or coercion. Why? Because they have seen the Lord of Hosts upon His throne and He is extending His scepter from Zion and ruling in the midst of His foes.

All over the earth the Holy Spirit is recruiting this warrior Bride. She is one who abandons herself into the service of her Beloved Bridegroom. She takes no thought for self-preservation or the applause of man. Her eyes gaze upon the face of the King of Kings and she is transformed from glory to glory. As she hears the voice of Her Lord saying, "Whom shall we send?" there is no hesitation in her response.

Just as the dew covers the whole earth in the morning, so too this Bride will appear all over the earth, in the beauty of holiness, bringing refreshing to all she comes into contact with. And the Lord at her right hand will slaughter kings in the day of His power!

Prayer: Lord, I too want to be found among these who offer themselves willingly. All I have to give you is myself. Here I am, Lord, amen.

June 25th

Heb 12:22 But you have come to Mount Zion and to the city of the living God, the heavenly Jerusalem, and to an innumerable company of angels, Heb 12:23 to the general assembly and church of the first-born who are written in Heaven, and to God the judge of all, and to the spirits of just men made perfect

This bridal company assembles on Mount Zion, not at an earthly location. They are those which make up the heavenly Jerusalem, the city where God dwells. We must remember that we are not part of an earthly company but a heavenly company. We are members of the church of the first-born. As long as we continue to consider ourselves members of separate factions of the Body on earth, we will never truly grasp the revelation of what God is doing in the heavenlies.

There is only one church known in Heaven and that is the church of the first-born. The spirit of religion desires to separate the Body, magnify differences and elevate one group above another. The Spirit of Christ seeks to unify the Body and glorify Christ alone. If we are truly part of the company on Mount Zion, we will live our lives from a different vantage point. We will relate to one another in the Body differently.

Prayer: Father, help me to live my life bringing heaven to earth and not just standing on earth gazing up into the heavens. Help me to see as You see and hear what You are saying so I can be about my Father's business, in Jesus Name, amen.

June 26th

Heb 12:27 MSG The phrase "one last shaking" means a thorough housecleaning, getting rid of all the historical and religious junk so that the unshakable essentials stand clear and uncluttered.

God intends to shake everything that can be shaken one last time. This is for our good, because it will remove everything which is not of Him. Everything in our belief systems which is part of the earthly Jerusalem instead of the heavenly Jerusalem will fall away in this shaking. The religious rituals which we find so hard to stop of our own accord, will be shaken loose and fall away.

So we must not dread the shaking but welcome it as coming from the hand of a kind and good Father. He knows what is essential and what is superfluous in our lives. It will be necessary to travel light in the coming days. All unnecessary baggage must be left at the roadside if we want to run and not become weary.

Do not fear the shaking, when it is the hand of your Father Who loves you causing it. All His plans for you are for good. You can trust Him completely.

Prayer: Father, I submit to Your wisdom. Spring-clean my spiritual house and take away anything I have hoarded that is not necessary for the coming journey, amen.

June 27th

Heb 12:28 Therefore, since we are receiving a kingdom that cannot be shaken, let us have grace, by which we may serve God

acceptably with reverence and godly fear, Heb 12:29 for also,
"Our God is a consuming fire."

Let us be comforted as all is shaken within and without. The Kingdom of God within us is unshakable. It does not even wobble in the midst of the most severe storm. No matter what else is removed in these shakings, that which has its origin in heaven is immovable.

God's last shaking is designed to make us streamlined and pure - no more mixture in our doctrines. The fire of God will consume all chaff and stubble in the religious systems of man. The wisdom of man will come to nothing in these days and those who operate in the wisdom of God will be sought out. The grace of God will be heavily upon those serving Him in godly fear.

Prayer: Father, I know the coming days will be uncomfortable, especially for those who try to hold on to their own kingdoms. Grant me grace to walk in the fear of God. Increase the deposit of Your kingdom within me, amen.

June 28th

Dan 12:10 Many shall be purified, and made white, and tried. But the wicked shall do wickedly. And none of the wicked shall understand, but the wise shall understand.

An angel informs Daniel that in the end-times, there will be shaking and trouble. It will be a time of refining and purifying. Those who are wise will understand what is happening and their faith will not be shaken because they know the kingdom of God will remain unshaken. They will continue in the fear of God no matter what happens in the world around them.

The Holy Spirit will bring to remembrance the things that Jesus has said and the Word will be a light to their feet, even though there is darkness around them. They know they are citizens of another kingdom; part of the bridal company on Mount Zion. From this place God is extending His scepter and ruling in the midst of His foes.

Beloved, don't focus on the wicked and what they are doing. Set your eyes on Jesus, the Author and the Finisher of your faith! He will give you understanding and make you a shelter for others in this time.

Prayer: Father, as the shaking comes, help me to remember Whose I am and use me to extend Your scepter even into the darkness and turmoil. Let Your kingdom come, on earth, as it is in heaven, amen.

June 29th

Isa 60:2 For, behold, the darkness shall cover the earth, and gross darkness the people: but the LORD shall arise upon you, and his glory shall be seen upon you.

In the time of greatest darkness, the bridal company will arise, resplendent with the glory of God. We will not function according to the natural, but will walk by the light of the heavenly city of which we are citizens. This will be clearly evident and people will notice that we are unmoved by the shakings and the dense darkness. They will be drawn to us as moths to the flame and as we share the reason for the hope within us, a great harvest of souls will be brought into the kingdom.

The difference between the darkness of religion and the vibrancy of a real relationship with Christ will be plain to see. Psalm 91 tells us that darkness and light are the same to God. So too will they be the same to the end-time Church. The state of the world around us will not intimidate or depress us. We will go from glory to glory, for we walk gazing upon His face.

Prayer: Lord, make my life a light-house that guides people safely through the stormy seas to You. You are the only safe harbor I know, amen.

June 30th

Rev 21:23 And the city had no need of the sun, nor of the moon, that they might shine in it, for the glory of God illuminated it, and its lamp is the Lamb. Rev 21:24 And the nations will walk by the light of it; and the kings of the earth bring their glory and honor into it.

This beautiful heavenly city that is descending out of heaven does not look to the earth's sources of light. She is lit up from within by the glory of God. Her lamp is the Lamb. Because He is within her, she becomes the light of the world. The coming days of shaking will cause every false source of light to be extinguished. Every messenger of satan that has masqueraded as an angel of righteousness will be so shaken that his charade will be exposed for what it is.

We are entering the days when the foundations will be exposed. Only that which is founded upon Christ, the solid Rock, will pass safely through the upheaval. Many will look to the citizens of the heavenly Jerusalem for guidance and counsel in the time to come.

Let us seek the spirit of wisdom and revelation that we may be those who have understanding of the times, to know what to do.

Prayer: Father, human wisdom is foolishness and will not get me through the season that is upon us. Grant me the spirit of wisdom and revelation in the knowledge of Christ, I pray, amen.

July 1st

2Pe 1:2 Grace and peace be multiplied to you through the knowledge of God and of Jesus our Lord,

Grace or favor comes upon our lives in increasing measure as we grow in our knowledge of the Father and of Jesus. This word 'knowledge' actually means 'full discernment and comprehension'. It is not referring to a vague head knowledge that the Godhead exists but rather speaks of an ever deepening relationship and discovery of who the Father and the Son are.

The other benefit of this growing closeness with the Father and Jesus is an accompanying increase of peace within our hearts. Though there may be storms raging externally, the rule of peace within our temples is ever multiplying. This word 'peace' is also translated 'prosperity' which means all-round wellbeing in body, soul and spirit! How vital it is to make our relationship with the Godhead of utmost priority.

This Light that lights the heavenly city also radiates grace and peace, or if you prefer, favor and prosperity, in rays that become stronger and stronger (they multiply). No wonder the Word teaches us that we go from glory to glory as we behold Him!

Prayer: Father, I want to know You more deeply. I want to really discover how You think and Who You are. I want to know Jesus in the same way. This will only happen as I fellowship with You both. Help me to prioritize my life correctly, amen.

July 2nd

2Pe 1:3 according as His divine power has given to us all things that pertain to life and godliness, through the knowledge of Him who has called us to glory and virtue,

Once again we find that the provision of everything we need for this life is directly linked to the depth of our relationship with God. He has already made this abundance available to us – we can tap into any resource we need, IF we are in a vital and vibrant relationship with God the Father AND Jesus. How tragic that many of us go through life feeling we do not have the necessary wisdom or revelation we need for our situation, when it is sitting there just waiting for us to press in and find it!

The Father has called us to 'glory and virtue'. This word 'virtue' is not one that is used much nowadays. It means 'manliness, valor' and is associated with strength and power to accomplish the task at hand. God never intended for us to flounder when faced with difficult situations or seemingly impossible problems. The full intimate knowledge of the Father and Jesus makes available to us His treasury of power – and this is the source of both glory and strength. Let us press in and get to know more intimately the parameters and extent of this power at our disposal!

Prayer: Father, everything I will ever need to equip me for any situation I encounter, is found in the depths of relationship with You. I want to press in deeper and further, amen.

July 3rd

2Pe 1:4 through which He has given to us exceedingly great and precious promises, so that by these you might be partakers of the divine nature, having escaped the corruption that is in the world through lust.

The Father intends us to be partakers of the divine nature – in other words, all of us should be sharing and steadily increasing in the kind of life-flow that produced resurrection. Jesus said 'I am the Resurrection and the Life' -It wasn't a different power source that was used to raise Jesus from the dead, but the very same one to which we are invited to drink from!

So how do we tap into this divine life-source? This verse tells us that the amazing promises we have been given are the tool we use to access this treasury. Peter calls these promises 'precious'. Have we treasured the promises given to us? Have we valued them and considered them to be of great worth or have we glossed over them, hardly giving them a second glance? If something is not considered precious to us, we will make no effort to prevent it being stolen or to hide it in our hearts.

Prayer: Father, I realize that sometimes I have not esteemed Your promises enough. Please forgive me for treasuring Your great promises to me, for treating them like any other common saying, amen.

July 4th

Psa 119:162 I rejoice at Your Word, as one who finds great spoil.

Do we pounce upon the promises of God as if discovering a great treasure? Are we filled with joy when we come across one of His statements of intent towards His children? For many of us in nations where freedom to worship is taken for granted and the Bible is readily available, we treat as common these 'exceedingly great and precious promises'. In other countries our brothers and sisters in Christ are tearing up and sharing single pages of the Word and hungrily devouring every syllable of the Father's communication to them. They suck every ounce of spiritual nourishment out of single verses; memorizing and meditating deeply upon each phrase. Such action causes the Word to become flesh in them. They can use a single written promise in the Word as a doorway into a deep and effective relationship with the Godhead.

Prayer; Father, forgive me for not valuing Your Living Word and treasuring Your promises. I want to regain a reverence and awe for the exceedingly great promises given me. Help me, I pray to recover what I didn't even realize had been stolen from me, amen.

July 5th

Psa 119:103 How sweet are Your Words to my taste! More than honey to my mouth!

We need to devour the Word of God, preferring its taste to any saccharine-sweet diet the world and its systems have to offer. Moreover we need to prefer the taste of the pure Word of God above the psychology-riddled humanistic sermons on most of the present-day Church's daily menu! Remember too that the religious spirit depicted as the strange woman in Proverbs offers us a meal of secret bread and stolen water. Her lips drip honey but turn bitter in your stomach.

Stick to the Word of God, explained by the precious Holy Spirit. Hunger and thirst for it because this is what man shall live by. Depend less on Christian books and CDs and more upon the sweet times of tasting the Word broken for you by the Spirit. This will truly nourish Your spirit. Memorize scripture and you will discover that the verses pop into your mind just as you need them, out of the rich storehouse you have conscientiously filled in past days.

Prayer: Father, restore to me the hunger I had for the Word when first I came to know You. Forgive me for allowing it to be eroded by a steady diet of entertainment and religion, amen

July 6th

Psa 119:99 I have more understanding than all my teachers: for Your testimonies are my meditation.

If we desire wisdom and understanding we must stop looking to man as our source and return to meditating upon the pure Word of God. Men of God can teach us only as much as they have discovered themselves. So if we rely totally upon others in the Body to feed us spiritually we are deliberately limiting our spiritual growth to the measure they have achieved.

This is not what the Father intended for us as His sons. He desires us to discover the depths of the wisdom and knowledge hidden within Christ for ourselves and has provided a teacher, the Holy Spirit, as our personal tutor. If we follow His personally designed curriculum for us, we will find that He reveals spiritual truths to us which others have not even accessed yet. The depths and heights of our discoveries in Christ are limited only by our own hunger! Rejoice in HIS Word as one who finds great spoil. Dig deep into the Word and ask the Holy Spirit to shine His light on the hidden treasure within.

Prayer: Holy Spirit, thank-you for sharing the riches of the Word of Christ with me. I want to go deeper and further, energized by the awesome nature of the Truth I discover, amen.

July 7th

Psa 119:98 Through Your Commandments You make me wiser than my enemies, for they are ever with me.

Not only does the meditation of the Word give us more understanding than our teachers, but also equips us to deal with those which oppose us. The Word of God is living and active – when it is hidden in our hearts, it is a continually bubbling source of life, ministering wisdom and counsel for every situation we meet.

The Word in us is continually weighing up and rightly dividing whatever is facing us and giving us strategic counsel in order to wage war and get victory. If satan had known God's plan, he would not have crucified the Lord of Glory. The strategy of the cross outwitted the enemy and brought him to his knees. Today, the Spirit is still using the wisdom of the cross as effective strategy in dealing with our enemies!

We do not need to prepare lengthy speeches when we are brought before authorities or legal benches for our faith. The

Holy Spirit gives us the suitable portion of the revealed Word for that situation right at the moment we need it.

Prayer: Father, I rejoice because my part is to soak myself in Your Living Word. Then I am equipped to face whatever comes and emerge victorious! Hallelujah!

July 8th

Psa 119:18 Open my eyes, so that I may behold wonderful things out of Your Law.

It is possible to read whole chapters of the Bible and get absolutely nothing life-giving out of them. Generations of religious organizations bear testimony to this. The key to obtaining the life and power of God from the written Word is receiving revelation from the Holy Spirit. We must not lean on our own understanding. Men who have done this have produced libraries full of the doctrines of man – bringing bondage to countless millions since the book of Acts.

It is the Spirit of Truth Who opens our eyes to behold wondrous things in the Word. Only He has been delegated the authority to unlock the wisdom of Heaven for the benefit of man. It would serve us well to entreat His help every time we eat a portion of the Bread of Life. Remember the two men at Emmaus whose eyes were opened to see Jesus in the breaking of bread? Let us ask the Spirit of Truth to open our eyes to see our Bridegroom ever more clearly as He breaks bread with us daily.

Prayer: Spirit of Truth, come and reveal to me the different facets of truth hidden in the verses I chew. Help me to glean all the available nourishment from them. Give me understanding, in Jesus Name I pray, amen.

July 9th

2Pe 1:3 according as His divine power has given to us all things that pertain to life and godliness, through the knowledge of Him <u>***who has called us to glory and virtue***</u>,

Beloved, the Father has called us to glory and virtue – this is the expected end He desires us to reach. This is the destination which He intends the discovery of the Word of Truth to lead us to! Glory and virtue – the manifestation of heaven's power and presence in our midst – no less is acceptable for the true believer!

We must lift our eyes and begin to see once again the destination which we are moving towards. We are heading for glory and virtue. We are moving towards a manifestation of God's power in us and through us. He has called us to this destination and for this purpose. Do we honestly believe it or are we just plodding on, going through the motions and trying to live good lives. We must begin to develop a hunger to see glory and virtue, not just on some far-off continent but right in our own lives and our own circumstances. He is a God Who shows Himself strong on behalf of those who earnestly wait for Him!

Prayer: Father, if You called me to glory and virtue, then it is not only possible but probable that I will experience both! I set my face like a flint towards this goal. Help me to attain it, amen.

July 10th

*Phi 3:12 Not as though I had already attained, either were already perfect, but I am pressing on, if I may **lay hold of that** for which I also was taken hold of by Christ Jesus.*

What are we supposed to lay hold of? Why did Jesus take hold of us? The Father has called us to glory and virtue. This is what we are possessed by Christ for!

The Greek word translated 'lay hold of' is 'katalambano' and actually means 'to eagerly seize for one's own possession'! Does that sound like hunger is involved? Are you hungry to see the virtue and power of God in your life? Do you long for His glory to be seen through you? Then you are in good company – this was the very thing that Paul pressed towards. He hungered for a deep intimate knowledge of Christ because he knew that glory and virtue were found there. And the key to laying hold of this prize was letting go of what had been before, in order to free his hands up to grasp what was still coming. Don't cling to the good of the past. Realise that what is still laid up in store for you is even better and greater than this!

Prayer: Lord, I also want to press on to eagerly seize this glory and virtue You have intended me to have. Lead me, I pray, amen.

July 11th

*Mar 5:30 And Jesus, immediately knowing in himself that **virtue** had gone out of him, turned him about in the press, and said, Who touched my clothes?*

It was virtue which healed the woman with the issue of blood and every other person who was made whole by Jesus. Do we desire to be custodians of His healing virtue? Are we hungry for His glory to be manifested in making men whole?

Virtue is a spiritual substance – we know this because Jesus felt some leave His body. The Bride of Christ should be full of the same life-giving virtue. To this we are called – but whether we lay hold of it is up to us. We must press on, no matter the hardships or obstacles; no matter whether we are rejected by men of the cloth and scorned by those who call themselves our brothers. Nothing must persuade us to deviate from this path or prevent us from taking hold of that for which we have been taken hold of!

You were born for a purpose and you must lay hold of that purpose. The Kingdom of Heaven is waiting for you to become part of its extension in the earth.

Prayer: Father, strengthen me in my inner man so that I may not be distracted from laying hold of the glory and virtue You have intended for me, amen.

July 12th

*2Pe 1:5 But also in this very thing, bringing in all diligence, filling out your faith with **virtue**, and with virtue, knowledge;*

Peter also encouraged the church to add virtue to their faith. He knew that the natural result of a man exercising faith was a corresponding increase in manifestation of the power of God! Faith without works is dead – but what are these works to be?

The Word tells us that we are His workmanship created to do good works, which He has prepared for us to walk in. We must not walk in our own dead religious works, but in those works that the Father has appointed us to walk in. The Pharisees were always filling their days with religious works, publicly praying long prayers and giving to the poor in order to gain the praise of men. In their own imaginations they excelled in good works – yet Jesus called them a brood of vipers! There was no evidence of the glory and virtue of God in their lives. Is there in ours? Have we added virtue to our faith?

Jesus only did what He saw the Father doing. Don't be busy with your own soulish endeavors. Ask the Spirit to help you see what the Father is doing. Then get involved there!

Prayer: Father, I don't want my life to full of empty religious works. I desire to be walking in the good works You have prepared for me to walk in. Show me what You desire me to do, amen.

July 13th

Joh 9:4 I must work the works of him that sent me, while it is day: the night cometh, when no man can work.

Jesus said this just before He healed the man who was born blind. In other words, this healing was one of the works of the Father and His desire is for us walk in similar good works! Jesus came to bring life to every area where death reigned, whether in body, soul or spirit. He was the first-born of many brethren and we, as children of God, are intended to do the very same thing – bring the life and power of God into every area where death has been at work.

169

This is the work of the Kingdom, when the life of Heaven invades the earthly realm and drives back darkness and disease. This is the will of God that must be done on earth. He is looking for vessels willing to co-labor with Him in letting the Kingdom come on earth.

Don't you want to be a part of driving back the kingdom of darkness? The way you do this is by working the works of Him Who sent you to be a blessing to the world.

Prayer: Father, I want to work Your works. I want to be a part of introducing the Kingdom of God to earth. Use me, Lord. Help me to add virtue to my faith, amen.

July 14th

Jam 2:26 For as the body without the spirit is dead, so faith without works is dead also.

If we say we believe that God heals the sick and sets the captive free, yet do not pray in full confidence when the opportunity arises, then our faith has no life. The natural outcome of the exercise of faith is the flow of God's power and virtue.

The mandate of Isaiah 61 is our mandate as the Bride of Christ. The Spirit of the Lord is upon us in order to preach good news to the poor, bind up the broken-hearted and proclaim liberty to the captive! Jesus re-emphasized this when He sent out His disciples after the resurrection. He said that believers would heal the sick and cast out demons amongst other things!

The church of Jesus Christ has become too comfortable with the presence of sickness and the working of death in our midst. It is time to rise up and begin to work the works of God, fully confident that we have the whole of Heaven's backing and God's power and virtue at our disposal!

Prayer: Father, forgive me for settling for mediocrity in my walk, for not rising up and boldly proclaiming the entrance of Your kingdom. Your Spirit is upon me for a purpose far beyond goose-bumps or comfort. Ignite my faith again, in Jesus Name, amen.

July 15th

Mar 16:20 And they went forth, and preached everywhere, the Lord working with them, and confirming the word with signs following.

The key here is obedience. Jesus said 'Go…and preach' and they went forth and did it. Because of their obedience, the Lord was there with them, co-laboring AND confirming what they said with signs manifesting. What signs were these? Simply those He had mentioned when He gave the commandment to go – 'In my name shall they cast out devils; they shall speak with new tongues; they shall take up serpents; and if they drink any deadly thing, it shall not hurt them; they shall lay hands on the sick, and they shall recover'.

For too long we have stayed instead of going, endlessly studying the theory and the principles but failing to just simply obey. It is in the going that we shall see the signs following! If we are afraid that we will step out and nothing will happen, remember that it is your part to step out. It is His part to work with you confirming

171

the Word with signs and wonders. Dare to believe for something wonderful.

Prayer: Lord, shake up my comfort zone and show me specifically where You want me to go. Fill me afresh with the power of Your Spirit. Light a fire in me, Father, amen.

July 16th

Isa 61:1 *The Spirit of the Lord GOD is upon me; because the LORD has anointed me to preach good tidings unto the meek; he has sent me to bind up the brokenhearted, to <u>proclaim</u> liberty to the captives, and the opening of the prison to them that are bound;*

The word 'proclaim' means 'to call out, to pronounce'. So often we pray and ask God to set people free, yet He calls us to proclaim or announce it! It is pointless to ask the Father to do something He has given us the authority to do ourselves. If I gave you a key to my front door, you would not need to ask me to unlock the door for you – the key is in your own hand!

It's time to rise up, Bride of Christ, and announce and decree liberty to all we encounter who are captive. Be confident in the delegated authority you possess! Less begging at the gates of Heaven and more decreeing is in order. Let every prison door be opened now in Jesus Name!

Prayer: Father, I have wasted so much time and prayed so many well-intended but powerless prayers for the release of family and friends. I will now rise up and use the authority You paid so dearly to purchase for me, amen.

July 17th

Isa 61:2 To proclaim the year of the Lord's favor, and the day of vengeance of our God; to comfort all that mourn;

Here is another decree we need to make over ourselves and others – this is the year of the Lord's favor! The original language carries within it the sense of debts canceled, reconciliation and pardon. Do we realize how powerful that proclamation is? Imagine a judge deliberating a sentence for an offender. Then he brings his hammer down and declares that every debt is from henceforth canceled and the prisoner is pardoned and must be instantly released! Can you see the joy that erupts in that prisoner's heart? See him being unshackled and the cell door opening. Watch him walking out into the sunshine, every weight of guilt and shame falling from his shoulders. See him reconciled to the Father.

This is the honor we have, Beloved – we have the delegated authority and anointing to proclaim pardon and favor over people who are weighed down by guilt and sin. The Blood of Christ has canceled every debt and paved the way home. All prisoners have received a royal pardon! Let's announce it everywhere we go!

Prayer: Father, I have been waiting for You to do things that You have assigned me to do. Now that I realize, I will not wait any longer. I will proclaim the year of Your favor, amen!

July 18th

Isa 61:3 To appoint unto them that mourn in Zion, to give unto them beauty for ashes, the oil of joy for mourning, the garment of praise for the spirit of heaviness; that they might be called trees of righteousness, the planting of the LORD, that he might be glorified.

'To appoint' – here is another word that carries authority. You as an ambassador of the Kingdom have been released with authority to appoint every good thing that the Kingdom embodies into the lives of others. Rise up and begin to release the goodness of God where darkness has reigned.

In the above verse there are exchanges that are described. Instead of ashes, heaviness and mourning (all associated with death), you must begin to appoint beauty, joy and new garments! All judgments which are passed begin with a decree spoken. Begin to boldly speak as a representative of the Throne.

Today, find someone sitting in the ashes of their loss and decree the year of the Lord's favor over them. Decree the oil of joy as a replacement for mourning. Be the one that opens prison doors by the words of Life in your mouth. Be the one that peels the bandages off and unwraps graveclothes.

Prayer: Lord, this excites me. I have waiting for You to do something. Meanwhile, You are waiting for me to do what you've authorized me to do! Hallelujah! I get it!

July 19th

Isa 61:3 To appoint unto them that mourn <u>in Zion</u>, to give unto them beauty for ashes, the oil of joy for mourning, the garment of praise for the spirit of heaviness; that they might be called trees of righteousness, the planting of the LORD, that he might be glorified.

We see that the ones primarily intended to receive this exchange are 'in Zion'. In other words they are in the Church. Why do God's people need to have the trappings of death removed? 2 Corinthians 3:6 tells us that the letter kills but the spirit gives life. In every place where the spirit of religion has held sway death will be evident. One of the main assignments of the Spirit of the Lord is to deliver God's children from religious bondage. Where the Spirit of the Lord is, there is liberty!

Perhaps the first place we need to proclaim and appoint is over our own lives. Are we experiencing ashes, mourning and heaviness of spirit? Arise and decree these exchanges over yourself today! Proclaim a change of atmosphere. Begin to breathe heaven's pure air!

Prayer: Father, I proclaim the year of Your favor over myself and the day of Your vengeance on my enemies. I command the removal of every vestige of death, ashes and mourning from my body, soul and spirit and I appoint beauty and the oil of joy to replace it. Let new garments be released from heaven's wardrobe for me today, in Jesus wonderful Name, amen.

July 20th

Isa 61:3 ...that they might be called trees of righteousness, the planting of the LORD, that He might be glorified.

Why are we given authority to proclaim these things? It is so that our lives and the lives of those we minister to may be living testimonies of His power and love. God desires to be glorified though us. He wants to make His people trees of righteousness. What does this mean?

Well, an apple tree produces apples. A tree of righteousness produces fruit of righteousness. This Hebrew word translated 'righteousness' can also mean 'justice'. God wants our lives and those we touch to display His justice.

God's version of justice is not like man's. The Message Bible puts it like this: *GOD sent me to announce the year of his grace-- a celebration of God's destruction of our enemies.* God's justice means a pardon for us and a destruction of the work of the enemy in our lives.

Prayer: Father, how amazing is this gift of grace and favor You freely give to us. May I bear fruit of righteousness for others to eat of, amen.

July 21st

12:22

Act 10:38 How God anointed Jesus of Nazareth with the Holy Ghost and with power: who went about doing good, and healing all that were oppressed by the devil; for God was with him.

Jesus was the first Tree of Righteousness. He went about doing GOOD and healing ALL who were oppressed by the devil. We are born of the incorruptible seed of this Tree of Life. It is time to stop sitting on all the potential within us to bring forth fruit of the same kind!

As Jesus doing good and healing, He told people that the kingdom of God had come to them; "*But if I with the finger of God cast out devils, no doubt the kingdom of God is come upon you*". Whenever life and joy and peace replace sickness and torment, it is evidence of the arrival of the Kingdom of God! You could say that the fruit we bear is full of the juice of Kingdom Life!

Prayer: Lord, because You are in me, I can bring forth Kingdom Life. Let us do good today and proclaim liberty to anyone we meet who is held captive. Let Your Kingdom come, amen *Amen!!!*

July 22ⁿᵈ

Mat 6:10 Your kingdom come. Your will be done, as in heaven, so on earth.

When Jesus taught his disciples how to pray, He was <u>not</u> giving a few sentences to recite like a mantra. He was showing them how to achieve results in their interaction with Heaven. 'Let Your Kingdom come' is a decree, not a tentative request. We already know that God's declared intention IS for His Kingdom to be manifested on earth. This is why He sent Jesus. So 'let Your Kingdom come' is more a proclamation for a feast to begin – a feast of His goodness.

The keys of the Kingdom, which have been handed to us, are for the purpose of releasing the Life and power of Heaven into earth's atmosphere. Don't let them just hang from your belt. Begin to proclaim the arrival of the Kingdom at every scene where death has been at work!

Prayer: Father, there are some announcements I need to make over myself and others. Thank you the Heaven's authority is behind my spoken words, amen.

July 23rd

Gen 1:2 And the earth was waste and void; and darkness was upon the face of the deep: and the Spirit of God moved upon the face of the waters Gen 1:3 And God said, Let there be light: and there was light.

Here we read the first proclamation God made on planet earth – Let there be Light! It is <u>exactly</u> the same kind of proclamation and decree we are authorized to make. Wherever we encounter a situation that is without form (desolate, confused) and void (an indistinguishable ruin, empty) we are authorized to announce 'let Your Kingdom come'. Wherever darkness (misery, destruction, sorrow) is blanketing a situation, we, as representatives of another kingdom, must decree, "let there be light".

When God made man in His own image, He intended us to be able to function just as He does. Now that Jesus has restored us to our former estate, we must be about our Father's business – which is decreeing an exchange of rule and a change of the prevailing circumstances in people's lives.

Prayer: What an awesome privilege we have, Father. I am beginning to understand what being a co-laborer with You means – and I can't wait to get to work, working the works of God!

July 24th

Isa 60:1 Arise, shine; for thy light is come, and the glory of the LORD is risen upon thee.

The Amplified Bible says 'arise from the depression and frustration in which circumstances have kept you; arise to a new life'. Bride of Christ, it's time. The days of purifying, the long fiery trial is coming to a close. Now lift yourself up out of that place of mourning. Emerge from your grave-clothes. The portion of Heaven's light appointed you before the foundation of the earth is here!

Recognize the changing of the season in your life. The rains are over and gone. The season of singing has come! Now arise and SHINE!

Prayer: Father, I had become so accustomed to the dim light of this tomb of preparation that I hadn't noticed You switched the light on!! It's time to get up!!

July 25th

Psa 110:1 The LORD said unto my Lord, Sit at my right hand, until I make your enemies your footstool. Psa 110:2 The LORD shall send the rod of your strength out of Zion: rule in the midst of your enemies.

We are seated in heavenly places in Christ, according to Ephesians 2:6 and God's intention is to make the enemies of Christ His footstool (and ours!). A footstool is something that enables you to reach higher than you could do in your own strength. It was prophesied in Genesis that the seed of Adam would crush the head of the serpent. Any attack that comes against you is for the purpose of providing you with a step up – a footstool- so that you are propelled to greater heights in God. The enemy may intend it for evil but God turns it for good as you follow His heavenly counsel in dealing with it. Out of Zion, the heavenly city, the scepter of Kingdom rule is extended. This is done through us, as we declare 'let Your Kingdom come' and use the keys provided to bind and loose. You are intended to be ruling in the midst of your enemies, not being pummeled to a pulp by them. Rise up and begin to really understand who you are in Christ.

Prayer: Father, many times I have allowed the enemy to ride right over me – but this day I determine to stand and use his attack as an opportunity to reach higher in Your purposes, amen.

July 26th

Est 6:11 And Haman took the royal clothing and the king's horse and dressed Mordecai, and brought him on horseback through the street of the city, and proclaimed before him, This is what shall be done to the man whom the king delights to honor!

Haman was Mordecai's enemy and had just built a gallows the night before because he intended to hang Mordecai. Yet the king had been going through the records and discovered that Mordecai had never been rewarded for saving the king from assassination. So Haman was ordered to honor Mordecai by dressing him in royal garments and helping him up onto the king's horse, before openly declaring that he was a man whom the King honored! Beloved, even though the enemy has plans to destroy you because you will not bow your knee to him, know that the King of Kings is reading the Book of Remembrance at this time - and you WILL receive the glory and honor due to you as His faithful servant. Just as Haman gave Mordecai a leg up to a higher place – a vantage point from which he looked down upon the enemy – so too will the Lord cause your enemy to become your footstool. You will be clothed in royal garments and openly declared to be one whom God has favored! And your enemy will be publicly humiliated!

Prayer: Father, thank you that everything the enemy intends for my destruction, You will turn to my good and his destruction. Hallelujah!

July 27th

Est 7:10 So they hanged Haman on the gallows that he had prepared for Mordecai. Then was the king's wrath pacified.

There is a day of vengeance of our God upon all that has come against His people. In the fullness of time, once the refining trial has produced a vessel fit for the Master's use, the King of Kings decrees judgment upon all that has been arrayed against you. No weapon formed against you shall prosper or achieve success. Once the fire has brought forth a weapon fit for its purpose, God puts it out!

The plots and plans of Haman drove Mordecai to intercession and fasting, not only for himself but for his people. He refused to bow his knee to the one who coveted the throne even though it could bring severe consequences to himself. Beloved, God sees every choice you have made for righteousness and the protection

181

and promotion of His kingdom. He is about to pass judgment in favor of the saints, that His wrath may be pacified!

Prayer: Father, You are a God of justice. You will contend with those who contend with me. Thank you for the decisions of the courts of Heaven over me in these days, amen.

July 28th

Est 8:2 And the king took off his ring, which he had taken from Haman, and gave it unto Mordecai. And Esther set Mordecai over the house of Haman.

Everything Mordecai faced, all the injustice he opposed at the expense of his own safety, served to fashion a vessel the King could use. His choices in difficult situations shaped him into a man who was fit to be promoted to a place of authority and governance. Once the enemy was dealt with, Mordecai was given the king's signet ring – a symbol of royal authority – because the King trusted his judgment. He was also placed over all of his enemy's former wealth.

In the same way, Beloved, God is about to release a much greater level of authority to you as you are appointed to a position of royal influence. You have proved yourself faithful and trustworthy and the Lord knows you do not seek power or wealth for yourself. The good of the kingdom is your concern. Therefore you will be appointed authority to make godly judgments and decrees over that which previously belonged to the enemy, be it the souls of men or houses or lands.

Prayer: Father, I want only the extension of Your Kingdom and the glory of Your Name. Grant me wisdom in the place You are taking me to, amen.

July 29th

Est 8:8 And you write for the Jews as it pleases you, in the king's name, and seal it with the king's ring. For the writing which is written in the king's name and sealed with the king's ring, no man may turn back.

Mordecai is given freedom to issue a decree 'as it pleases you'. The king has such confidence in the purity of his motives and the intentions and desires of his heart that he releases him with authority to decree whatever is upon his heart.

Once the goldsmith can see his own face in the molten surface of the gold in the furnace, he knows it is pure and ready to be forged into a vessel of honor. It is the same with us – when the Father can see His character and likeness clearly in us, He ends the fiery trial and we emerge as vessels he can trust with Kingly authority. We are fit to issue royal decrees that will not only affect our own families but peoples and nations!

Prayer: Father, I am almost grateful for the fiery trial because it has purged me of much dross. Thank you for Your ways which are so much higher than ours – You know exactly what You are doing! Thank you for allowing me to write and speak things in Your Name and accompany them with the seal of Your powerful Name, amen.

July 30th

Dan 3:16 ,17,18 Shadrach, Meshach, and Abednego answered and said to the king, O Nebuchadnezzar, we have no need to return a word to you on this matter. If it is so that our God whom we serve is able to deliver us from the burning fiery furnace, then He will deliver us out of your hand, O king. But if not, let it be known to you, O king, that we will not serve your gods nor worship the golden image which you have set up.

These three men were not prepared to bow their knee to the gods of Babylon or the golden image which the king had set up. They were wholly faithful to God, no matter what the consequences were. They knew God was able to deliver them but they did not demand that He do so. <u>Their faithfulness to God was not dependent on Him coming through for them!</u>

So often we are prepared to defend our faith IF God moves on our behalf. We will remain faithful IF He comes through for us. How many have turned their backs on God because He didn't perform according to their expectations, not realizing that their hearts were being tested in the process of the delay or absence of His visible workings. Beloved, we must determine to align ourselves with Truth because it IS Truth, no matter what the personal consequences are for us.

Prayer; Father, too many times I have threatened to walk away if You will not move on my behalf. Forgive me for my wavering commitment, amen.

July 31st

Dan 3:19 Then Nebuchadnezzar was filled with wrath, and the form of his face was changed against Shadrach, Meshach, and Abednego. He spoke and commanded that they should heat the furnace seven times more than it was usually heated.

Seven times hotter – a complete refining is commanded because of these young men's' unwillingness to bow the knee in idolatry. The king's face was changed towards them – in other words, his attitude toward them changed. Previously they had been set up in positions of authority in the business world of Babylon (v 12). Now suddenly they went from a position of favor and influence to being in disfavor.

In the church, there are those who have been put in positions of authority, ruling in the Babylonian religious system. However, they are true servants of God. There comes a day when they are faced with a choice – enter into idolatry and remain in favor *OR* remain faithful to the King of Heaven and lose position and influence in the religious system.

This choice is the preliminary test of those desiring to become vessels of gold in the Master's House. On making the right choice in God's eyes, they are not then rewarded (as is the way of man) but rather plunged into a refining fire seven times hotter than is considered a normal trial. Perhaps, Beloved, this will help you understand the journey you have traveled!

August 1st

Dan 3:21 Then these men were tied up in their slippers, their tunics, and their mantles, and their other clothes, and were thrown into the middle of the burning fiery furnace.

These men were not tossed into the furnace naked. Every vestige of clothing they wore also entered the fiery flames. In the same way, everything connected to you – your spiritual giftings, mantles of authority and every area in which you function in the kingdom – is also destined to pass through a refining and testing process.

Remember that the clothing these young men wore was the clothing of Babylon. They had been functioning in delegated positions of power in the business sector of the Babylonian empire. Beloved, in order to be transformed into a vessel of gold, it has to be determined whether the garments you wear are truly God-appointed or bestowed by man. As Paul teaches, 'each one's work shall be revealed. For the Day shall declare it, because it shall be revealed by fire; and the fire shall try each one's work as to what kind it is' (1 Cor 3:13). Their garments came out without the smell of smoke so they could continue to wear them and operate in their appointed positions.

Prayer: Father, the refining fire appointed me does so much more than I realized. Not only is it testing my heart but also my garments – a complete refining. Thank you.

August 2nd

Dan 3:22 Then because the king's commandment was urgent, and the furnace exceedingly hot, the flame of the fire killed those men who took up Shadrach, Meshach, and Abednego.

The mighty men of Babylon were the ones to throw these three into the furnace. They represent principalities and powers who are appointed to harass and torment the servants of God, just as satan was given permission to attack Job.

However, the wonderful thing about the heat of the fiery furnace you have been thrown into, Beloved, is that it will destroy all those who have been arrayed against you. Every demonic messenger whom satan has assigned to bring about your destruction will be burnt up by the heat of the fire. And the ironic thing is that it was the king of Babylon who chose the measure of heat in the furnace! That which he intended for evil, God turned for good! Everything the enemy throws at you boomerangs and destroys those he has sent to destroy you! Now that is a reason for rejoicing this day!!

Prayer: Father, thank you that every enemy assignment against me shall be destroyed by this refining fire I am in. Hallelujah! I never thought I would thank You for the exceeding greatness of the heat but I see it has its benefits! Amen.

August 3rd

Dan 3:23 And these three men, Shadrach, Meshach, and Abednego, fell down bound into the midst of the burning fiery furnace.

187

These three faithful servants went into the fire bound. Not only were they bound but they fell down and were unable to help themselves. They must have experienced a moment of sheer terror and helplessness, being unable to do anything to shield themselves from the heat. However, Psalm 37:24 tells us that when a righteous man falls, 'he shall not be utterly cast down: for the LORD upholds him with his hand'. The flames dealt with the ropes binding them and they were lifted back onto their feet by an unseen hand.

Beloved, every form of bondage that the enemy has put on you before entering this fiery trial will be removed. He intended for the ropes to prevent you from helping yourself but the flames will deal with them. Every form of restriction that prevents you moving freely in your service of God will be dealt with during this time. You will emerge from this season with every fetter on your hands and feet completely destroyed. If the enemy had known what the fire would accomplish, he probably wouldn't have thrown you in or made it so hot! It is time to thank God for the results of this fiery furnace season.

Prayer: Father, thank you that every form of bondage is being progressively removed as I am in this fire. Your ways are so amazing. Amen.

August 4th

1Pe 4:12 Beloved, think it not strange concerning the fiery trial which is to try you, as though some strange thing happened unto you: 1Pe 4:13 But rejoice, inasmuch as you are partakers of Christ's sufferings; that, when his glory is revealed, you may be glad also with exceeding joy.

We all know the old saying 'the proof is in the pudding'. It is all very well to have a wonderful sounding recipe but until it has been tried and tested, one is unable to confidently recommend it.

Well, Beloved, until we pass through the fiery trials we are no more than a recipe! Theoretically, we can state what we believe and who we are, but only the heat of the fiery trial will bring out the true character hidden within. For us to have the fragrance and flavor of Christ forged within our bones, we must pass through the oven. Our lives are to be living letters not just words on a page. Therefore we should not be shocked at the fiery furnace.

Prayer: Father, thank you that the result of the time in the fire is the revelation of Your glory. I am glad You did not stop after creating the recipe in my life! Others must taste and see Your goodness through me. Amen.

August 5th

Isa 43:1,2 ... I have called you by your name; you are Mine. When you pass through the waters, I will be with you; and through the rivers, they shall not overflow you. When you walk through the fire, you shall not be burned; nor shall the flame kindle on you.

Not 'if' you pass through the waters, but 'when'. Not 'if' you walk through the fire, but 'when'. Trials of different kinds are an expected part of our journey in God and without them we are destined to remain spineless and characterless. Just as a great tree grows strong when buffeted by stormy winds, so we must look back over our lives and recognize the value of the storms and trials in building strength within.

189

During them, we can think only of the blessed day of release, of the calm that will follow the storm. However, there is value in pausing and acknowledging the amazing spiritual growth that has emerged as a direct result of opposition and trial. There has to come this moment when we make peace with the route that God has taken us – otherwise we will never be able to close the chapter and leave it behind.

Prayer: Father, I am Yours, You have called me by name and You have chosen the long torturous road I have traveled to this point. Help me to make peace with all that I do not understand about Your choices. I must take one last look back and let it all go before moving forward into all You have for me, amen.

August 6th

Mat 27:34 they gave Him vinegar mixed with gall to drink. And when He had tasted, He would not drink.

Gall is associated with bitterness. When Jesus was being crucified, he was offered vinegar with gall because it would act as a painkiller. However he refused to drink it. He was not prepared to partake of bitterness – even though it would ease his own suffering and reduce the amount of pain he felt.

In the same way, Beloved, as we are in the midst of our fiery trial, we must choose not to partake of bitterness because it will defile us. Bitterness towards man is easily enough dealt with but the bitterness we feel towards God for leading us right into this furnace is less easily identified and expelled. We trusted Him to lead us in green pastures and beside still waters and instead we have found ourselves in the valley of the shadow of death! Just like Job, our confidence in His character can be severely shaken at these times because we do not see as He sees. He sees us emerging from the tomb in resurrection power. He sees the binding ropes burned off. He sees the glorious afterward. We see the height of the flames and feel their heat.

Prayer: Father, if I am honest I have muttered about Your choice of road to my future. Forgive me for criticizing Your judgment and wisdom. I repent for thinking I know a better road to my destiny. Restore trust to my heart, I pray, amen.

August 7th

Dan 3:24 Then Nebuchadnezzar the king was amazed. And he rose up in haste and spoke and said to his advisers, Did we not throw three men bound into the middle of the fire? They answered and said to the king, True, O king. Dan 3:25 He answered and said, Behold! I see four men loose, walking in the middle of the fire, and there is no harm among them. And the form of the fourth is like the Son of God.

When the fiery trial has done its work then the fourth man is seen in the fire. The purpose of the fire is to bring forth Christ in you and even your enemies will testify that they can see Him in your life. Beloved, this is what we are predestined for – to be conformed to the image of Christ. Even though the conforming involves situations in which we are 'pressed beyond measure', we must be aware that the purpose is to manifest the life of Christ in these earthen vessels.

If we fix our eyes upon the end result, we are able to be full of joy in the fire because the schemes of the enemy to destroy us actually result in him bowing his knee and acknowledging the manifestation of Christ within us! Hallelujah!

191

Prayer: Father, Your ways are definitely not our ways but the results are so superior! Thank you for using the fire heated seven times by the enemy to bring forth the image of Christ in me, amen.

August 8th

Dan 3:26 Then Nebuchadnezzar came near the door of the burning fiery furnace. He answered and said, Shadrach, Meshach, and Abednego, servants of the Most High God, come forth and come here. Then Shadrach, Meshach, and Abednego, came forth from the middle of the fire.

Now this verse holds an amazing secret. It is the enemy, the one who had the fire heated seven times hotter, the one who tried to lure you into idolatry and sin, who announces the end of the trial. When he sees the Christ in you and the fact that your bonds have been destroyed, he issues a command, "come forth". Out of the fiery womb of the furnace, the sons of God are birthed and come into plain view. Manifestation time is Here!

The night of adversity is over and from the womb of the morning spring forth His young men who are as the dew (psalm 110). The enemy has been made a servant for their good. He has been the one who stoked the fire and rained the blows that have made a weapon fit for its purpose. Now the time has come for the inspection parade of God's mighty hidden army. God will cause even the enemy to acknowledge His superior power.

Prayer: Father, You amaze me, using the enemy to call me forth from the refiners fire! How like You to cause him to be the first one to view Your handiwork! I praise You for the mysterious wisdom of Your ways, amen.

August 9th

Dan 3:27 And the satraps, the prefects, the governors, and the king's advisers gathered and saw these men on whose bodies the fire had no power (and the hair of their head was not scorched, nor were their slippers changed, nor had the smell of fire clung on them).

Beloved, in the day you emerge from the flames, every principality and power arrayed against you will gather and acknowledge that the fire has no power over you. More than that, the smell of the fire will not have clung to you. In other words, everything you have experienced in the refining process will remain in the closed previous chapter. Your hair, which represents the anointing on your life, will be in no way diminished or damaged. In fact, it will probably have grown during the trial! There will be no vestige or residue of the trial upon you – so much so that people will find it hard to believe that you actually went through those terrible trials. You will be whole. There will be no sign of damage upon you.

All those who saw you enter the fiery trial and know the details of your circumstances will stand amazed at what they see before their eyes - just as the disciples were dumbfounded when they saw Jesus in His resurrected whole body because they had seen the gory details of the crucifixion and the wounds inflicted upon him.

Prayer: Father, all the glory goes to you that I emerge whole from this place of trial for it was Your hand that healed my wounds even in the midst of the fire!.I love You, amen.

August 10th

*Dan 3:28 Nebuchadnezzar spoke and said, Blessed be the God of Shadrach, Meshach, and Abednego, who has sent His Angel and has delivered His servants who trusted in Him, and has **changed the king's words** and have given their bodies that they might not serve nor worship any god except their own God.*

Beloved, there were decrees of death and destruction issued over your life by the enemy just before you entered the furnace. They were powerful and the elements were put in place for them to be carried out. However, God Almighty holds the power to change decrees issued in the spiritual realm. This is why no weapon formed against you can prosper – God uses the legal decrees issued against you and turns them for your good. The words of the king of darkness are changed in order to bring forth light in and through you! Therefore there is never any need to fear the might of the enemy.

Every judgment issued against you, you will show to be in the wrong (Isaiah 54:17 AMP). How? By the character you display in the furnace, by the life and virtue of Christ which is visibly seen in you even while you are in the midst of the fire. Therefore there is a day of vindication for you, a glorious afterward – a day when the enemy bows his knee and acknowledges that God loves you.

Prayer: OH Father, how glorious are your deeds. I stand amazed at the works of Your hands in my life. My life is a testimony that Your Word is indeed Truth at every level and in every circumstance!

August 11ᵗʰ

Dan 3:30 Then the king made Shadrach, Meshach, and Abednego prosper in the province of Babylon.

Following the fire there is a time of recompense, a time of restoration and prosperity manifested in your life – and God uses the enemy to bring it about! In just the same way as Mordecai was placed in a position of rule over the house of Haman and all his wealth, so too will the Lord bring you into a place of influence and cause you to prosper in the very realm where the enemy has ruled previously! You are going to be taking ground for the Kingdom of God and plundering the province of the enemy. He will have no option but to restore to you seven times what he stole in the previous season. In the same measure with which he heated the fire (seven times hotter) so will he be made to deliver recompense seven times more that you have lost. This covers every area of your life – emotional, relational, physical, financial, spiritual.

Prayer: Father, thank you that even like Job, I will experience restoration in increased measure. I bless you for it, amen.

August 12ᵗʰ

Dan 1:7 to whom the ruler of the eunuchs gave names. For he called Daniel, Belteshazzar; and Hananiah, Shadrach; and Mishael, Meshach; and Azariah, Abednego.

These men of God were given names in Babylon by the ruler of the eunuchs. In other words the enemy attached labels to them which were intended to render them incapable of bringing forth fruit. Eunuchs had the appearance of masculinity but had no ability to father children. However God knew their real names and the plans He had for them. Daniel means 'God has judged'. Hananiah means 'God has favored'. Mishael means 'who is what God is?'.Azariah means 'God has helped'. Their original names were a declaration of the work God would bring forth in their lives through the fiery furnace. They are a vivid depiction of judgment being given in favor of the saints! Beloved, it doesn't matter what labels have been attached to you. It doesn't matter what words of death have been spoken over your potential to bear fruit. God will use the trial of the fiery furnace to break every limiting word over your life and bring forth your full potential in full sight of your enemies! They will be forced to acknowledge that their labels have not stuck! You are not who the enemy says you are.

Prayer: Father, thank you for the day of emerging from the furnace. Thank you for the fruit that will be seen. Thank you that I will be a living memorial to prove You are faithful to bring forth Your intended declaration over my life, amen.

August 13th

Isa 55:11 So shall my word be that goes forth out of my mouth: it shall not return to me void, but it shall accomplish that which I please, and it shall prosper in the thing whereto I sent it.

Do you realize that you are the manifestation of a word spoken by God? You shall not return to Him without accomplishing the purpose for which He sent you. The word void means 'empty or ineffective'. The Father says you will not be ineffective but prosper in the thing to which He has sent you. The spoken word from His mouth which became flesh and created you is still in the process of unfolding and manifesting the DNA of His intended purposes.

Like an arrow shot from the bow of an archer, you are still on course . David was catapulted from the obscurity of the sheepfolds to a place of power and influence, shepherding God's people. Many things came against him but ultimately he fulfilled the intended purpose for his life; the purpose that was declared the day Samuel anointed his head and decreed the plan of God for the young boy. No weapon that is formed against you shall prosper and you will walk in all that God has intended for your life. Press on and continue to let your life 'speak', Word of the Lord.

Prayer: Father, I never realized before that I am part of Your living message in the earth. May the tone of Your voice be clearly heard in me, amen.

August 14th

Mar 14:3 And He being in Bethany, in the house of Simon the leper, while He reclined, a woman came having an alabaster jar of ointment of very costly, pure spikenard And having broken the alabaster jar, she poured [it] over His head.

The shattering of the alabaster jar signifies the end of a season; a time when what has been stored up and prepared within a previous season is now poured out. The jar will never be seen in its previous form again. The costly perfume born out of the sufferings and trials of the preparation season is released for all to savor the perfume and the vessel itself is irrevocably changed. There is no going back; no return to the place of hiddenness.

The breaking of the jar announces the beginning of a new season – a season of being known openly and recognized for who you are in Christ. Jesus said, "Wherever this gospel shall be proclaimed in all the world, *this* also that she has done will be spoken of for a memorial of her". The company that releases their costly ointment in this coming season will be known, not by their names but by their deeds – the anointed word they release will minister to and bless the Body of Christ and Jesus, the Head of the Body will affirm them openly and rebuke any who speak against them.

Prayer: Father, may the ointment You have prepared within me by many crushings, minister to You as I pour it forth. May I be broken and spilled out for You, amen.

August 15ᵗʰ

Isa 61:3 to appoint to those who mourn in Zion, to give to them beauty for ashes,

Out of the ashes, the breakings and the crushings, the loss and the incinerated dreams, beauty is released. Out of the separate whole spikenard roots, an ointment was made by crushing and grinding and mixing with oil – and a beautiful fragrance came forth. The fragrance cannot be poured forth without the crushing. In the pouring forth of the precious revelation within, even the broken vessel itself is aware of and is touched by the fragrance of Christ that permeates the room. This is the fruit of the travail of your soul and it will satisfy you as it satisfied Jesus that day.

Medicinally, spikenard is used to ease birth difficulties and for people with deep-seated emotional pain or ancient grief. The release of the ointment of Spikenard from your belly will bring a corresponding release in the area where ancient heaps of ashes lie buried in your past. Beauty will be your portion in place of these losses and griefs. It has been appointed you!

Prayer: Father, thank you that the days of mourning are over and the time of beauty and rejoicing is at hand. The season of the making of this ointment was awful but I know it will be worth it when I smell the fragrance released from my life.

August 16th

Isa 61:7 MSG Because you got a double dose of trouble and more than your share of contempt, Your inheritance in the land will be doubled and your joy go on forever. Isa 61:8 "Because I, GOD, love fair dealing and hate thievery and crime, I'll pay your wages on time and in full, and establish my eternal covenant with you.

Recompense and restoration are part of the beauty that we receive in exchange for our ashes. In every instance where the thief has marauded, the Father says you will receive double. Just as Job was raised up from the ashes and all he had lost, restored, so too will you see a return of all that was lost. Every wage that the enemy has held back in times past will be paid in full and on time. The oil of joy will flow from your heart and cause your face to shine!

God hates robbery and executes a judgment from His throne that awards you double what has been stolen from your life. Perhaps you need to expand your mindset to make space for all that God intends to restore to you!

August 17th

Psa 110:3 Your people shall be willing in the day of your power, in the beauties of holiness from the womb of the morning shall spring forth your young men who are as the dew.

The night of affliction and trial have served as a womb – and from this dark place, fruit is brought forth in the morning. A holy people, set-apart and ready for the Bridegroom are released to work the works of God in the earth. They are like the dew. Dew falls all over the earth. In the very early morning it appears and refreshes and waters the earth.

The word for 'dew' also means 'to plate'. The ark of the Covenant was plated or overlaid with pure gold and the presence of God was contained within it. So too, those who are as the dew are vessels of pure gold, carrying the presence of God within them. They cover the earth and bring the presence of God into every situation they encounter.

Prayer: Father, I understand that this womb of preparation has been to bring forth a people radiant with the beauty of holiness. May I be a vessel of pure gold, profitable for any good work, amen.

August 18th

Mar 14:10 And Judas Iscariot, one of the Twelve, went to the chief priests in order to betray Him to them.

The event of the ointment poured forth announced a change of season for the vessel, a day of release. However it also triggered another release. Judas was so disgusted with the extravagant outpouring of love and worship that he began negotiations with the chief priests in order to betray Jesus.

The season which we are entering will contain a marked increase in persecution and betrayal for the Body of Christ. Judas was one of the disciples; he had fellowshipped and walked with Jesus. So too, for us, the betrayers will come from within our ranks. Brother will turn against brother and our enemies will be the members of our own households. It is imperative for us to always walk in love and forgiveness towards those the enemy uses against us, no matter how close they are, and how much it hurts.

Prayer: Father, these days will be hard days for us as the Body amidst all the glory. Grant me the grace to love well and forgive fully, in Jesus Name, amen.

August 19th

Mat 26:49 And coming up to Jesus immediately, he said, Hail, Master! And he kissed Him. Mat 26:50 And Jesus said to him, Friend, why are you here? Then they came and laid hands on Jesus and took Him.

Jesus addressed Judas, "friend". He is demonstrating how to love your enemies well. He has no bitterness in His heart towards His betrayer because He understands that there are certain steps that must occur in order to fulfill the Father's plan and bring forth life for many. Every son of God who desires to walk in resurrection power will have a Judas. It is part of being conformed to the image of Christ.

We must always remember that a Saul can become a Paul if we, like Stephen, can pray, "Father, forgive them" even while the stones are raining down upon our heads. Stephen means 'crown' and the Bride of Christ as the crown of her Husband will respond in the same spirit as He did at Calvary. This is how she will be recognized.

Prayer: Father, fill me with the love that is able to love its enemies and even release them into their appointed destinies, amen.

August 20th

Isa 66:5 Hear the word of the LORD, you that tremble at his word; Your brethren that hated you, that cast you out for my name's sake, said, Let the LORD be glorified: but He shall appear to your joy, and they shall be ashamed.

The eyes of the Lord have been running to and fro throughout the whole earth looking for those who are wholehearted towards Him; those who tremble at His Word. These saints have suffered much persecution, mocking and rejection at the hands of certain people in the Body. Throughout these trials they have remained faithful and walked in the fear of the Lord.

However the time comes when God moves His hand on their behalf and their weeping is replaced by joy! In instances where they have been poorly treated in the name of the Lord and supposedly for the cause of the Church, the tables will be turned and the Lord will render recompense. In the coming days, it will be clearly seen which people have God's favor on their lives and which are under His discipline. However, it is not a time to walk in presumption and pride – rather let us be those who tremble at His Word and make the change necessary as soon as the Spirit convicts us

August 21st

Isa 66:6 A voice of noise from the city, a voice from the temple, a voice of the LORD that rendering recompense to his enemies.

Here Isaiah sees in the spirit a time when the Lord is dealing with His enemies – but where are they to be found? Surprisingly not only in the city but in the temple His voice rings out. There are some who assume they are friends of God but their lives tell a different story and the stance they have taken has set them as enemies of God. Verse 4 gives us a clue as to their behavior: 'they did evil before my eyes, and chose *that* in which I delighted not'. Furthermore, verse 3 tells us 'they have chosen their own ways, and their soul delights in their abominations'.

For what seems like an interminable time God seems to tolerate the wayward behavior of His people and then suddenly a new dispensation is entered and judgment begins with the household of God. He draws a clear dividing line between those who fear Him and those who are lovers of their own ways. Then He deals with the two groups according to their ways. For those who have endeavored to choose the life He delights in, there will be recompense in the form of reward. For those who have gone their own way and shut their ear to His voice, recompense comes in the form of fiery judgments.

August 22nd

Isa 66:14 And when ye see this, your heart shall rejoice, and your bones shall flourish like an herb: and the hand of the LORD shall be known toward his servants, and his indignation toward his enemies.

Not only will His hand be shown towards you but it will be KNOWN towards you. In other words, there will be a testimony that comes from the hand of the Lord moving on your behalf that will be common knowledge. Conversely it will be clear when the hand of the Lord renders His wrath and deals with stubborn rebellion and waywardness in His church. He disciplines those He loves when they choose their own way.

For those who have patiently waited to see the hand of the Lord moving on their behalf, it will be a day of flourishing and rejoicing even in the midst of that which is coming upon the earth. They will arise and shine amidst the dense darkness, as jewels which are more clearly displayed against a black velvet background! Faithfulness to the Lord has its reward in Hid appointed day.

Prayer: Lord, thank you that those who went out weeping, will come again with rejoicing, bearing sheaves, amen.

August 24th

Isa 66:15 For, behold, the LORD will come with fire, and with his chariots like a whirlwind, to render his anger with fury, and his rebuke with flames of fire.

Jesus said that He came to send fire on the earth and how He wished it was already kindled. However he had a baptism to go through first – this referred to the crucifixion. Psalm 104:4 tells us that He makes His ministers flames of fire.

In just the same way as Jesus had to go through the experience of the cross before the fire could be kindled, so too His ministers must face their Calvary in order to be made a flame of fire. Then they will be vessels that can be trusted to minister in the fear of the Lord and not of man. God requires His flames of fire to minister rebuke in order to deal with the impurity and chaff in the church.

The day of seeker-friendly services is drawing to a close as God cleanses His temple. It is more important to create an environment where God feels welcome than to pander to the soulish whims of a backslidden Church – that is if we really desire His presence in our midst!

Prayer: Father, the presence of Your Spirit is more important to me than any measure of sensory satisfaction or vain pleasure. Make me a flame of fire that can set others aflame, amen.

205

August 25th

Mal 4:1 For, behold, the day comes, that shall burn as an oven; and all the proud, yes, and all that do wickedly, shall be stubble: and the day that comes shall burn them up, says the LORD of hosts, that it shall leave them neither root nor branch. Mal 4:2 But to you that fear my name shall the Sun of righteousness arise with healing in his wings; and you shall go forth, and spring about as calves let from the stall.

Here once again we see two distinct groups of people – those who do wickedly and those who fear the Lord. The fear of the Lord is an inner garment, an undergarment if you will. It acts as a foundation for all we think and do but is not immediately apparent to others. Yet the day is coming when God is going to make a clear distinction between those who wear the undergarments of pride and those who walk in humility and the fear of the Lord.

For the latter, there is recompense, healing and fullness of joy! There is a performance of all the Lord has promised during the dark days of the refiner's fire. The day of the Lord is both great and terrible. It all depends on where your heart lies.

Prayer: Father, grant me a visitation of the Spirit of the fear of the Lord so that I may be fully ready for the day that burns like an oven, amen.

August 26th

Isa 66:16 For by fire and by his sword will the LORD plead with all flesh: and the slain of the LORD shall be many.

The Lord comes to deal with all flesh. This not only refers to all men but also to areas where the flesh is ruling in His people. He uses fire and the sword of His Word and those who are not bowed in humility will find themselves 'beheaded' by the sweep of His strong right arm. It is a fearful thing to fall into the hands of the Living God. For too long, large sectors of the church have treated God like their financial advisor or benign and harmless grandfather. They are about to discover just Who the Lord of Hosts really is.

The fire deals with dross and all built from wood, hay and stubble. The sword divides between soul and spirit. None shall escape this end-time dealing. From the mighty to the obscure, all are being measured for reward in this season which has just begun.

Isa 3:10 Say to the righteous, that it shall be well with him: for they shall eat the fruit of their doings. Isa 3:11 Woe unto the wicked! it shall be ill with him: for the reward of his hands shall be given him.

Prayer; Lord, show me clearly where I need to attend to unfinished business. Work humility in me, amen.

August 27th

Isa 62:11 Behold, the LORD has proclaimed to the end of the world, Say to the daughter of Zion, Behold, your salvation comes; behold, his reward is with him, and his recompense before him. Isa 62:12 And they shall call them, The holy people, The redeemed of the LORD: and you shall be called, Sought out, A city not forsaken.

Reward and recompense are on the way for the faithful ones, those who have set themselves apart as holy vessels. This will cause those who observe their lives to recognize that they are the redeemed of the Lord and many will seek them out in that day. For all who have felt ashamed because their life holds no great testimony, only trials and tribulations – this is your turning point.

The day is coming when men will acknowledge that you are a people the Lord Himself has favored and blessed! The days of reproach will be a dim memory as you minister to others using the wisdom gleaned in the refiner's fire and the secret place.

Prayer; Father, thank you that the day of the completion of my testimony is at hand. Men will hear of Your faithfulness to me. You are the Alpha and the Omega and You will complete that which You began. I worship You, amen.

August 28th

Mat 16:27 For the Son of man shall come in the glory of his Father with his angels; and then he shall reward every man according to his works.

The rewards Jesus brings always fits the works -Gal 6:7 says *'Do not be deceived, God is not mocked. For whatever a man sows, that he also will reap'*. There is also the principle of increase. You sow one seed but it grows into a plant bearing many seeds. If these seeds are then allowed to fall into the soil of your heart, they in turn bear more of the same kind of harvest. In a sense one sows the wind and reaps the whirlwind (Hosea 8:7).

This is why it is imperative to weed out (by the root) any sin-bearing plants growing in the gardens of our hearts AS SOON AS WE BECOME AWARE OF THEM!! Then we save ourselves the whirlwind harvest of many seasons of unrepented sin. Beloved, we are entering a season of unprecedented and quick reaping of the seeds of hidden sin. Judge yourselves that you may not be judged openly.

Prayer: Father, so often I have just removed the visible parts of the plant that shouldn't be growing in my life, instead of dealing with the roots which keep it coming up over and over again. I have no desire to reap the whirlwind in these areas. Help me to have the strength and determination to fully repent and turn from these things, amen.

August 29th

Gal 6:8 For he sowing to his flesh will reap corruption from the flesh. But he sowing to the Spirit will reap life everlasting from the Spirit. Gal 6:9 But we should not lose heart in well-doing, for in due season we shall reap, if we do not faint.

In the same way as fleshly weeds multiply if left unchecked, so too is there a multiplication seen in harvest of righteous acts born of the Spirit of God. This is why we must persevere – because there is a DUE SEASON of reaping!

What harvest is about to be brought in, in our lives? Are we to reap honor and glory or corruption? Whatever seeds we have been tending in the soil of our hearts are about to come into plain view! By the time it is harvest time, it's too late to change your mind about the kind of seed you want to sow! Better do some weeding before it's too late and begin to sow good seed, sow to the Spirit while there is still time for it to grow and bear fruit!

Weeds also just sprout after their seed is blown in by the wind. Keep checking your heart-garden for alien invaders!! Guard your heart for out of it flow the issues of life.

Prayer: Lord, help me to be patient as I wait for the early and the latter rains. And give me tenacity in the pulling out of weeds in my heart so they don't choke my good seed, amen.

August 30th

Psa 24:3 Who shall ascend into the hill of the LORD? or who shall stand in his holy place? He that hath clean hands, and a pure heart; who hath not lifted up his soul unto vanity, nor sworn deceitfully.

The hill of the Lord is where Mount Zion, the true Church of Jesus Christ, is found. Only those who have clean hands and a pure heart can ascend to this place. No wonder David cried out, "search me, o God, and know my heart. Find any wicked way in me". The works of our hands, that with which we are involved for the Kingdom, spring from the contents of our hearts.

So a pure heart, a heart wholly after God and His glory, is one of the first prerequisites for being able to stand in His holy place. Deception and idle pursuits have no part in the life of a son of the Light.

Prayer: search me, O God, amen.

August 31st

Isa 5:20 Woe to those who call evil good and good evil; who put darkness for light and light for darkness; who put bitter for sweet and sweet for bitter! Isa 5:21 Woe to those wise in their own eyes, and bright in their own sight! Isa 5:22 Woe to those mighty to drink wine, and brave men to mix strong drink; Isa 5:23 who justify the wicked for a bribe, and take away the righteousness of the righteous from him! Isa 5:24 So, as the fire devours the stubble, and the flame burns up the chaff; their root shall be like rottenness, and their blossoms shall go up like dust, because they have cast away the Law of the Lord of Hosts, and despised the Word of the Holy One of Israel.

The fear of the Lord is to hate evil. The Church of Jesus Christ has for too long called that which is evil, good and accepted darkness as being light. Now the fire which refines is sweeping His Body and He is dealing with all who have despised His Word and His holy standards.

Let us allow the Spirit to put His divine plumb-line upon our hearts and check that that which we have built so far is according to His blueprint, and not according to the architecture of Babylon.

September 1st

Rth 3:2 .... Behold, he winnows barley tonight in the threshing-floor. Rth 3:3 Therefore wash yourself, and anoint yourself, and put your clothing upon you, and go down to the floor.

The Bridegroom is winnowing barley. This is the first of the grain crops to come in and is harvested at Passover. Jesus was the first-fruits offering of the barley harvest, presented to the Father as a wave offering.

Barley has no gluten content and therefore can only be made into unleavened bread. Jesus was without sin and is looking for a first-fruits company that have washed themselves in the water of the Word and, fully prepared, have descended to the threshing floor. It is here He finds His Bride, who is bone of His bone and flesh of His flesh.

The barley harvest comes in before the wheat harvest. He harvests the harvesters who then go in and bring in the great end-time harvest of souls.

Beloved, have we washed and prepared ourselves for this appointment with the Bridegroom? The church is at the threshing floor being winnowed and those who are part of the first-fruits company from among the dead are being presented as a wave offering.

September 2nd

Num 15:18 Speak to the sons of Israel and say to them, When you come into the land where I bring you, then it shall be that when you eat of the bread of the land, you shall offer up a heave offering to the Lord. You shall offer up a cake of the first of your dough, a heave offering, as the heave offering of the threshing-floor, so you shall lift it up.

One of the stipulations from the Lord upon entering the Promised Land, was the presentation of a cake made from the first grain threshed at the threshing floor during the wheat harvest. It was not enough to offer the grain in its raw state, like at Passover. The Father expected them to grind the wheat flour, make the dough by adding water, then bake it and present it to the Lord. Herein is a picture of the preparation undergone in the wilderness. After the first Passover, the Israelites traversed the wilderness while God tested their hearts. Sin in the camp was dealt with and finally a remnant crossed the Jordan. Beloved, we are the cake which is offered up as an offering to the Lord, having been through much preparation – grinding and crushing, followed by the addition of the water of the Word. We have been in the refiner's fire and now we are emerging and being presented to The Father. We are the fruit of the travail of the Bridegroom's soul.

Prayer: Lord, thank you for all the preparations You have subjected me to. I am glad I am ready, amen.

September 3rd

Lev 23:15 And you shall count to you from the next day after the Sabbath, from the day that you brought the sheaf of the wave offering; seven Sabbaths shall be complete. Lev 23:16 To the next day after the seventh Sabbath you shall number fifty days. And you shall offer a new food offering to the Lord. Lev 23:17 You shall bring out of your homes two wave loaves of two-tenth parts. They shall be of fine flour. They shall be baked with leaven, firstfruits to the Lord.

The firstfruits loaves presented after the wheat harvest were baked with leaven. This does not represent the leaven of sin but the leaven of the Kingdom mentioned in Matthew 13:33. The wilderness period is to ensure that we do not possess the wrong kind of leaven. Jesus warned against the leaven of the Pharisees and Sadducees, by which He meant their doctrines (Matt 16:12). In Luke 12 He also equated their leaven with hypocrisy.

The threshing floor deals with the chaff. The grinding stone deals with rigid mindsets and pride. The dough-making process adds just the right amount of revelation of the water of the Word. The fire brings to completion and full stature and solidifies the work which has been wrought within. Then the firstfruits loaves are ready to come out of the oven and presented to the Lord. Thereafter they are eaten and nourish many.

Prayer: Lord, help me to identify which part of the process I am in and to work with You, instead of against You, amen.

215

September 4th

Gen 47:12 And Joseph nourished his father and his brothers, and all his father's household, with bread, for the mouth of the little ones.

Joseph was Himself the prepared loaf that emerged from the prison of fiery preparation in order to meet the need of a nation. When the family of God is malnourished and the true Word of the Lord is rare, the Joseph Company are brought forth and from the storehouse of heavenly wisdom within, they minister the bread of the Kingdom to the Father's household, who receive it as little children.

The family of God does not know when they set out to look for bread that one of their own will be dispensing it. They have long since written the Josephs off and set up their gravestones. They remember Joseph as a young boy, still with all the chaff present in his life. No wonder they do not recognize him clothed in the garments of maturity and occupying a position of authority.

Prayer: Father, thank you that You have wrought such change in me that I am virtually unrecognizable! I look forward to the reunion with those who formerly considered themselves my enemies! May You be glorified! Thank you for working humility and grace in my heart in the prison years. May they see Jesus in me as I share the words You give me, amen.

September 5th

1Ch 13:9 And when they came unto the threshing-floor of Chidon, Uzzah put forth his hand to hold the ark; for the oxen stumbled. 1Ch 13:10 And the anger of the LORD was kindled against Uzzah, and he smote him, because he put his hand to the ark: and there he died before God.

Uzzah means 'the strength of man'. At the threshing floor God deals with those who attempt to use the strength and wisdom of man to steady the ark of His presence. The Hebrew words used to describe Uzzah's laying hold of the ark carry within them the idea of laying hold of for one's own possession.

All those who attempt to possess the glory of God for their own ends will come to a sticky end as the Church meets this appointment at the threshing floor. The ark had been staying at Uzzah's father's house until the cart was made and Uzzah probably became very familiar with it. Those treating God with familiarity and possessing no fear of the Lord will be severely dealt with. God's dealings in these days will leave the David's chastened and send them running back to the Word to find out where they went wrong. The day of man-made carts is over!

September 6th

2Sa 24:17 And David spoke unto the LORD when he saw the angel that smote the people, and said, Lo, I have sinned, and I have done wickedly: but these sheep, what have they done? let

Your hand, I pray thee, be against me, and against my father's house. 2Sa 24:18 And Gad came that day to David, and said unto him, Go up, rear an altar unto the LORD in the threshing floor of Araunah the Jebusite.

The threshing floor is also the place where men of God recognize their sin and the repercussions it has had on others. It is the place of re-consecration and of building altars to the Lord.

Araunah offered to give David the threshing floor and the oxen to make the sacrifice but David knew that he could not just go through a process which cost him nothing. The altar we build at this threshing floor is at great personal cost. David saw the angel of the Lord with His sword drawn and knew that God meant business with him. He could not play games any more. Innocent people were paying the price for his own sin and he knew it was time to return to the Lord with all his heart. Beloved, we are in a time where those who have wandered from God's plumb-line will see the error of their ways. As the winnowing process continues, chaff will be separated from the nutritious kernel, just as in David's case, and altars of reconsecration will be built.

September 7th

2Ch 3:1 Then Solomon began to build the house of the LORD at Jerusalem in mount Moriah, where the LORD appeared unto David his father, in the place that David had prepared in the threshing floor of Ornan the Jebusite.

Solomon built the temple on the very site where David built his alter of repentance and reconsecration. Remember that David collected the material for the building of the temple but because of mistakes he had made, the Lord assigned the building of the temple to Solomon. The same place where David was chastened by the Lord and realigned himself to God's plumb-line became the place where his son completed the work David had begun many years before. Beloved, the name 'Solomon' comes from a root word meaning 'to be at peace, to complete, make whole, restore, compensate'.

The point in our spiritual journey where we re-align and re-consecrate our lives becomes the very spot upon which God can finish the purposes that He designed for our lives. For a while it seemed that David had derailed his eternal purpose because of foolish decisions and sin. His first child died as a consequence. However, from the grave of his mistakes, wisdom (typified by Solomon) was brought forth. Through Solomon came completion and restoration of all that the enemy had stolen from David's destiny. What God had purposed was accomplished in the end but it took a dying and the wisdom of God coming forth to accomplish it.

September 8th

Gen 50:7 And Joseph went up to bury his father: ...Gen 50:10 And they came to the threshing-floor of Atad, which is beyond Jordan, and there they mourned with a great and very sore lamentation:

The last hours of Jacob's life were taken up with an impartation and prophetic declaration over all the seed he had brought forth. The place where Jacob was buried was beyond the Jordan in the land of Canaan. The next chapter in God's timetable must lay to rest the bones of the movement from which they sprang. The old must pass away before the new can come into its fullness.

As Joseph carried the dead body of his father across the Jordan into Canaan he depicted the dying that must come to the Body in order to plant one's feet upon the land of promise. There is an honoring of that from which they have sprung but a laying to rest of that which is now over. The threshing floor of Atad also tells a story. 'Atad' means 'piercing' and speaks of the cross. It is at this place of the cross that the Church must undergo 'a great and very sore lamentation' as they bid farewell to the expression of all that has gone before. The dawn of a new day has risen for God's people and 'Jacob' with all his dualism (his scheming, supplanting ,competitive nature enmeshed with his desperation to lay hold of his inheritance) must now be laid to rest. It is time for a new dispensation, the Joseph era to fully emerge. Joseph, prepared in the pit and the prison, can only take center stage once that which has fathered him is laid to rest.

September 9th

Deu 15:12 If your brother, a Hebrew man or a Hebrew woman, is sold to you and serves you six years, then in the seventh year you shall let him go free from you. Deu 15:13 And when you send him out free from you, you shall not let him go away empty. Deu 15:14 You shall richly bestow on him from your flock, and from your grain floor, and from your winepress; with what Jehovah your God has blessed you, you shall give to him.

The threshing floor is also the place where every brother we have held in bondage must be released with blessing. The issue of unforgiveness and the chains it places on others must be thoroughly dealt with. When we hold something against our brother, we place him in a prison. God says that in the seventh year, we are to release him. Seven speaks of completion, of the end of a matter. The Father says it is time for the issues you have held against your brother to be over.

Moreover, it is not enough to forgive and release. God requires His people to richly bless those forgiven. How do we do that? In whatever way the Lord has blessed you, a portion of that is to be given as a blessing to your brother. The threshing floor is the place where the chaff of unforgiveness and grudges part company with the nutritious kernel of Christ in you!

September 10th

Jdg 6:36 And Gideon said to God, If You will save Israel by my hand, as You have said, Jdg 6:37 behold, I will put a fleece of wool in the grain-floor. And if the dew is on the fleece only, and dry upon all the ground, then I shall know that You will save Israel by my hand, as You have said.

The threshing floor is the place where we discover God's mind on a matter. Gideon was unclear as to God's will and was not prepared to move forward leaning upon his own understanding. He had the support of men – many tribes had come to join him should he decide to attack the enemy but Gideon did not want to rely upon the confirmation of man. He asked for a completely supernatural sign – and upon receiving it, asked once again for a confirmation. Only then did he step forward with confidence, knowing that the power of heaven backed his movement. The threshing floor is a place to receive supernatural confirmation and clarity concerning God's will for you. It is a breathing space where you can check your spiritual compass; a heavenly pause before throwing all your weight into the path that lies before you. It is the place where your own natural understanding of situations is threshed and the chaff removed so that you may clearly understand the Lord's will. From this threshing floor, you move forward to certain victory as you follow every detail of His instruction, no matter the size of the enemy encamped against you!

September 11th

Hos 9:1 O Israel, rejoice not for joy, like the peoples. For you have gone lusting away from your God; you have loved a reward on every grain floor. Hos 9:2 The floor and the winepress shall not feed them, and the new wine shall fail in her.

The threshing floor is also the place where God examines heart motives. Those who have hearts full of covetousness, seeking promotion and reward at the floor will be disappointed. God declares no wine will come forth from them – they are not chosen to be vessels dispensing the wine of the third day. Nor will they will not be nourished by the proceeds of the threshing floor. Ruth, on the other hand, embodies the company who go to the threshing floor seeking the Bridegroom and not His rewards. She lies down at His feet, in the place of a servant. She wants Him not His benefits. As a result, He pours six measures of barley into her widow's mantle. Those who go with clean hands and a pure heart to the threshing floor come away full. Those who come with hidden agendas are sent away empty-handed. The hidden motives of the heart are brought into plain sight as God separates with His winnowing fan. What is in our hearts – do we know what is motivating us from deep within?

Prayer: Father, search me and know my heart. Find out if there is any wicked way in me and lead me in the way everlasting, amen.

September 12th

Mic 4:11 Now also many nations are gathered against thee, that say, Let her be defiled, and let our eye look upon Zion. Mic 4:12 But they know not the thoughts of the LORD, neither understand they his counsel: for he shall gather them as the sheaves into the floor.

Not only is God threshing His Church in this day. He is also dealing with the nations. He is gathering them as sheaves to the floor as they gather against natural Israel. He is winnowing and bringing to the surface that which has been hidden in the boardrooms of government. He declares that they do not understand His counsel or know His thoughts.

Can we as His people say that we do understand His counsel and know what He is thinking? How we need the ministry of the Spirit of Revelation and the Spirit of Counsel in these days. If we do not receive it, we are doomed to using our natural understanding to try and fathom the hand of God in the earth in these days. This will lead to presumption and fleshly interpretation. Just as many of the nations assume that natural Israel should be harshly dealt with, so too there are some who assume that God is coming to judge and destroy His Church. In actual fact He comes to winnow in order to separate and preserve that which is good, the kernel of Christ within – only destroying with fire that which is chaff or fleshly. Fire deals with wood, hay and stubble but that which is gold, silver and precious stones comes through unscathed.

September 13th

Mic 4:13 Arise and thresh, O daughter of Zion; for I will make your horn iron, and I will make your hoofs bronze; and you shall crush many peoples. And I will give their gain to the Lord and their wealth to the Lord of the all the earth.

The daughter of Zion refers to the Bride. She is appointed the task of threshing the harvest of the nations. Great strength and endurance will be imparted to her for the task of bringing souls into the kingdom. The gain that she threshes out from the nations are souls. God considers people to be the wealth of nations, not perishable gold or silver. His storehouse is to be full of the proceeds of the threshing floor – multitudes who have been separated from the chaff of the world system and gleaned for the Kingdom.

Prayer: Give me the strength to gather in the true wealth of the nations, that I may fill Your treasuries with the souls of men, amen.

September 14th

Mat 3:12 whose fan is in His hand, and He will cleanse His floor and gather His wheat into the storehouse; but He will burn up the chaff with unquenchable fire.

He will gather His wheat into His storehouse- that speaks of the expression of Christ in us. All that has been deposited in us by the Spirit is for the feeding of the nations and when the chaff has been removed from our lives we are able to be useful in the Master's hand.

The threshing floor is not a place of comfort but a place of upheaval, for the sons of God - a place of being dealt the rod of His Word which speaks of discipline. It is a place of separation within our heart as we let go of that which is fleshly or chaff. It is a place of being tossed in the air by His winnowing fan and allowing the wind of His Spirit to blow the chaff from our lives. It is an up and down experience, a time of not knowing which way is up for a while. However each successive dealing from the Lord's hand removes more of the chaff that has been weighing us down and holding us back. A lightness of spirit is experienced as the weights are set aside and we are freed to run with perseverance the race set before us.

September 15th

Jdg 7:13 And when Gideon had come, behold, a man told a dream to his fellow, and said, Behold, I dreamed a dream, and lo, a cake of barley bread tumbled into the host of Midian, and came to a tent, and struck it so that it fell, and overturned it, so that the tent lay along.

What tumbled into the camp of the enemy was not a sheaf of barley but a barley cake. In other words, it was in a prepared state. In the interpretation of the dream we are told that the barley cake was Gideon. So Gideon was used as a weapon against the enemy once he had been through the process of preparation.

So often we think we are ready to be used when we are just a sheaf of freshly harvested barley. After all we have reached the stage of fruitfulness! However God knows there is still much preparation to be done before we can be released into the middle of the enemy camp to bring destruction. There is a difference between fruitfulness and effectiveness. We must allow the hand of the Lord to work both in our lives. Effectiveness for the kingdom involves the visit to the threshing floor and time in the fire. Then we can be released to tumble without hindrance straight into the enemy camp.

September 16th

Rth 3:15 Also, he said, Bring the veil on you, and hold it. And when she held it, he measured six measures of barley and laid it on her.

Ruth had gathered one measure of barley by her own effort in the fields of Boaz. However her time at His feet brought in six more measures, so she had seven in all. Seven is the number of completion. For the Bride to lay hold of the rest of the harvest, she must be found at His feet at the threshing floor.

The final six measures were given to her without sweat or fleshly effort on her part. She received them from a position of rest. More is accomplished for the Kingdom through worship and waiting upon the Bridegroom in secret than by laboring in the heat of the day using our own strength. Our appointment at the threshing floor not only removes the chaff from our lives. It also ensures that our widow's veil becomes a receptacle overflowing with the fullness of harvest.

The Lord of the Harvest is able to release to us the fruit of the travail of His soul and the results of His finished works if we will only seek the place at His feet and the place near His heart.

September 17th

Heb 12:1 Therefore since we also are surrounded with so great a cloud of witnesses, let us lay aside every weight and the sin which so easily besets us, and let us run with patience the race that is set before us,

The threshing floor is a place for laying aside the weight of the chaff in our lives. Those who cling to fleshly ways only ensure that the Lord winnows them for longer. We often don't realize that the chaff in our lives is weighing us down. It is so well-attached to us that only threshing will loosen it. Once the Lord has managed to bring a separation then the wind of the Spirit blows it from our lives.

227

Then we are able to run the race set before us effectively. No-one runs a race weighed down with overcoats and heavy combat boots. It is far more effective to run wearing His robe of righteousness and the shoes of the gospel of peace.

Prayer: Father, thank you that You help remove the fleshly outer garments I hide myself behind. I want to cooperate with what You are doing in my life, releasing those behaviors which only hide Christ in me. Then I can run with the wind of Your Spirit in order to get a prize, amen.

September 18th

Heb 12:2 looking to Jesus the Author and Finisher of our faith, who for the joy that was set before Him endured the cross, despising the shame, and sat down at the right of the throne of God.

Jesus was the Author and the Finisher. He showed us how to run the race of faith. He did it with His eye on the finish-line. It was there He saw the joy set before Him. His trophy was a Bride who would be in His own likeness. Having this vision before Him empowered Him to endure the suffering appointed Him.

Just as a mother endures travail because she knows that at the end she will hold her child in her arms, so too we are empowered by reminding ourselves constantly of the joy set before us. The birth pangs are a necessary detail of the journey to fruitfulness and the completion of what God has started in the womb of our spirits. A mother doesn't care who sees her or how much clothing she has on when she is in the throes of giving birth. She is so focused on bringing that baby forth. She is not concerned with the opinions of others. In the same way, at the time of birthing God's promises, we look not to the right or the left but with fixed purpose, despising the shame, we co-operate with the Spirit in writing the finishing chapter.

September 19th

Heb 12:3 For consider Him who endured such contradiction of sinners against Himself, lest you be weary and faint in your minds. Heb 12:4 You have not yet resisted unto blood, striving against sin.

The contradiction of sinners, the criticism, the tongue-lashings, the mockery and cruel treatment must be endured as an expected part of the valley of travail. Whatever we have faced, it pales in comparison to that which Jesus faced as His blood poured out at Calvary.

The time when people are opposed to us is not the time to be weary and become faint in our minds. We must understand that the coming forth of the purposes of God in the earth will always be opposed and resisted by sinners and satan himself. Thrust any form of self-pity from your thinking. Only those in travail bring forth fruit. The mocking bystanders with their theological arguments are not even with child! Focus on the joy set before you.

Prayer: Father, help me to keep looking forward to the joy set before me. Let me not be moved by the mockers and scoffers on the sideline watching my race – they are not even running! amen.

Christine Beadsworth

September 20th

Heb 12:5 And you have forgotten the exhortation which speaks to you as to sons, "My son, despise not the chastening of the Lord, nor faint when you are rebuked by Him; Heb 12:6 for whom the Lord loves He chastens, and He scourges every son whom He receives."

Anyone who has been a parent knows that children have to be rebuked in order to realign them to the standard of godly behavior. A child left to himself comes to ruin, Proverbs tells us. We must expect the Father to chasten or correct us because it is a sign of His love.

In these days, God is weighing hearts and bringing correction. We have the choice of setting aside the weights He points out to us and forsaking the sin He convicts us of – or we can harden our hearts and continue stubbornly on in the path of rebellion to His Word.

Our first response as humans is 'who, me? Surely not!' when He puts His finger on an area. We justify and try to wriggle out from under the spotlight because we feel so naked and uncomfortable. Instead of being ruled by pride, let us in this season humbly acknowledge what His light has revealed and then repent and leave it at the foot of the cross.

Prayer: Father, deliver me from self-justification and pride. Grant me the grace to admit my failings to You and others – **even** if You use my enemy to point out my weakness, amen.

September 21st

Heb 12:9 Furthermore we have had fathers of our flesh who corrected us, and we gave them reverence. Shall we not much rather be in subjection to the Father of spirits and live? Heb 12:10 For truly they chastened us for a few days according to their own pleasure, but He for our profit, that we might be partakers of His holiness.

Submission to the Father's chastening produces life. Rebellion leads us in the path of death. The strange woman in Proverbs allures, flatters and strokes our egos and it seems far more rewarding to follow her wherever she leads. However, her victims do not realize 'Her house *is* the way to hell, going down to the chambers of death (Prov 7:27).

Even though it hurts when God chastises us through His Word, we can be certain that He does it for our good. He wants us to be partakers in His holiness. Why? Because without holiness, no-one can see the Lord. Being thankful for the one who has the courage to rebuke is a learned art – much easier attained when humility is present.

Prayer: Father, thank you that You love me enough to tell me my faults. Help me to have the humility to embrace the truth and so be changed, amen.

September 22nd

Heb 12:11 Now chastening for the present does not seem to be joyous, but grievous. Nevertheless afterward it yields the peaceable fruit of righteousness to those who are exercised by it.

Heb 12:11MSG At the time, discipline isn't much fun. It always feels like it's going against the grain. Later, of course, it pays off handsomely, for it's the well-trained who find themselves mature in their relationship with God.

A young tree must be bound to a straight stake so that it doesn't begin to grow crooked as a result of contrary winds. In the same way, while we are immature in our walk with God, He straightens us using the constant presence of the plumb-line of His Word. Just as children chafe against the restraints placed upon them by wise parents, so too we baulk against some of the areas where God requires us to conform to His standard of righteousness. Be comforted in the knowledge that willing submission to the chastenings of the Father result in quick growth to maturity. Cooperation is the quickest route from A to B!

September 23rd

Heb 12:12 Because of this, straighten up the hands which hang down and the enfeebled knees. Heb 12:13 And make straight paths for your feet, lest that which is lame be turned out of the way, but let it rather be healed.

From these verses we can see that areas which are not in conformity to God's ways cause us to limp. This is why Paul starts the chapter calling us to lay aside every weight and the sin which so easily entangles us. When we tolerate sin in our lives it affects our ability to run the race before us because our ankles are held by its octopus tentacles..

However, be encouraged because we are not helpless. Paul says **we** are able to make straight paths for ourselves, to carve them out by our choices. When we stop feeling sorry for ourselves and resisting the chastening of the Father, suddenly our change in attitude empowers us to take the steps which are straight ahead of us. Call the octopus by its real name and shake it off you. There is healing when we submit to the Holy Spirit's rebuke and make the necessary changes. So we have a choice – denial and disease or humility and healing!

Prayer: Father, I want to run with the wind of Your Spirit. Show me the choices I need to make to produce straight paths before me, amen.

September 24th

Heb 12:14 Follow peace with all, and holiness, without which no one shall see the Lord; Heb 12:15 looking diligently lest any fail of the grace of God, or lest any root of bitterness springing up disturb you, and by it many are defiled,

233

Walking in peace essentially means we hold nothing in our heart against another person – it means we have dealt with the issue of forgiveness. If we fail to do this, unforgiveness leads to bitterness and our hearts become full of justifying arguments and mental battles instead of focusing upon God. To be holy means to be fully set apart for the Father and His desires. When our hearts are not at peace with men, our thoughts are not wholly set apart. When we are not at peace with all and bitterness has invaded our hearts then the words which come forth from our mouths are tainted and defile those who hear us. We underestimate the power of a few cynical words. It is necessary to come to a place of peace with all men – even those we do not agree with – if we desire to see God. This means practically that there are things that need to be spoken of with those who have hurt us; issues to be brought to a conclusion and then the power of forgiveness released.

Prayer: Father, I still want to run this race unimpeded. Give me the courage to have the conversations I need to have. Grant me the grace I desperately need to forgive and walk in peace with all, amen.

September 25th

Heb 12:25 See that you do not refuse Him who speaks. For if they did not escape, those who refused him that spoke on earth, much more we shall not escape if we turn away from Him who speaks from Heaven, Heb 12:26 whose voice then shook the earth; but now He has promised, saying, "Yet once more I will not only shake the earth, but also the heavens."

The voice of the Father is resounding over us in these days as He shakes both the earth and the heavens. The question is – will we respond or will we refuse Him? There are many in the valley of decision at this present time. Hearts are being weighed and the Father is watching to see our responses. Economic systems are shaking, storms are pounding in both the natural and the spiritual arena and the heart of man is at a crossroads.

Only that which is of Christ will survive this shaking. Only the shadow of the Almighty is a safe shelter in the coming days. Choosing the shelter of earthly wealth or the citadel of our own strength will prove foolish. The things which we have thought were our supports in the past may actually be revealed to be weights that need to be cast aside. Let us become people who boast only that we know and understand Him who is the fountain of Life and True Wealth.

September 26th

Jer 9:23 Thus says the LORD, Let not the wise man glory in his wisdom, neither let the mighty man glory in his might, let not the rich man glory in his riches: Jer 9:24 But let him that glories glory in this, that he understands and knows me, that I am the LORD who exercises loving-kindness, judgment, and righteousness, in the earth: for in these things I delight, says the LORD.

In the days that lie ahead, the wisdom of men, the might of men and the wealth of men will prove to be unreliable shelters. The word 'exercise' above means 'to accomplish, produce and appoint or bestow'. There are some upon whom the Lord will be appointing loving kindness in these days and others who will be appointed judgment. For those of God's people who have walked in idolatry and vain pursuits there will severe shakings in order to bring them to a place of righteousness and holiness again.

For others who have been refined in the fire and chosen the fear of the Lord, a time of recompense is appointed. Is our delight and greatest desire to know Him or do we still seek after the things of this world? Our hearts are being weighed.

September 27th

Jam 4:4 MSG You're cheating on God. If all you want is your own way, flirting with the world every chance you get, you end up enemies of God and his way. Jam 4:5 And do you suppose God doesn't care? The proverb has it that "he's a fiercely jealous lover." Jam 4:6 And what he gives in love is far better than anything else you'll find. It's common knowledge that "God goes against the willful proud; God gives grace to the willing humble." Jam 4:7 So let God work his will in you. Yell a loud no to the Devil and watch him scamper. Jam 4:8 Say a quiet yes to God and he'll be there in no time. Quit dabbling in sin. Purify your inner life. Quit playing the field. Jam 4:9 Hit bottom, and cry your eyes out. The fun and games are over. Get serious, really serious.

The things the world seeks after are self-realization, money, power, fame and fortune. To a large extent these goals have crept into the Body of Christ and set us on a path of enmity with God. He IS a fiercely jealous lover, wanting to possess our whole hearts and allegiance. Beloved, it is time to thoughtfully examine our lives for evidence of these worldly ideals in 'Christian' guise.

Let us return to the Lover of our souls with all our hearts and repent of placing our trust in useless things like silver and gold or positions of power, even in a Christian context.

Prayer: Lord, you are looking for faithful lovers, not business managers. Straighten up any crooked understanding I have of Your plan for Your Bride, amen.

September 28th

Heb 12:27 And this word, "Yet once more," signifies the removing of those things that are shaken, as of things that have been made, so that the things which cannot be shaken may remain. Heb 12:28 Therefore, since we are receiving a kingdom that cannot be shaken, let us have grace, by which we may serve God acceptably with reverence and godly fear, Heb 12:29 for also, "Our God is a consuming fire."

The reason for the shaking is to remove that which can be shaken – in other words all that is not founded upon the Rock, Christ. This means that financial systems run by the greed and ambition of men will be shaken. It means governments founded upon the wisdom and political ambition of men will be shaken. It also means the theories and doctrines of men will be severely rattled. The shaking will unearth hidden corruption and the works of darkness that have been going on unimpeded in the wings. The day of shaking is a day of revelation and exposure, a day when the refuge of lies is swept away by the hand of God. The kingdom of God cannot be shaken. Its government is stable and unable to be toppled. Therefore those who are seated in heavenly places in Christ, resting in the power of the cross and the wisdom of God, will be above the shakings.

Prayer: Father, may I be seen as a true son of the Light in dark days. Glorify Your Name through my surrendered life. I hide myself under the shadow of Your wings, amen

September 29th

Rom 5:3 There's more to come: We continue to shout our praise even when we're hemmed in with troubles, because we know how troubles can develop passionate patience in us, Rom 5:4 and how that patience in turn forges the tempered steel of virtue, keeping us alert for whatever God will do next.

The storm and the shaking serves to remove from us all the unnecessary weights and debris which clutter our thinking and our lives. In a time of crisis, we simplify in order to survive. Suddenly things which would have rocked our foundations just a short time previously, hardly ruffle our feathers and we realize that God is building strength and endurance into our spirits. We become focused on what is really important and strain our ear to hear His still small voice.

We seek the peace to be found in the eye of the storm because we so desperately need to know what course to take and there is no other way to hear clearly. The shaking and the storm makes us more dependent, less self-assured. It forces us to choose that which is of value because that which is worthless has crumbled away under our weight. It brings us to the state of mind that God desires of us – surrender and trust. It drives us into the cleft of the Rock.

Prayer: Father, how wise you are to bring the shaking. Thank You for streamlining my Christian profile and getting me to focus on what is really important, amen.

September 30th

Mal 3:16 Then they that feared the LORD spoke often one to another: and the LORD listened, and heard it, and a book of remembrance was written before him for them that feared the LORD, and that thought upon his name. Mal 3:17 And they shall be mine, says the LORD of hosts, in that day when I bring forth my jewels; and I will spare them, as a man spares his own son that serves him.

The Lord has taken note of those who have continued to walk in the fear of the Lord. He has recorded their names in His Book of Remembrance. At the appointed time the book is opened and read and those who have been faithful in affliction and have not turned aside to idolatry will be rewarded.

Just as God remembered Hannah and gave her a son; just as God remembered Noah waiting in the ark, God will remember those who fear Him and fulfill His purpose in their lives. Never think that God has forgotten you or discarded your prayers.

October 1st

Est 6:1 On that night could not the king sleep, and he commanded to bring the book of records of the chronicles; and they were read before the king. Est 6:2 And it was found written, that Mordecai had told of Bigthana and Teresh, two of the king's chamberlains, the keepers of the door, who sought to lay hand on the king Ahasuerus. Est 6:3 And the king said, What honour and dignity hath been done to Mordecai for this? Then said the king's servants that ministered unto him, There is nothing done for him.

It had been recorded in the books what Mordecai had done to protect the king and the kingdom – but seemingly it had been forgotten! However, at the appointed time the books were opened and the King remembered Mordecai. His faithfulness was rewarded.

At the very moment the enemy was constructing a gallows for Mordecai, the King was reading the books. Beloved, never focus on what the enemy is plotting concerning your life. All the days of your life are written in God's book and He WILL remember you and recompense you. He will overturn the enemy's plan for destruction and use him for your elevation! Rest and be peaceful. God has it all in hand!

Prayer: Lord, thank You that You read the books of our lives and You are faithful to give honour where honour is due! My future is in your hands, not in the hands of my scheming enemies, amen.

October 2nd

Luk 1:45 And blessed is she that believed: for there shall be a performance of those things which were told her from the Lord.

Mary believed before there was any sign of the manifestation of that promise from the angel. She put her trust in the word of God and said, "be it unto me according to Your Word". Beloved, you too have believed. When the Father dropped that vision of His purpose in your heart, you received it without protest, never considering the price you would pay to bring forth that promise. Whatever it was what the Father wanted to do through you. you were willing.

However, now many days have passed and the persecution, the loneliness, the alienation have all taken their toll on you. Receive fresh strength from this verse – 'there shall be a performance of those things told you by the Lord'. You believed before any outward manifestation had come your way. Now today receive a fresh confirmation – you have not believed in vain. Press through to the finish-line. The performance is almost in sight. Now is not the time to lose heart and fall by the wayside! His Word never returns void!

October 3rd

Luk 1:41 And it came to pass, that, when Elisabeth heard the salutation of Mary, the babe leaped in her womb; and Elisabeth was filled with the Holy Ghost: Luk 1:42 And she spoke out with

241

a loud voice, and said, Blessed art thou among women, and blessed is the fruit of thy womb.

Whenever God plants something in the womb of your spirit, he will connect you to others who are also experiencing similar things. This is for the process of confirmation and encouragement. There is a witness spirit to spirit.

Let us be grateful today for those the Lord has drawn alongside us to mentor and encourage us in our unique journey with God to bring forth His purposes in the earth. Without them we would be lonely and craving some sort of input that confirms to us we have not believed in vain.

October 4th

Luk 1:46 And Mary said, My soul magnifies the Lord, Luk 1:47 and my spirit has rejoiced in God my Savior. Luk 1:48 For He looked on the humiliation of His handmaiden. For, behold, from now on all generations shall count me blessed. Luk 1:49 For the Mighty One has done great things for me; and holy is His name.

All Mary had in her womb was the beginnings of what God was going to do, when she made this declaration. The DNA had been deposited and in due season it would bring forth the fullness of what God had decreed over her. Yet right here at this juncture she speaks as if the fullness is already accomplished. She is praising God for His finished works and decreeing that all shall see and know that God has mightily blessed her.

She was seeing by faith the outcome and the manifestation of the spoken word over her life and praise erupted from her lips. So often we wait for the manifestation before we magnify the

Lord. Beloved, let us open our mouths and begin to magnify and glorify God for the substance of what we see with the eye of faith. If the Word has been released, it CANNOT return void and the position of our hearts is to be settled assurance and joyful praise because what He has spoken, He will fully perform.

October 5th

Luk 1:51 He has worked power with His arm, He has scattered the proud in the imagination of their heart. Luk 1:52 He has put down rulers from their seats and exalted the lowly, Luk 1:53 He has filled the hungry with good things, and He has sent away the rich empty. Luk 1:54 He has helped His servant Israel, in remembrance of His mercy, Luk 1:55 as He spoke to our fathers, to Abraham and to his seed forever.

Hear the language of Mary's mouth – He HAS worked power, He HAS scattered, He HAS put down, He HAS filled – every sentence is in the past tense. Mary sees the work completed before even the Savior is born . When only the spoken Word, carrying the DNA of a complete plan of action, has been deposited in her womb, Mary speaks of an accomplished fact and all its outworkings. That is settled faith and confidence in the power of God's spoken intention.

Let us repent of all our wavering and align our tongues confidently with God's spoken promise, which is UNABLE to fail. Let confidence return to our hearts. The Word has already been sent and even now He works unseen to bring forth every detail of His plan. As Mary said – His plan is to scatter the proud and put down principalities that have assaulted you. His plan is to lift you up and fill your hungry heart and souls with good things. We are children of Abraham by faith and therefore His covenant to

Abraham extends to us. The finished works of Christ speak over your life. Begin to rejoice and declare what you see by faith!

October 6th

Luk 1:59 And it happened that on the eighth day they came to circumcise the child, and were calling it Zacharias, after his father's name. Luk 1:60 And his mother answered and said, No, but he shall be called John.

The thing that God is bringing forth in this day will not follow old patterns or traditions. It will not be according to the expectation of man nor the ways of earthly fathers. It will not even be after the pattern of those who have gone before us in the Church. God has declared a new day and is doing a new thing. Now it springs forth. Be aware of it and its differences. It is so different that God will not even allow it to carry the same name as the last season.

It was strange to all that Zacharias was rendered dumb during the pregnancy. He knew it was because of the unbelief he expressed as to God's ability to do what the angel had spoken. Silently he observed his wife's growing belly and his heart must have repented many times but God only released him to speak of it on the 8th day, the day of circumcision and naming. Beloved when you see the face of what God has spoken, you will know that is indeed doing a new thing. Old ways and things have passed away and you will toss old traditions and the ways of man to the wind and joyfully embrace the embodiment of a new season in your life. Get ready to be the herald of a new day. God will release you to speak again in power to confirm what He is doing!

October 7th

Luk 1:59 And it happened that on the eighth day they came to circumcise the child, and were calling it Zacharias, after his father's name. Luk 1:60 And his mother answered and said, No, but he shall be called John.

Zacharias means 'God has remembered'. John means 'God has favored'. God was declaring a change in season. No longer was God only going to remember His faithful people but a season of favor was now decreed upon them. Judgment is being passed in favor of the saints.

As John grew, people marveled at the favor of God upon him even as a child. In the same way, Beloved, the message that comes forth from your life will no longer be 'God hasn't forgotten me' but now you will enter into a new dispensation when the judgment in favor of you will begin to be carried out - where the favor of God upon you will be openly displayed for all to see.

The season when John was in the womb was a silent season for Zacharias but on the 8th day when the time of naming God's manifestation was at hand, Zacharias' tongue was loosed as he confirmed the name of the new season.

Do not make the mistake of assuming that the next season, the season of manifestation, will have all the same labels attached. A new day is at hand and your tongue will be loosed to declare the purposes of God to all who watch.

Prayer: Lord, Help me not to have rock-hard mindsets about the next season. You will remember me and Your plans for me are for good and not for evil, amen.

October 8th

Luk 1:67 And his father Zacharias was filled with the Holy Ghost, and prophesied, saying,

The previous generation prophesies over the following one. A word from the throne is spoken by the power of the Holy Spirit which releases the next season for the Church. Until this eighth day, Zacharias was silenced and could only see and hear. Then the day came when he wrote on the tablet, confirming the will of God and lining himself up with the purposes of God. Because of this, the Spirit was able to use him to bring a powerful word at the junction of two different seasons in the purposes of God.

Obedience and acknowledgment of God's purposes in the unusual thing manifesting will always cause the power of the Spirit to be released in and through us. When we are prepared to put aside the way things have always been done and walk in the fear of God and not man, then we become a useful instrument in the hand of God. He puts His words in our mouths and covers us with the shadow of His hand as we boldly speak His intentions.

October 9th

Luk 1:71 That we should be saved from our enemies, and from the hand of all that hate us; Luk 1:72 To perform the mercy promised to our fathers, and to remember his holy covenant; Luk 1:73 The oath which he swore to our father Abraham, Luk 1:74 That he would grant unto us, that we being delivered out of the hand of our enemies might serve him without fear, Luk 1:75 In holiness and righteousness before him, all the days of our life.

Zachariah was not prophesying about John's life here but about Christ. He was speaking a forerunner word which would only begin to be fulfilled when Jesus came to be baptized by John. This was about thirty years later! God sees the end from the beginning. We are so concerned with immediate needs and our comfort but God is looking ahead and already beginning to speak creative words which will in time manifest in the natural realm.

So often God speaks a Word to us and we expect its fulfillment in days or weeks or at the most months. John was the forerunner who would prepare the way for Christ. He was not the Christ - yet his life and ministry were a vital bridge between the old and the new. John formed the juncture at which the shadow met the reality and his father Zacharias saw past the shadow to the face of the reality.

Prayer: Father, open my eyes to see past the immediate – help me to recognize the bridging seasons and not mistake them for the final manifestation. Show me Your full purposes and use me to begin to proclaim them with the eye of faith. Amen.

October 10th

Luk 2:7 And she brought forth her son, the First-born, and wrapped Him, and laid Him in a manger-- because there was no room for them in the inn.

There is no room for the manifestation of Christ in today's busy business-model Church. Our programs are full, just as the innkeeper's rooms were. There are budgets to be met and people to be satisfied – the Church is today part of the Hospitality Industry. We are seeker-friendly and we don't want people being upset by the sounds of a woman in labor coming from the next-door room! Heaven forbid that we should shuffle around our schedule and make room for Christ to be brought forth in our midst!

How many times have we turned away those who carry within them the answer we so desperately need? How often we have protected the reputation of our establishment at the expense of giving shelter to those God has chosen to bring forth His purposes? How often have we answered the knock at the door but not recognized the face of God's purposes standing before us, because of our own prejudices and preferences?

Prayer: Father, forgive us for not making room for the fruit of Your purposes to come forth in our midst. We have only impoverished ourselves without realizing it. Open our eyes, God, to see as You see and to recognize Your arrival in the unexpected and the inconvenient, amen.

October 1st

Luk 2:7 And she brought forth her son, the First-born, and wrapped Him, and laid Him in a manger-- because there was no room for them in the inn.

For those who have long carried this God-given vision, there is only the lonely place, outside the warmth of the general gathering. There is no comfortable bed or midwife to assist them in their arduous labor. They are comforted by the Holy Spirit and the word that when God brings to the birth, He will also bring forth. He will not block the womb or cause the death of this Christ-child. In the midst of a lonely labor, those with the honor of being forerunners are comforted by the knowledge that the fruit of their travail will benefit all those still caught up in the feasting and revelry within the inn.

Obscurity is the birthplace God chooses to introduce His answer. There is no fanfare or celebration on earth as the manifestation of Christ quietly makes its entrance – but in heavenly realms angels are singing and rejoicing!

Prayer: Father, open my ears to hear the angels singing over me as I labor to bring forth Your purposes in the earth. Let me not look for the support of man or the confirmation of man, but let me hear Your voice coaching me, amen.

October 12th

Joh 19:38 And after this Joseph of Arimathaea, being a disciple of Jesus, but secretly for fear of the Jews, besought Pilate that he might take away the body of Jesus: and Pilate gave him leave. He came therefore, and took the body of Jesus. Joh 19:39 And there came also Nicodemus, which at the first came to Jesus by night, and brought a mixture of myrrh and aloes, about an hundred pound weight. Joh 19:40 Then took they the body of Jesus, and wound it in linen clothes with the spices, as the manner of the Jews is to bury.

Just as Joseph cared for Mary and protected her as she brought forth Jesus, so too another Joseph later cared for the body of Jesus and prepared and ministered spices in preparation for coming forth of Firstborn from among the Dead. Two Josephs - both given stewardship of God's secret plans; both trusted with the responsibility of doing what was needed in order to make a safe delivery of God's Son from the womb and from the tomb. Both do not stay in the spotlight for long because all focus is upon what God is doing but God knew He could trust them to fulfill their part in the story, without fanfare or desire to seek center stage. There are those who seem to work in the wings at the edge of God's unfolding plans – or so it seems from man's point of view. May God help us to see from His perspective those who have been found trustworthy and courageous enough to spurn the fear of man and walk in the fear of God, whether it involves joining oneself to something that is scandalous in society's eyes and causes loss of one's own reputation.

October 13th

Luk 2:8 And in the same country there were shepherds living in the field, keeping watch over their flock by night.

We are living in times that are growing darker and many are milling around like sheep without a shepherd. However, thankfully, there are some faithful shepherds keeping watch over their flocks by night.

Notice these shepherds were living in the field, right at the level of their sheep – no comfortable warm beds while their sheep faced the evening chill alone. They are not hirelings who flee at the first sign of trouble. They are the shepherds with the heart of David, willing to slay a lion and a bear to protect those they care for. This is why God finds them worthy to be the receivers of the good news of the manifestation of Christ.

He does not send the angelic messengers to the king in his palace or to the priests busy at their religious duties. He chooses those who have laid down their lives in the pattern of the Chief Shepherd to be the ones who first receive the revelation of Christ. Those who are hirelings flee at the first sign of discomfort or danger but shepherds with a heart like David's are hand-picked to be messengers of His glory. As Job said, "I had heard of you, but now my eyes have seen You". Then they could return and share the good news with the sheep in their care.

Prayer: Father, thank you that in these difficult times you have raised up shepherds after Your own heart, and that You release the revelation of Christ to them that they may share it with others, amen.

October 14th

Zec 2:5 For I, says the LORD, will be to her a wall of fire round about, and will be the glory in the midst of her.

Once more, according to this scripture, God promises to be present in the midst of His people. Long ago, the prophet said His name would be called 'Emmanuel' meaning 'God with us' and in the fullness of time Christ came and tabernacled amongst us. He was also present by the power of the Holy Spirit at Pentecost and was clearly evident working with the disciples as they preached the Word.

Then sadly, the Church began to descend in the ways of Babylon and after a while, it was difficult to distinguish the believer from the worldly-wise. No wonder the Lord needs to come as a consuming fire, devouring all dross and purifying His beloved Body. In the latter days, the glory of His presence will again be seen in her midst and the protection of His fiery love will surround her and deal with every attack. But His glory will not be in a building made with hands but in a Body, a living temple, holy and set-apart for her Bridegroom.

251

Just as He tabernacled with the lowly and was born in a stable and first seen by shepherds, so too, this time, He comes to those who are humble of heart; those not involved in the trafficking of Babylon. He comes forth in those who were willing to say 'be it done to me according to Your Word'; those willing to lose their reputations in order to be counted as one of His.

October 15th

Joe 2:17 Let the priests, the ministers of the LORD, weep between the porch and the altar, and let them say, Spare Your people, O LORD, and give not Your heritage to reproach, that the heathen should rule over them: why should they say among the people, Where is their God? Joe 2:18 Then will the LORD be jealous for his land, and pity his people. Joe 2:19 Yeas the LORD will answer and say to his people, Behold, I will send you corn, and wine, and oil, and you shall be satisfied therewith: and I will no more make you a reproach among the heathen:

In large measure, the world is saying to the Church, "where is your God?" We say much but produce little result and the power of God is seldom seen in our midst. However, when the royal priests begin to intercede and repent on behalf of the Body for their sin and idolatry, then God takes pity on His people. He declares He will send them corn, wine and oil to satisfy their souls.

The corn represents souls entering the kingdom. The wine depicts heavenly revelation of the Word, where water has been turned into wine. The oil represents the anointing. When corn, wine and oil are present, it signifies that Tabernacles is manifesting once more and God is in our midst!

Prayer: Father, forgive us for going astray after other gods. Remove our reproach and manifest Yourself in our midst once again. Send us corn, wine and oil in abundance, amen.

October 16th

Deu 11:14 I will give the rain of your land in its due season, the first rain and the <u>latter rain</u>, that you may gather in your grain and your wine and your oil.

In order for the fields of corn, grapes and olives to become ready for harvest, the latter rain is needed. There is a 'due season' or an appointed time for the latter rain to fall. It comes as the crops come to maturity and it originates with the Lord. There is no other place where we can receive the necessary latter rain. The first or former rains are light showers and ensure germination but the latter rains are heavy.

They speak of an outpouring of the revelation of Christ which causes the Church to come into the full experience of what was intended when Christ first came and tabernacled among us. The Hebrew word translated 'latter rain' also means 'eloquence'. The heavy latter rain will cause the voice that comes forth from the Church to be fluent and eloquent. No longer will there be a stammering and a stuttering because of poor understanding. There will be an impartation of revelation, understanding and wisdom through this heavy latter rain. The voice of the Church will no longer be a clanging cymbal but go forth in authority, accompanied by a demonstration of the Spirit and power.

Prayer: Lord, how desperately we need this heavy latter rain; the revelation and manifestation of the presence of Christ in the midst of us. We ask You to release the rain that brings the harvest to completion, amen.

October 17th

*Jer 3:1 They say, If a man put away his wife, and she go from him, and become another man's, shall he return unto her again? shall not that land be greatly polluted? but you have played the harlot with many lovers; yet return again to me, says the LORD... Jer 3:3 Therefore the showers have been withheld, **and there has been no latter rain;** and you had a harlot's forehead, you refused to be ashamed.*

When there is idolatry and harlotry amongst God's people, then one of the results is the withholding of both the first showers and the latter rain. In other words, not only is there little germination of seed sown; the crops also fail to reach maturity. Unless the Church of Jesus Christ stops making excuses for it's' love affairs with the world, it will never come into the corporate fulfillment of Tabernacles, where the presence and glory of God is evident in their midst. Individuals can repent and walk in holiness and experience the latter rain personally because of their relationship with God. However the Body by and large will die in the wilderness without setting foot in the promised land of their full inheritance, unless they deal with their 'harlot's forehead'. Proverbs 30:20 tells us 'Such *is* the way of an adulterous woman; she eats, and wipes her mouth, and says, I have done no evil'.

Prayer: Father, forgive us for being lured away by the deceptive dainties of other lovers. Cause Your people to 'come to themselves' like the prodigal son so that we may return to our Father's house, amen.

October 18th

Hos 6:1 Come, and let us return unto the LORD: for he hath torn, and he will heal us..... Hos 6:3 Then shall we know, if we follow on to know the LORD: his going forth is prepared as the morning; and he shall come unto us as the rain, as the latter and former rain unto the earth.

There has to first be a tearing of the veil of blindness and self-deception over the Church's eyes before she can come to herself and return to the Lord. God does this in order to bring us to healing. However, the tearing of the veil can be painful. Sometimes it involves the exposing and toppling of idols in the life of the Church. Once the prodigal son realized where he was and that he was eating pig's food, it was the start of a journey back to Father's house.

Once we turn from our harlotry and idolatry, God can set in motion the plan He has been keeping on ice all the time we were in the land of uncleanness – His going forth is prepared and He comes as the rain to His thirsty wilted Body. When the father caught sight of his son on the road home, he ran to embrace him and then issued the instructions to get the banquet ready. How God longs to release the fullness of all that is stored up in heaven for us. However we must forsake every other lesser lover and begin the journey home to His embrace!

Prayer: Father, tear every veil over the eyes of my heart that is keeping me in any form of idolatry or harlotry. I earnestly desire to receive the latter rain of Your presence, amen.

October 19th

Joe 2:19   the LORD will answer and say to his people, Behold, I will send you corn, and wine, and oil, and you shall be satisfied therewith: and I will no more make you a reproach among the heathen:

Corn is harvested with a scythe but both oil and wine are produced by crushing. The processes God brings to bear in our lives to produce the fullness of harvest are often painful. True revelation often comes forth during periods of great pressure and extremity as God breaks the Bread of Life with us and prepares a table for us in the presence of our enemies. He does not always remove our enemies before feeding us the meat of the Word. In full view of our enemies, He invites us to sit down and sup with Him .

There is a continual flow of oil to the candlesticks in Zechariah's vision. However the process of producing the continual power of the Spirit in our lives involves crushing and breaking and dying to self. In order to dispense oil and wine to both the Church and the world, the valley of the shadow of death is the pathway appointed. Paul said 'death is at work in me, but life is at work in you' – and so it is with us. The inner pressure and crushing brings a continual impartation of the life-giving revelation of Christ to others!

Prayer: Father, thank you for the privilege of becoming a door for others to taste and experience oil and wine. I thank you that You were wise enough to work death in me, so that Your life could have room to flow from me, amen.

October 20th

Joe 2:23 Be glad then, ye children of Zion, and rejoice in the LORD your God: for He hath given you the former rain moderately, and He will cause to come down for you the rain, the former rain, and the latter rain in the first month. Joe 2:24 And the floors shall be full of wheat, and the vats shall overflow with wine and oil. Joe 2:25 And I will restore to you the years that the locust hath eaten, the canker worm, and the caterpillar, and the palmer worm, my great army which I sent among you. Joe 2:26 And ye shall eat in plenty, and be satisfied,

God's promise is that once He has dealt with the enemy coming against His people, the latter rain will be poured out and the harvest will come forth in full measure. The floors shall be full of wheat and the vats will overflow! How heart-rending it is for a farmer to sow precious seed and water and tend it, only to come out one morning and find that caterpillars have annihilated every green shoot. In contrast what joy there is when a field full of grain comes to maturity and is harvested.

Tabernacles is a time of great joy because the fullness of the harvest has been brought in. In the same way, in the prophetic fulfillment of Tabernacles, the seed of the Word which we have received and confessed, watered and tended through a long hot summer, will bring forth abundant fruit. There will no longer be broken dreams, shame and hope deferred; . God's people will enter into a time of fullness of joy and it shall be known that God Almighty is in the midst of us.

Prayer: Lord, You are the restorer, the sender of rain which brings the harvest to fullness. Thank you for Your goodness, in spite of our tendency to wander at times, amen.

October 21st

Psa 126:5 Those who sow in tears shall reap in joy. Psa 126:6 He who goes forth and weeps, bearing precious seed, shall doubtless come again with rejoicing, bringing his sheaves with him.

The time of weeping precedes the time of reaping. The seed of the Word is sown in the fertile soil of our earthen vessels and we carry it undetected for a season as it takes root and begins to grow, watered by our tears of intercession.

Sometimes the season of weeping and travail seems so long and one can almost lose hope of ever seeing the fruit of one's prayers manifest in the earth BUT God promises that those who sow in tears shall reap in joy! The times of Tabernacles does indeed come in the fullness of time. We will hold in our arms the sheaves of our harvest and dance for joy before the Lord.

These sheaves represent the full manifestation of the Word of Promise sowed many days before in the soil of our hearts. His Word is unable to return void or unfruitful. It WILL accomplish the purpose for which He sent it. We WILL rejoice in the Word and hold in our arms the fruit of His promise, just as Sarah held Isaac and laughed with joy because of God's unsurpassed faithfulness! The time of mourning and travail will be replaced by the flow of the oil of joy as we experience our own personal Tabernacles feast.

October 22nd

Pro 16:15 In the light of the king's countenance is life; and his favor is as a cloud of the latter rain.

When we live and dwell before His face or continually aware of His presence, the light of His countenance shines upon our lives and His favor is poured out upon us. Solomon says that God's favor has the same effect as a cloud of latter rain. In other words, it brings fullness of fruitfulness in the fields we labor in and visible manifestation of the fruit of the seed of promise planted in our hearts. How we need the evidence of God's favor in our lives in order to have a testimony before the heathen.

Hosea 6:1-3 calls the people of God to return to the Lord fully so that in the third day we may dwell before His face and know Him intimately. The reward of a deep love relationship with the King is an outpouring of favor, the heavy latter rain.

Prayer: Father I desire face to face relationship with my Bridegroom. Bring me to the place where I dwell fully in the light of Your countenance, amen.

October 23rd

Isa 60:1 Arise, shine; for your light is come, and the glory of the LORD is risen upon you.

'Your light has come' - what light? The light of His countenance is upon you. Here is a fulfillment of the Aaronic blessing given to the children of Israel- ' The LORD bless you, and keep you. The LORD make his face shine upon you, and be gracious to you; the LORD lift up his countenance upon you, and give you peace'. There is something profound released upon our lives when we know the Lord face to face. It speaks of there being no obstacles between you and Him, no baggage obscuring your view of His beauty. As He gazes upon you, His beloved, His light and glory fill you and overflow.

This is the blessing which God instructed His priests to speak over His people. The Hebrew word for 'peace' is 'shalom'. It can be translated more fully as ' completeness (in number), safety and soundness (in body), welfare, health, prosperity, peace, quiet, tranquility, contentment, peace, friendship with God especially in covenant relationship'. What more do we need other than this 'shalom' which comes when His face shines upon us?

Prayer :Father, may the light of Your face shine upon me and my family. Let Your peace, Your Shalom manifest in our lives, amen.

October 24th

Isa 60:2 For, behold, the darkness shall cover the earth, and gross darkness the people: but the LORD shall arise upon thee, and his glory shall be seen upon thee.

The amazing thing is that this light that arises upon God's people does not come in a time of safety and outward peace. It comes when there is darkness over the earth and gross darkness over the people who do not know Him. This word 'darkness' has a figurative meaning in the Hebrew - ' misery, destruction, death, ignorance, sorrow, wickedness'. What an accurate description of the state of the world at this present time.

This is the very time God chooses to cause His light to arise upon His beloved faithful saints. Diamonds are always displayed best against a black velvet backdrop and God will display His jewels throughout the earth during a time of great darkness and trouble. This is why He calls us to arise and shine. As the darkness grows deeper, it is not a time for His saints to go into hiding for fear of what is approaching. It is a time to stand and allow the light He is pouring out within you to shine as never before!

October 25th

Isa 60:3 And the Gentiles shall come to thy light, and kings to the brightness of thy rising.

In a time of darkness and turmoil all over the earth, the Bride radiates the light of God and draws people to Him. Even those in places of authority will acknowledge that God's people have something they do not at this time – wisdom and direction. When people are running to and fro desperately seeking answers and stability and shelter, the Bride of Christ will be found to be the source of the words of Life and Light. Her heart will be at peace in the midst of the stormy seas of the nations and she will draw the desperate to her like bees to a honey pot.

Even as this happens, persecution will also increase against those who hold out the Word of Truth. Demoniacally inspired hatred will stir up violence against the people of God. However, this is not a time to run and hide your identity but a time to be strong and courageous, knowing you have been brought to the Kingdom for such a time as this. Stand and shine in your home, your workplace, your community with the light of God's favor upon you. Love your enemies. Do good to those who hate you. Pray for those who persecute you that you may be seen to sons of your Father who is in Heaven.

Prayer: Lord, give me courage to arise and shine, even when the persecution begins to assault my life. May I be a lighthouse that is unaffected by the force of the waves pounding at its walls, amen.

October 26th

Zec 4:7 Who art thou, O great mountain? before Zerubbabel thou shall become a plain: and he shall bring forth the headstone thereof with shoutings, crying, Grace, grace unto it.

Are you facing a mountain that seems to stand squarely in the path of your progress? God will turn it into a plain. He will make the rough places smooth and level every steep place before His Bride as she moves forward in His purposes. The word 'headstone' above is feminine in the Hebrew, indicating that the Bride, operating in the same level of authority as her Groom (the Cornerstone), will be brought forth in the latter days.

This manifestation will be accompanied by a shout. The Hebrew word for 'grace' is also translated 'favor'. So we see that this crowning stone of the building God has been building; the Bride of Christ, shall be brought forth with a Royal command to release a double portion of favor upon her. Favor will open double doors for those the Lord is causing His face to shine upon in these days. All the painful years of preparation will be worth it as we arise, radiant with His glory.

Prayer: Father, thank you for a double portion of recompense poured out in my life through Your overflowing favor, amen.

October 27th

Psa 44:3 For they did not get the land in possession by their own sword, neither did their own arm save them; but it was Your right hand, and Your arm, and the light of Your face, because You favored them.

It is neither the strength of man nor the arsenal of man's weapons which will bring us into the experience of the Promised Land of the revelation of Christ. Everything depends upon the strong right arm of God working on our behalf AND the outpouring of His favor upon our lives.

Just as the Jordan River rolled back, opening up a way for the Israelites to enter Canaan on dry ground; so too the favor of God opens doors of influence and opportunity. However we must remember that these opportunities are not for the purpose of self-fulfillment but the extension of the Kingdom. He will bring His trusted saints before kings and men in authority in order for us to speak the words He gives us. This why we are required to be bold and courageous – we will be coming face to face with ungodly systems and mindsets. This is the time to speak the anointed word that brings light and supernatural wisdom to bear on situations. Open your mouth wide and God will fill it!

October 28ᵗʰ

Luk 21:12 But before all these, they shall lay their hands on you and persecute you, delivering you up to the synagogues and prisons, being brought before kings and rulers for My name's sake. Luk 21:13 And it shall return to you for a testimony. Luk 21:14 Therefore settle it in your hearts not to meditate beforehand what you shall answer. Luk 21:15 For I will give you a mouth and wisdom which all your adversaries shall not be able to gainsay nor resist.

Persecution is already an expected part of everyday life for many believers worldwide. For those who have not yet tasted it, we can be sure that it will come, probably not too many days from now.

263

If the captain of our salvation was made perfect through suffering, we cannot expect anything different for ourselves.

Yet, in the midst of this prospect there are words of comfort – we are not to fret about what to say in these instances. Jesus Himself has promised to supply us with every word we need to speak right at the moment it is required. The wisdom of Heaven that confounds the worldly-wise is to be our portion. Furthermore He says that the experience of this persecution will supply us with a testimony; a testimony of His provision and greatness; a testimony of His power! So let our hearts be settled and at peace. No matter what we are required to face, the resources of Heaven are at our disposal.

October 29ᵗʰ

Luk 21:16 And you shall be betrayed also by parents and brothers and kinsmen and friends. And they will cause some of you to be put to death. Luk 21:17 And you shall be hated by all for My name's sake. Luk 21:18 But there shall not a hair of your head perish.

Is this not a painful thing – that those we love and trust and have eaten bread with, shall in the latter days betray us? However, in this too, we walk the path that Jesus walked. Judas walked closely with Jesus for three and a half years, ate at the same table, laughed and cried and prayed with Him. Yet, on the appointed day, he betrayed Him.

How we shall need the grace of God to continue responding in love when the day of betrayal comes. For many of us, we have already been in training, suffering smaller rejections or betrayals by other believers. We have been learning to respond in the Spirit and not according to our flesh. We shall be grateful for these rehearsals in coming days for when the greater betrayals come, we will find our hearts responding easily, having learnt the lessons privately in our closets. We shall be seen to be sons of our Father in heaven, who rains on both the just and the unjust.

Prayer: Father, thank you that nothing can separate me from Your love. When the tests come, thank you that the grace needed to forgive and release will be there for me to access, amen.

October 30th

Luk 21:25 And there shall be signs in the sun, and in the moon, and in the stars. And on the earth will be anxiety of nations with perplexity; the sea and the waves roaring; Luk 21:26 men fainting from fear, and expecting those things which have come on the earth. For the powers of the heavens shall be shaken.

We are already seeing the anxiety of nations. Government leaders are gathering and trying to find solutions to financial shakings. They do not realize it is God himself who is doing the shaking and they cannot prevent its completion! Jesus speaking here just confirmed the prophesy of Isaiah who said, " In that day a man shall cast his idols of silver, and his idols of gold, which they made *each one* for himself to worship, to the moles and to the bats; Isa 2:21 To go into the clefts of the rocks, and into the tops of the ragged rocks, for fear of the LORD, and for the glory of his majesty, when He arises to shake terribly the earth"(Isa 2:20).

God is determined to deal with pride and idolatry and the shaking we feel in the financial markets will precipitate a domino effect, resulting in the toppling of every idol man has bowed his knee to.

His purpose is to bring man to the end of his own wisdom. Let us make sure we are walking in the fear of the Lord and giving Him His due place in our lives.

October 31st

Luk 21:34 MSG "But be on your guard. Don't let the sharp edge of your expectation get dulled by parties and drinking and shopping. Otherwise, that Day is going to take you by complete surprise, spring on you suddenly like a trap, Luk 21:35 for it's going to come on everyone, everywhere, at once. Luk 21:36 So, whatever you do, don't go to sleep at the switch. Pray constantly that you will have the strength and wits to make it through everything that's coming and end up on your feet before the Son of Man."

Pray constantly – here is one of the keys to safety and strength in the days we face. Prayer causes us to acknowledge God's superior wisdom and strength. When we cease praying and start plotting we return to leaning on our own limited understanding. If we acknowledge Him in all our ways, He will direct our paths. However, this is not a casual two minute prayer as we rush about our social schedule. Denial will not get us through. We must be alert and spiritually awake and ready.

Waiting upon the Lord for counsel and direction also takes time and will be of paramount importance in the days ahead. We cannot afford to make the mistake of leaning on the arm of flesh if we want to come through the storm unscathed. Only the secret place of the Most High is immune to the effects of the roaring waves and shaking heavens. Here we can discern His still small voice. We must hide ourselves in Him and await His instruction – and then be instantly obedient. Herein is our safe passage through great tribulation.

Prayer: Lord, I take refuge under the shadow of Your wings. Keep me awake and alert and aware of the dangers of complacency, amen.

November 1st

Romans 5:11 AMP ' Moreover let us be full of joy now! Let us exult and triumph in our troubles and rejoice in our sufferings, knowing that pressure and affliction and hardship produce patient and unswerving endurance. 5:4 And endurance develops maturity of character. And character of this sort produces the habit of joyful and confident hope of salvation.

The troubles and sufferings we have undergone produce endurance in us. This is vitally necessary for the days that lie ahead. We are in a long-distance race, not a sprint and unless we have developed endurance, we will not cross the finish-line. Endurance causes us to push past the pain, past the discomfort, past the signals screaming from our flesh and propels us determinedly towards the prize awaiting us. Those who have come through much, have much endurance and are not swayed by upheavals and shakings. They have come to know personally the character of their God in the valleys and up the long mountain passes and are joyfully confident that they serve a God who is faithful. They have been tested and tried in the furnaces of affliction and have spiritual backbone. It is these ones who will be shelters for the fearful in the days ahead as they offer encouragement and counsel.

Prayer: Father, thank you for training me and pushing me and building endurance in me in the seasons that have passed. I know You were equipping me so that I would lack nothing I need for the days ahead. Your wisdom is perfect even if I don't like Your training schedule!

November 2nd

Psa 84:5 Blessed is the man whose strength is in You; in whose heart are the highways to Zion. Passing through the valley of weeping, they make it a place of springs; the early rain also fills the pools with blessing.

Those who know where their strength is found will pass safely through the valley of weeping. Not only that but they change it into a place where fresh living water springs up. They have learnt to dig deep in God and tap into a supernatural strength and supply that is not dependent on their outward circumstance. They may be in a valley but they turn it into a place where those who come after them find refreshing – even in the midst of their own weeping.

There is no shelter like our God. He is a rock that stands sure and unchanging and the place where this truth is mined is in the valley of weeping. Once a saint taps into this life-giving revelation and receives an impartation of God's supernatural strength to go the distance, he himself becomes a spring of living water, satisfying the thirst of many a weary traveler. In the days that lie ahead, those forerunners who have safely traversed this valley will be sought out because they hold out the Word of Life and know the keys to safe passage through the turmoil ahead. Blessed is the man whose strength is in Him!

November 3rd

Jam 1:2 My brothers, count it all joy when you fall into different kinds of trials, Jam 1:3 knowing that the trying of your faith *works patience. **Jam 1:4** But let patience have its perfect work, <u>so that you may be perfect and entire, lacking nothing</u>.*

The Greek word translated 'patience' here also means 'endurance'. Once again we see that the purpose of trials is to build endurance. Beloved, this is going to be one of the most needed qualities during the shakings which have already begun.

For those of us who look back on a seemingly unending season of trial after trial, we can now be thankful because the Father's purpose in allowing them was to equip us completely for the days we are entering. How great is His love in not wanting to send us unprepared into what lies ahead. He sees the end from the beginning and every day of our lives was written in His book before one of them came to be. This is why He has put us through weight training and resistance training and spiritual aerobic workouts. He needs us to be spiritually fit and ready for the obstacle course in front of us. He has been training us to be overcomers. There will be rejoicing in the tents of the righteous in the coming days as we realize we possess within us all we need to successfully navigate the course.

November 4th

Jam 5:10 Take, my brethren, the prophets, who have spoken in the name of the Lord, for an example of suffering affliction, and of patience 5:11 Behold, we count them happy which endure. Ye have heard of the patience of Job, and have seen how the Lord blessed him in the end;

The prophets spoke out God's message and were often not well received. Yet they practiced patience and ENDURED, often not even seeing the manifestation of what they had spoken in their own lifetimes. Sometimes we have given others a word from the Lord and been ridiculed and scorned as there is no sign of its fulfillment. In our instant society we often expect a promise from the Lord to be fulfilled within a week or, at the very most, a year. It causes us great distress when time continues to march on and the fruit of the promise remains unseen.

Job also suffered much and when all had been stripped away from him and it seemed impossible that he should even survive his ordeal, God chose to give him a fresh revelation of His greatness. Job's knowledge of God moved from hearing to seeing and he also received double recompense after the trial was over. Remember, Beloved, as you press on and develop greater levels of endurance during the dark hours of your trial, that the day of recompense is coming. Weeping endures for a night but joy comes in the morning.

November 5th

Heb 12:1 Therefore since we also are surrounded with so great a cloud of witnesses, let us lay aside every weight and the sin which so easily besets us, and let us run <u>with patience</u> the race that is set before us, Heb 12:2 looking to Jesus the Author and Finisher of our faith, who for the joy that was set before Him <u>endured</u> the cross, despising the shame, and sat down at the right of the throne of God. Heb 12:3 For consider Him who <u>endured</u> such contradiction of sinners against Himself, lest you be weary and faint in your minds.

Jesus was the pattern Son; the One who went before us setting an example for us to follow. He endured suffering, persecution and finally the cross. Through all these things, He remained unswayed, His eyes fixed upon His goal. He was so aware of the

271

assignment the Father had given Him that it did not matter what men said or did to Him. He pressed on. Paul calls us to run the race before us with the same endurance and patience. How do we manage this? By looking unto Jesus, our example. He is both the author and the finisher of our faith. When weariness and faintness assails us, we must meditate on the sufferings and endurance of Jesus. Because of His sacrifice, we are able to be seated in heavenly places now, far above any persecution or suffering. This is the reason we can rejoice in our sufferings.

Prayer: Father, thank you so much that I can withdraw into the secret place of Your presence any time I need to. Here I find strength to press on. What a great salvation we possess!

November 6th

Rom 8:35 Who shall separate us from the love of Christ? shall tribulation, or distress, or persecution, or famine, or nakedness, or peril, or sword? ...No, in all these things we are more than conquerors through him that loved us. Rom 8:38 For I am persuaded, that neither death, nor life, nor angels, nor principalities, nor powers, nor things present, nor things to come, Rom 8:39 Nor height, nor depth, nor any other creature, shall be able to separate us from the love of God, which is in Christ Jesus our Lord.

Absolutely nothing we will ever face has the power to separate us from the love of God. Let these verse not only be letters on a page for you. Let them sink in and become part of the foundation stones of your heart. It does not matter whether you are facing persecution, attack, lack of food, emotional distress or the point of a sword. Let the ever-present love of God be a continual revelation to your soul. Nothing in the future can separate you from Him. Nothing going on presently in the world can prise you from His loving arms.

So don't listen to the lies of the enemy when he whispers that you are all alone and God doesn't care. Don't believe him when he tells you that you have been abandoned and must face your giants alone. Eat the words of these verses, chew on their nourishment and be strengthened by Truth. He is with you right now, right where you are. Close your eyes and soak in His life-giving presence.

November 7th

Rev 3:10 Because you have kept the Word of My patience, I also will keep you from the hour of temptation which will come upon all the habitable world, to try those who dwell upon the earth.

Here we see that patience or endurance and perseverance in remaining faithful to the Lord has a reward – God Himself promises to keep these ones safe during the time of great trial that the whole earth is appointed to suffer. These are those who have been counted worthy to escape the things coming upon the earth (Luke 21:36).

So, Beloved, do not resent the fiery trials which have prepared you for this day. By continuing to remain faithful no matter what you have endured, you have been found worthy. The trial was to test your quality, to see if you could be counted worthy to escape what is coming. Just as Noah, a preacher of righteousness, was counted worthy to escape the flood and was hidden in the ark until the danger was past, so too will His faithful ones be sheltered in the hour of temptation. Even though Noah was ridiculed and mocked for being obedient to God for many years while the ark was being built, when the flood came he was no doubt grateful that he had persevered and endured and finished the assignment!

As you are obedient to the Lord, He will shut the door behind you and no man will be able to open it and cause you harm. You will be carried safely above the coming judgments.

November 8th

2Ti 3:12 Yea, and all who desire to live godly in Christ Jesus will be persecuted.

Paul warns us that all who really desire to live devout God-fearing lives WILL suffer persecution. This is not a 'maybe' but a 'definitely'. When we live the way God intends us to, we stand out from the crowd and make those living in compromise or wickedness feel very uncomfortable. They will attempt to find occasion to cause us to stumble. We will be ridiculed and called names. There will even be times when we are prosecuted for standing up for what we believe to be right and just.

This can be a painful experience and so we must arm ourselves with the words of Jesus beforehand in order to see everything from an eternal perspective when it happens to us:

Mat 5:10 Blessed are they who have been persecuted for righteousness sake! For theirs is the kingdom of Heaven. Blessed are you when men shall revile you and persecute you, and shall say all kinds of evil against you falsely, for My sake. Rejoice and be exceedingly glad, for your reward in Heaven is great. For so they persecuted the prophets who were before you.

Prayer: Lord, persecution is an occasion for rejoicing!! Help me to remember this when it happens and thank you for the honour of fellowshipping in Your suffering, amen

November 9th

Act 8:1 And Saul was consenting unto his death. And at that time there was a great persecution against the church which was at Jerusalem; and they were all scattered abroad throughout the regions of Judea and Samaria, except the apostles. And devout men carried Stephen to his burial, and made great lamentation over him. As for Saul, he made havoc of the church, entering into every house, and hauling men and women out, committed them to prison. Therefore they that were scattered abroad went everywhere preaching the word.

The result of persecution is that saints are thrust out into other regions to preach the Word. Before this great persecution broke out, the Acts church was having a lovely time fellowshipping in Jerusalem but they had not fulfilled the prophesy of Jesus who said they would be His witnesses to the ends of the world (Acts 1:8). It took the assault of Saul and persecution to galvanize the believers into fleeing to other regions.

Sometimes comfort is the enemy of evangelism. The Father in His wisdom brings times of discomfort – much like the mother eagle who thrusts sticks through the bottom of the nest to propel the eaglets into flight! So let us not fear persecution. In every instance in history it has only served to purify and strengthen, energize and grow the Church of Jesus Christ.

November 10th

Mat 5:43 You have heard that it was said, "You shall love your neighbor and hate your enemy." Mat 5:44 But I say to you, Love your enemies, bless those who curse you, do good to those who hate you, and pray for those who spitefully use you and persecute you, Mat 5:45 so that you may become sons of your Father in Heaven. For He makes His sun to rise on the evil and on the good, and sends rain on the just and on the unjust.

God wants us to display His character to the world. Real character does not emerge during sunny days but during dark times. Only when an orange is pressed on every side, does the juice run out and prove that it is actually the fruit that the outer appearance indicated. In the world, people are kind to those who are kind to them or who can benefit them in some way. It goes completely against the grain of HUMAN nature to respond in love to someone who hates you or wishes you harm.

Every instance of persecution and mistreatment is an opportunity for DIVINE nature to be exhibited. One of the first steps to doing this is – 'PRAY for those who persecute you'. As we bring our hearts before God in prayer, any motive for revenge soon brings the conviction of the Spirit as He purifies our prayers on the golden altar before the throne.

As we begin to pray the prayers God would have us pray for our enemies, we find our hearts are softened towards them because we begin to see them as God sees them. Then the spring of love begins to trickle towards them.

November 11th

Mat 5:46 For if you love those who love you, what reward do you have? Do not even the tax-collectors do the same? Mat 5:47 And if you greet your brothers only, what do you do more than others? Do not even the tax-collectors do so? Mat 5:48 Therefore be perfect, even as your Father in Heaven is perfect.

The word 'perfect' used here means 'of full age, manhood, complete'. Do you remember that James told us that the trials we have undergone are for the purpose of bringing us to a state of being '<u>perfect</u>', where we lack nothing? So we can see that the preparation we have undergone has also been in order to equip us to be able to love those who hate us and greet those who are opposed to us. We have to stick out in the crowd as being radically different in our attitudes and responses.

The church in the West has not experienced much open hatred up to this point. However, things are about to change radically. God knows this and has therefore been preparing His faithful ones in the fiery furnace so that they may stand and help the rest of the Church in these days. They have been brought to a stage of maturity and perfection through the things they have suffered, just as Jesus was.

November 12th

Joh 15:18 If the world hates you, you know that it hated Me before it hated you. Joh 15:19 If you were of the world, the world would love its own. But because you are not of the world, but I have chosen you out of the world, therefore the world hates you. Joh 15:20 Remember the word that I said to you, The servant is not greater than his master. If they have persecuted Me, they will also persecute you. If they have kept My saying, they will also keep yours. Joh 15:21 But all these things they will do to you for My name's sake, because they do not know Him who sent Me.

We should not be surprised if the world hates us. What shocks us is when those we considered to be brothers turn on us and begin to hate us. Jesus greatest persecution came from the religious establishment of the day. It proved they did not know God as they professed to. In the same way, in the days that are ahead, we will be surprised at the quarters from which attack and persecution comes. Many who have previously displayed an outer appearance of spirituality will suddenly begin to say and do things which are totally contrary to godliness. The dividing line will be Jesus Christ. He is the plumbline and those who have been deceived into believing there is more than one way to the Father (even in the Church) will begin to attack those who swear that there is no other name under Heaven by which we might be saved. The world has infiltrated the Church in a greater measure than we realize. We must prepare our hearts to walk in the blood-soaked footsteps of our Master.

November 13th

Rom 12:14 Bless those who persecute you; bless, and do not curse.

The power of life and death is in the tongue. Jesus warns us not to release words of death in retaliation to attack. We must continue to release words of blessing and life into the atmosphere, remembering that we are not wrestling against flesh and blood, but principalities and powers. If we will respond this way, we leave room for God to work.

Rom 12:19 not avenging yourselves, beloved, but giving place to wrath; for it is written, "Vengeance is Mine, I will repay, says *the* Lord."

God's declared intention is to deal with the powers of darkness that comes against us so we must not begin to operate in the flesh according to our own understanding. The highest form of spiritual warfare is not calling down curses upon the enemy camp but rather responding in the opposite spirit – releasing light in response to darkness.

November 14th

Mar 4:16 And these are they likewise which are sown on stony ground; who, when they have heard the word, immediately receive it with gladness; **Mar 4:17** *And have no root in themselves, and so endure but for a time: afterward,* <u>*when affliction or persecution arises*</u> *for the word's sake, immediately they are offended.*

Jesus taught that the condition of our hearts is paramount to reaping a good harvest. Here we also see that a stony hard heart can receive the Word but when affliction or persecution comes because of the Word, they become offended. This word 'offend' comes from a Greek word which is also translated ' to trap, ensnare or cause to stumble'. These people then fall away from the Truth.

So we see that persecution actually reveals the condition of the soil of our hearts. Up to this point, all looks well on the outside but the moment any affliction arises because of Jesus, the Word, it becomes apparent that there is no real root to their faith. Paul was shown that in the end-times, there would be a great falling away. I believe it will be caused by the level of persecution that arises against the Church. Let us pray that we may be granted the strength to stand faithful in the face of whatever comes.

November 15th

1Co 10:12 So let him who thinks he stands take heed lest he fall. 1Co 10:13 No temptation has taken you but what is common to man; but God is faithful, who will not allow you to be tempted above what you are able, but with the temptation also will make a way to escape, so that you may be able to bear it. 1Co 10:14 Therefore, my dearly beloved, flee from idolatry.

The word 'temptation' used here also means 'to put to the proof, adversity'. Whatever adversity we may have to face, we have the promise that God knows the extent and limits of our ability to endure. He has an exit door planned and an end to the trial on His schedule. This is why we are able to bear it.

It is interesting that Paul immediately after this warns against idolatry. The Israelites in the wilderness became victims of the things they idolized and God was not pleased with them. Therefore they were overcome and many died in the desert. An idol is anything in our lives which we allow to usurp the place of Christ, be it our carnal appetites, other people or our even our own opinions! The key to standing in adversity is keeping Christ as our central focus and greatest love.

Prayer: Lord, deliver me from the delusion that I am above temptation. That in itself is a form of pride that I need to be rid of! Cleanse my heart of arrogance, amen.

November 16th

1Co 16:13 Keep watching! Stand firm in the faith. Be acting like a man [fig., Be brave]. Continue becoming strengthened. 1Co 16:14 Let all your* [deeds] be taking place in love.

God intends for His saints to <u>stand</u> in the end-time trials. To stand firm in the faith we must be clear about what we believe. Our whole faith must be in the finished works of the cross of Christ and no other wishy-washy doctrine of works. We are also required to keep watching and not fall into a slumber. Then Paul admonishes believers to be brave. Fear will an enemy that will continuously try to creep into our hearts in these days. Banish it with declarations of Truth and of your faith in Christ's all-sufficiency to fulfill His Word.

We must act like men, and put away childish things in these days. The hour demands maturity of spirit and soul.

We must also continually strengthen ourselves in the Lord, drawing power and life from His indwelling presence. Finally, all our actions must be launched from a foundation of love. Jesus was God in the flesh and God is love. Therefore we may learn how Love behaves by observing the actions of Jesus. Love is not weak and does not delight in evil but rejoices in the Truth. Love always perseveres! Love speaks out against injustice. Love shows mercy.

November 17th

2Ti 2:4 No soldier on service entangles himself in the affairs of this life; his aim is to please the one who enrolled him as a soldier.

Are we living our lives to please the One who has enlisted us? Or are we entangled in the affairs of this life? Entanglement describes someone who has become almost ensnared in a thicket – like the lost sheep whom the Shepherd went to find. The parable of the lost sheep is often used regarding the salvation of the lost but we must realize that this was a sheep and not a goat that was lost. So the parable of the lost sheep is more accurately a picture of one of the Lord's children who has wandered off and become entangled and is now unable to extricate itself from the thicket.

The affairs of this life have that effect upon us when we become too involved in them. Instead of being able to serve as a soldier, obedient to the One who enlisted us, we can find ourselves so involved in the 'affairs' of life, that we are unable to respond. The word 'affair' comes from a root word meaning ' busyness, trading, business, work'. Where is our focus? What is our aim? Is it to please the One who enlisted us in His service? Do we have a single eye? Or are we entangled? If so, only the Good Shepherd is able to extricate us from our predicament. He removes the thorny branches that ensnare us so we can emerge. As we repent of over-involvement in the affairs of this life, there is much joy in heaven and we can return to active service – wholly consecrated and set-apart for Him.

November 18th

Joe 2:31 The sun shall be turned into darkness, and the moon into blood, before the great and the terrible day of the LORD come. Joe 2:32 And it shall come to pass, that whosoever shall call on the name of the LORD shall be delivered: for in mount Zion and in Jerusalem shall be deliverance, as the LORD hath said, and in the remnant whom the LORD shall call.

Mount Zion and the heavenly Jerusalem are the only place where deliverance and safety are available on the great and terrible day of the Lord. When upheavals are taking place on every side, the only place to run to is Mount Zion. His remnant, who carry the road-map to Zion in their hearts will be able to show the way to others.

Psa 84:5 Blessed is the man whose strength is in You; In whose heart are the highways to Zion.

You cannot guide anyone on a journey you have not traveled yourself. Printed tourist guides are written by people who have been to the places described. In the same way, in these end times, only those who know the pathway to Zion will be trustworthy travel-guides. The remnant who has been prepared in advance, often walking the difficult path without other human company, will be sought out in the days ahead. They know by personal experience every step on the path to Zion and will teach others. In the remnant whom the Lord shall call, there will be deliverance found.

November 19th

Isa 4:1 And in that day seven women shall take hold of one man, saying, We will eat our own bread, and wear our own apparel: only let us be called by thy name, to take away our reproach.

In the day when the Lord comes with His refining fire to His church, seven women (representing His complete church) will realize that they are actually not under the covering and protection of His name because of their worldly behavior. They will not longer want to be joined to the Lord for what they can get, like food and clothing, but will desire to be truly known as

His and bear His name so that their reproach amongst the heathen may be removed.

This marks a whole change in mindset for the church at large. No longer are they interested in what they can get out of the Lord, as if He is a giant slot machine, but rather their desire becomes to be in legitimate and legally recognized relationship with Him. To be called by His Name requires that one begins to take on His nature and character. Those called 'Christian's' will truly be Christ's ones and in an intimate relationship with Him. The fire of the Lord will accomplish this refining. It will deal with the chaff as He cleanses His threshing floor.

Prayer: Father, if there is any vestige of the desire for selfish gain in my relationship with You, may your refiner's fire burn it to ashes, in Jesus' Name. I want to carry Your Name out of love for You, amen.

November 20th

Isa 4:2 In that day shall the branch of the LORD be beautiful and glorious, and the fruit of the earth shall be excellent and comely for them that are escaped of Israel. Isa 4:3 And it shall come to pass, that he that is left in Zion, and he that remains in Jerusalem, shall be called holy, even every one that is written among the living in Jerusalem: Isa 4:4 When the Lord shall have washed away the filth of the daughters of Zion, and shall have purged the blood of Jerusalem from the midst thereof by the spirit of judgment, and by the spirit of burning.

The spirit of judgment and the spirit of burning operate during the baptism of fire that is coming upon the church. This refining purging fire purges and cleanses the people of God. Some will not be able to stand the dealings of the Lord in this refining process and will fall away. Others will find their works of wood, hay and stubble burnt up and only they themselves have emerged on the other side of the process. The refiner's fire separates the real from the counterfeit and the holy from the hypocrite. There is a remnant who, having built with gold and silver and precious stones upon the foundation of Christ, will stand during the application of these two fiery spirits and emerge beautiful and glorious in Christ as they make up the branch of the Lord.

Mal 3:17 And they shall be mine, says the LORD of hosts, in that day when I bring forth my jewels; and I will spare them, as a man spares his own son that serves him.

November 21st

Isa 33:14 The sinners in Zion are afraid; fearfulness has surprised the hypocrites. Who among us shall dwell with the devouring fire? who among us shall dwell with everlasting burnings? Isa 33:15 He that walks righteously, and speaks uprightly; he that despises the gain of oppressions, that shakes his hands free from holding bribes, that stops his ears from hearing of blood, and shuts his eyes from seeing evil;

Our God is a consuming fire. Mount Zion is place of everlasting burnings because His presence is continually there. Only those with a lifestyle of godliness and holiness can dwell in the midst of the fire and not be consumed. Those who are walking in sin and hypocrisy are afraid when the baptism of fire comes to the Church because they know that fire has the effect of exposing hidden impurities in the metal of the Body. The fire of the Lord brings separation of the holy from the unholy. Those who serve the Lord in name only and harbor abominations in their hearts will be in serious trouble when the Lord makes manifest the counsels of the heart through His fire.

Prayer: Father, You know the thoughts and intents of my heart. Show me any hidden wicked way in me and increase the fear of the Lord in me. I desire to be able to dwell with Your everlasting burnings,amen.

November 22ⁿᵈ

Dan 3:25 He answered and said, Lo, I see four men loose, walking in the midst of the fire, and they have no hurt; and the form of the fourth is like the Son of God.

Here are three men who were able to dwell with the everlasting burnings without being consumed. Why was this? Simply because when those in the world looked at them they saw the fourth man, Christ, as well. For us to be able to dwell with the everlasting burnings and carry the fiery flame of the Lord within us, the character of Christ has to come forth in us in such a way that the world can see Him. The refiner's fire does no harm to those who fear the Lord – its purpose is burn off any ropes that the enemy has bound them with. We should welcome the work of His fire in our hearts for it enables us to walk with Him in the midst of the everlasting burnings.

Moses gazed at a bush that was aflame yet not consumed. Little did He realize that he himself would become in effect a 'bush' burning with the fire and zeal of God for His people as He stood before Pharaoh. There is a fiery commissioning coming for many who have been quietly walking on the backside of the desert for many years. Get ready. Get ready to be equipped for the task with signs and wonders. Get ready to leave the place you have become so used to. He makes His ministers a flame of fire!

November 23rd

Dan 3:27 And the princes, governors, and captains, and the king's counselors, being gathered together, saw these men, upon whose bodies the fire had no power, nor was an hair of their head singed, neither were their coats changed, nor the smell of fire had passed on them. Dan 3:28 Then Nebuchadnezzar spoke, and said, Blessed be the God of Shadrach, Meshach, and Abednego,

The key to coming forth from the fire without even the smell of smoke upon us is contained in the words of Nebuchadnezzar above. These three men trusted God and refused to enter into any form of idolatry – even if it meant they would be killed. They declared that God was able to save them but even if He chose not to, their stand concerning idolatry remained firm. As a result the decree of the king was changed over them. Before the passage through the fire, there was a death sentence over their heads. After they emerged unscathed, the king's decree was that everybody in his kingdom was to honor the God of these young men for He was above all gods. Here we see a depiction of the verse in Revelation, 'and they overcame him by the blood of the Lamb and the word of their testimony and they loved not their lives even unto death'.

Is our stand concerning idolatry firm? Or will we compromise if our lives are at stake? The refiner's fire comes to purge any idolatry from our hearts. If we cling to our idols, we will perish along with them in the heat of the flames. We must once and for all time choose whom we will serve!

November 24th

Deu 4:23 Take heed to yourselves, lest you forget the covenant of the LORD your God, which he made with you, and make yourself a graven image, or the likeness of anything, which the LORD your God has forbidden you. Deu 4:24 For the LORD your God is a consuming fire, even a jealous God.

WE 'make' our idols. We give things the place in our lives which belongs to God alone. We allow them to steal our time and demand our attention - and God, the jealous Lover of our souls watches and waits for us to come to our senses. If we do not, however, He steps in with His consuming fire. The greatest idol in our lives can be ourselves. When our choices are governed by what will make us feel good, we have wandered from the fear of God. This self-worship is a hallmark of the last days:

2Ti 3:1 But know this, that in the last days perilous times will come. 2Ti 3:2 For people will be lovers of themselves [or, self-centered], ... lovers of pleasure more than lovers of God,

Let us, as the Bride of Christ, no longer indulge in any form of spiritual 'masturbation'; where we will rather do anything that gives us pleasure and satisfaction - while robbing the One with whom we are in covenant of adoration and attention. Let us rather live to give Him pleasure. Then the fire of His jealous love will do us no harm.

November 25th

Mal 4:1 For, behold, the day comes, that shall burn as an oven; and all the proud, yes, and all that do wickedly, shall be stubble:

and the day that cometh shall burn them up, says the LORD of Hosts, that it shall leave them neither root nor branch. Mal 4:2 But unto you that fear My name shall the Sun of righteousness arise with healing in his wings; and you shall go forth, and frisk about as calves let from the stall.

Here we see that the fear of the Lord is the quality which separates those who suffer loss from those who receive reward when the Refiner's fire comes. Where there is pride and wickedness, there will be destruction. Where there is the fear of the Lord, an entirely different scenario unfolds! The Sun of Righteousness, Jesus, comes to minister healing and restoration. These ones have been in stalls up to this point, shut in and restrained, lacking freedom. Then suddenly the stall door is opened and they can come forth with joy. Anyone who has seen a calf released into a meadow will know how they kick up their heels and frisk joyfully!

The word 'stall' also indicates a situation where something has been put on hold or 'stalled'. Are you in a place where your spiritual progress has been impeded by closed doors and a feeling of being shut-in? Well, the day is coming when you will be released from this 'stall' and the Lord will bring to completion that which concerns you. The fiery dealings of the Lord remove all hindering ropes and shut doors and full freedom is restored to those who fear the Lord! Expect a restoration of the joy of your salvation!

26th November

Isa 4:5 And the LORD will create upon every dwelling place of mount Zion, and upon her assemblies, a cloud and smoke by day, and the shining of a flaming fire by night: for upon all the glory shall be a defense. Isa 4:6 And there shall be a tabernacle for a shadow in the daytime from the heat, and for a place of refuge, and for a covert from storm and from rain.

After the spirit of judgment and the spirit of burning have cleansed the daughters of Zion, the manifest presence of God will be seen in the form of a cloud and fire, just as in the journey of the Israelites through the wilderness. The cloud provided protection and shelter from the heat and the pillar of fire provided direction and light at night. In the same way, as the end-time church flees to the wilderness (Revelation 12), His messengers who have been made a flame of fire will provide direction and light to those who have come out of the slavery of the Babylonian religious system.

Notice also that this cloud and fire will be both in the dwelling places and the assemblies on Mount Zion. Whether we are just one or two gathering at home or in larger gatherings of true believers, there will be a manifestation of our Father's protection and guidance. The question is – are we dwelling in the secret place of the Most High or are we choosing the flimsy shelters of the protection of man? Only on Mount Zion , the Jerusalem above, is true protection and provision provided.

27th November

Jer 20:9 Then I said, I will not mention Him, nor speak in His name any more. But His Word was in my heart like a burning fire shut up in my bones, and I was weary with holding in, and I could not stop.

It is one thing to hide the Word of God in our hearts, it is quite another for it to burn like a fire within us. It was said of Jesus that zeal for God's house consumed Him. There was nothing else that claimed His attention or warranted His focus. We have all hidden portions of the Word in our hearts and at times the Holy Spirit brings them to remembrance as a word of encouragement. However, when the baptism of fire comes, those Word stores within become ignited and we understand their content as never before and are then inspired to act according to that revelation. Peter, on the day of Pentecost, spoke under the direct inspiration of the Spirit with such eloquence that people were amazed. The words just tumbled out of him like a pent-up river released in power.

The Word and attached understanding may be lying quietly, almost dormant, in your heart at present but there is coming a mighty outpouring of the Spirit and fire to those waiting in the upper room. You will be equipped and propelled into the highways and byways, moving in the power of the Spirit.

28nd November

Dan 7:9 I beheld till the thrones were cast down, and the Ancient of days did sit, whose garment was white as snow, and the hair of his head like the pure wool: his throne was like the fiery flame, and his wheels as burning fire. Dan 7:10 <u>A fiery stream issued and came forth from before him</u>: thousand thousands ministered unto him, and ten thousand times ten thousand stood before him: the judgment was set, and the books were opened.

There is a fiery stream or river flowing forth from the throne of God. It is the release of His Spirit-quickened Word to His saints. This fire upon His Word deals with any thought or belief within us that is contrary to the Truth proclaimed. It cleanses and purifies and deals with the chaff in our belief systems and our character. (*Jer 23:29*) *Is not my word like as a fire? says the LORD.* It judges and divides between the thoughts and intents of the heart.

Isa 66:15 For, behold, the LORD will come with fire, and with his chariots like a whirlwind, to render his anger with fury, and his rebuke with flames of fire. Isa 66:16 For by fire and by his sword will the LORD plead with all flesh: and the slain of the LORD shall be many.

The baptism of fire both cleanses and empowers. The Lord will have for Himself a holy people that can be used in every corner of the earth for His glory!

29ᵗʰ November

Joh 21:8 And the other disciples came in a little ship; (for they were not far from land, but as it were two hundred cubits,) dragging the net with fishes. Joh 21:9 As soon then as they were come to land, they saw a fire of coals there, and fish laid thereon, and bread.

Jesus already had a fish on the fire before the disciples came to shore with their catch. A fish represents a man (Jesus said He would make the disciples fishers of men). So here we see a picture of a corporate Man made up of forerunners. This company has been lying on the coals in the refiner's fire for some time before the haul of other fish is brought to shore by the other six disciples. This fish has been prepared in advance by Jesus and will be presented along with the bread of the Word.

The flesh of this fish will also provide a meal for the disciples. This is a picture of the Word becoming flesh in this forerunner company. Once they have been removed from the fiery coals, they will share true meat (breaking the Bread of the Word) with a church hungry for the revelation of truth.

Prayer: Father, thank you for the refiner's fire which is preparing me to minister true meat with those you bring me into contact with. Help me to lie still on these coals until I am 'done'! Amen.

30ᵗʰ November

Joh 6:5 When Jesus then lifted up his eyes, and saw <u>a great company come unto him</u>, he said to Philip, where shall we buy bread, that these may eat? ...Joh 6:8 One of His disciples, Andrew, Simon Peter's brother, said to Him, Joh 6:9 <u>There is a boy here</u> who has five barley loaves and two small fish, but what are these among so many?

When the systems of the world as we have known it collapse, there will be a great company who come to Jesus as they hunger for Truth in the midst of chaos. At this time of crisis, those who have long in preparation for this very moment, will come to the forefront. They will not be the learned and the educated religious leaders of the previous season but rather those who have been with Jesus, walking and talking in intimacy, feeding on His body and drinking His blood.

The little boy with fish and loaves represents the manchild company who, in a time of the famine of the Word, share their own nourishment to feed a multitude. When the doctrines of man have at last been found to be without real nutrition or applicability in the world situation, the true meat of the Word will be presented in the simplest way. This manchild company possess within their earthen vessels the full council of God represented by the FIVE and the TWO, SEVEN being the number of completion. The food they offer will bring the Body of Christ to maturity, to the measure of the stature of the FULLNESS of Christ. Then we will reach mature manhood, no longer tossed by every wind of doctrine. Barley loaves contain no leaven and the ministry shared will be without the leaven of the Pharisees, which is hypocrisy.

Prayer: Lord, make me ready for the day I must share my lunch with the multitude. Remove any leaven from my understanding and nourish me with true meat, amen.

December 1ˢᵗ

Eph 6:11 Put on the whole armor of God so that you may be able to <u>stand</u> against the wiles of the devil. Eph 6:12 For we do not wrestle against flesh and blood, but against principalities, against powers, against the world's rulers, of the darkness of this age, against spiritual wickedness in high places. Eph 6:13 Therefore take to yourselves the whole armor of God, that you may be able to <u>stand</u> in the evil day, and having done all, to <u>stand</u>.

God desires His Bride to be able to stand in the evil day. We are not appointed to fall and be overcome. However, there are some important steps we need to take in order to ensure that we DO stand in the times that lie ahead of us. We need to make sure we have the WHOLE armor of God on. The very first thing we need to attend to is the understanding of what putting on the armor of God means. For years many well-meaning saints have gone through a prophetic ritual every morning of putting on the various parts of the armor as if they were getting dressed spiritually.

Unfortunately this has very little real effect in the spiritual realm because the armor of God actually describes a lifestyle, not an outfit hanging in your spiritual wardrobe! Once we understand this, we are equipped with knowledge of the necessary behaviors which will provide us with spiritual immunity.

Prayer: Good grief, Father, sometimes I wonder what on earth I have been doing all these years. Help me to move from play-acting to operating in power, in Jesus Name, amen.

Christine Beadsworth

December 2nd

Eph 6:14 Therefore <u>stand,</u> having your loins girded about with truth, and having on the breastplate of righteousness

The loins are responsible for fruitfulness. Whatever our spiritual loins are supported by will determine the kind of fruit we bring forth. Truth is a Person, not a principle or doctrine. If we are born of the seed of Christ, Who is Truth, then we will bring forth fruit after the same kind. Jesus 'gave birth to us by the word of truth for the purpose of our being a kind of first-fruits of His creatures'(James 1:18). Seed always produces after its kind. This is why the introduction of demonic doctrines is so damaging to the Church. Paul warns against those who preach twisted doctrines which are devoid of truth, one of which involves prosperity - 1Ti 6:5 Perverse disputings of men of corrupt minds, and destitute of the truth, <u>supposing that gain is godliness</u>: from such withdraw .

It is time to examine ourselves to make sure we are in the faith. The mixture of tares and wheat in God's field will be separated - we must make absolutely sure that what we are putting our faith in, has its origin in Christ and not the halls of hell. Many of the so-called Church have yet to be truly born again. The entry point to God's kingdom is a cross where we die and Christ from that point on, lives in us. Any sermon containing seed that encourages Self to be pandered to, does not issue forth from the Word of Truth. Spit it out!

1Jo 1:6 If we say that we have fellowship with Him and walk in darkness, we lie and do not practice the truth.

December 3rd

Eph 6:14 Stand therefore, having your loins girt about with truth, and having on the breastplate of righteousness;

The breastplate covers and protects the heart from which flow the springs of life. There is a righteousness which is received by faith in Christ but it must also lead to a righteous lifestyle; a life lived in the light where we have nothing to do the fruitless deeds of darkness. True righteousness bears fruit, displayed in a life that stands out like a light in the darkness. It is not sufficient to appropriate the robe of righteousness purchased by Jesus if we then live as the heathen do. We are only deluding ourselves. The Church has for too long adopted the ways of the world. We blend in so well that it is often difficult to discern the difference between saints and sinners. The Church's breastplate is severely compromised and there is a time of chastening appointed her.

Heb 12:11 Now chastening for the present does not seem to be joyous, but grievous. Nevertheless afterward it yields the peaceable fruit of <u>righteousness</u> to those who are exercised by it.

The scepter of the Kingdom is a scepter of righteousness (Heb 1:8) and righteousness and justice are the foundations of His throne. If we desire to rule and reign with Him, we must have the breastplate of a righteous life firmly in place.

December 4th

Eph 5:5 For you know this, that no fornicator, or unclean person, or covetous one (who is an idolater), has any inheritance in the

297

kingdom of Christ and of God. Eph 5:6 Let no man deceive you with vain words, for because of these things the wrath of God comes upon the children of disobedience. Eph 5:7 Therefore do not be partakers with them. Eph 5:8 For you were once darkness, but now you are light in the Lord; walk as children of light

The work of the Spirit in our lives brings forth goodness, righteousness and truth. The Spirit of Truth is also the Spirit of Holiness and will urge us to flee darkness and wholly set ourselves apart for the King's purposes. When we walk in the Spirit, obedient to His leading, we do not get led astray by the lusts of the flesh. In order to be able to stand in the evil day, we have to develop a heightened sensitivity to the voice of the Spirit and learn what grieves Him. The Church has become so used to functioning in half-darkness that many times we are not even aware that what we are eating is unclean. We must sit with the Spirit and learn again what is acceptable to the Lord for we have become used to a standard which is acceptable to the world.

Prayer: Precious Holy Spirit, would You come and show me where my standards have slipped. I don't want to live by torchlight but by the light of the Son of Righteousness, amen.

December 5th

Eph 6:15 and your feet shod with the preparation of the gospel of peace.

These are the shoes Jesus was wearing when He came to die for us. John tells us that He didn't come into the world to condemn the world but that through Him the world may be saved. When He was born, the angels proclaimed, "glory to God in the highest,

PEACE and goodwill to men on earth". He did not come to accuse men but to lay down His life for them.

In order to stand in the evil day, we must make sure we are wearing the right shoes. The message we bring is not a message of judgment but a message of peace because of the sacrifice of Jesus. The message of the Kingdom of God is a message of righteousness, PEACE and joy even in the midst of the worst shakings. We have the same commission as Jesus when He came. WE carry within us a message that people can have peace with God even when there are wars and rumors of wars raging around them. Let us make sure we are fully prepared for encountering people in a day in which true peace will be unobtainable, except in Christ. It is not a peace which the world gives, but a peace which enables one to stand, no matter what storm is raging. Get rid of any other gospel for it does not have the power to transfer people out of the kingdom of darkness.

"How beautiful are the feet of those who preach the gospel of peace and bring glad tidings of good things!"

December 6th

Eph 6:16 Above all, take the shield of faith, with which you shall be able to quench all the fiery darts of the wicked.

No matter how accurately our armor is worn, it is capable of being pierced by a flaming arrow from the enemy's bow. This is why we need the shield of faith. We are able to move it to protect any area that is under attack. However, the shield in itself is of no use unless we are able to see the arrow moving towards us or even to hear it whizzing through the air. It is extremely important to pray for eyes that see and ears that hear in the spiritual realm. We are not wrestling against flesh and blood and we must hone our ability to discern our enemy lying in wait for us. The Spirit of Revelation must minister information to us which is not apparent in the natural realm. We have to be forewarned in order to be fore-armed. Faith comes by hearing the spoken word from the mouth of God (Romans 10:17 speaks of a rhema word as opposed to logos or written word). Often the Spirit will quicken a certain scripture to us although it may seem to have no relevance at the time. However, what He is doing is equipping us to have the word in season when the attack comes. As the word is dropped into our hearts, we can then speak it with our mouths in faith and stop those fiery arrows in their tracks. Whether the arrow flies toward us using the mouths of those near to us or comes from a more hidden source, God is able to see the enemy's plans before they are enacted. The Spirit of God warns us ahead of time so that we can lift up our shield of faith and nullify the planned attack.

December 7th

Eph 6:17 And take the helmet of salvation, and the sword of the Spirit, which is the Word of God,

Remember the armor of God is a lifestyle, not a spiritual garment. The helmet of salvation is intended to protect our minds. How does it do this? When we understand what our salvation really means and what was accomplished for on the cross of Calvary, it will eliminate many of the mental battles that rage within. Our salvation is far greater and more encompassing than we realize. Revelation of this will be key in the times we are facing.

We have been fed such a watered-down version of the victory of the Blood of Jesus that we are tricked into facing accusations and grappling with issues that have already been dealt with. There has already been a court case over your life. You were found guilty on all charges and a sentence was handed down. However, Jesus took the sentence upon Himself when He went to the cross for you. When you received the substitution of Jesus for you by faith, the power of His Blood went into action And is still daily delivering you from the power of sin! Just remember it is no longer you who live but Christ who lives in you and you have access to His mind, His thoughts!

December 8th

Eph 6:18 praying always with all prayer and supplication in the Spirit, and watching to this very thing with all perseverance and supplication for all saints.

Do you notice there are three 'all's in this verse? All prayer with all perseverance for all saints – sounds like a full-time occupation to me! This speaks of prayer and communion with God becoming as natural as breathing in and breathing out. We are to pray ALWAYS – not only at appointed times of official prayer but our lives should be a continual communing with our Father. If we live our lives like this, it protects us from leaning on our own understanding because we are always bringing situations before His face and not only requesting but also listening for advice from the Spirit of Counsel on how to pray and proceed further.

Notice that our prayer must be 'in the Spirit' if we are to wrestle effectively against principalities and powers. It is useless to pray from a natural viewpoint because we need to take into account the things that are unseen. When the Spirit of Counsel shares the Throne's strategy with us, we are equipped to operate in the Spirit of Might. When the Spirit offers His counsel, it is far above our ways because His thoughts are not our thoughts! We need to breathe in His counsel before we breathe out our supplication! In the unseen realm a powerful victory takes place as light repels darkness! The church needs to go back to the drawing board and take another look at Jesus' warfare manual – it looks very different to much teaching on warfare circulating today!

December 9th

Eph 6:19 And for me, that utterance may be given unto me, that I may open my mouth boldly, to make known the mystery of the gospel, Eph 6:20 For which I am an ambassador in bonds: that therein I may speak boldly, as I ought to speak.

Paul was already sitting in prison as a result of his preaching of the gospel; yet he does not ask them to pray for his release, his comfort or any other personal need. He is consumed with his mission to spread the gospel, no matter what personal cost he may have to pay. He was dead to self. How the church needs more who are in Paul's mold.

He asked them to pray for boldness to speak because without boldness one is aware of the consequences that will follow your speaking and may draw back and close your mouth to protect yourself. Let us pray for boldness for ourselves and the right words to say, whether we are out in the neighborhood supposedly free but in the prison of our own fear of man!

Prayer: father, help me to pray not for my own comfort but for the strength and boldness to make use of every situation to extend Your kingdom, amen.

December 10ᵗʰ

Psa 68:9 You, O God, sent a plentiful rain, by which You upheld Your inheritance when it was weary. Psa 68:10 Your flock has dwelt in it; You, O God, have prepared in Your goodness for the poor.

Many saints are experiencing great weariness at this time. The journey has been long and difficult and sometimes it is almost too much to keep putting one foot in front of the other on this road of faith. Take comfort that the Father sees where you are and His solution is to send a plentiful rain to you. You can ask God for rain in the time of latter rain. Ask Him to rain on your heart. Then lift your tired face to the heavens and receive the glorious water of life as it falls upon you.

Verse 10 tells us that His flock can dwell in the rain. Picture that – a heavy black rain cloud over you as you keep walking towards the goal, showering much rain upon you wherever you are! Beloved, we can dwell in the plentiful rain. It doesn't have to be an occasional refreshing experience. The cloud of His presence causes the heavy rain will fall upon your life.

Prayer: Father, I am so dry and weary. I ask You for rain in the time of latter rain and, more than that – I want to dwell in Your rain! I never want to leave the place of continual soaking. Teach me how to dwell here, amen

December 11th

Gen 28:11 And he came on a certain place, and stayed there all night, because the sun had set. And he took of the stones of that place, and placed them at his head. And he lay down in that place to sleep.

When the journey of our life brings us to a place where there is darkness and the light of the Son of Righteousness is nowhere in sight, we must follow Jacob's example. A stone can either be a stumbling block or a stepping stone in our spiritual progress – and yes, the enemy definitely has placed it in our path in order to trip us up! Jacob, however, took the stone in front of him and used it as a pillow for his weary head. If we will lay our head upon the stone that seems to block our path and rest in the knowledge that all our steps are ordered of the Lord, peace will replace frustration and that place of darkness will become a place of refreshing and revelation, just as it did for Jacob

Gen 28:12 And he dreamed, and behold a ladder set up on the earth, and the top of it reached to heaven: and behold the angels of God ascending and descending on it.

Prayer: Father, it is good to realize that the stumbling block which I have found in this place of darkness is intended by You to be a place where my mind can rest and my spirit receives life-giving revelation. I rest in the knowledge that You know my path and this situation is appointed to lift me not crush me, amen.

December 12th

Gen 28:13 And behold! The Lord stood above it, and said, I am the Lord, the God of Abraham your father, and the God of Isaac! The land on which you lie I will give to you and to your seed. Gen 28:14 And your seed shall be like the dust of the earth, and you shall spread abroad to the west, and to the east, and to the north, and to the south. And in you and in your Seed shall all the families of the earth be blessed.

As Jacob found rest in the hard place he had come to, God began to give him revelation. He showed him angels carrying out God's commands in that very place which seemed so dark. He also promised him that the land he was lying on would belong to him and his children; that there would be increase in every direction and that his family would bless every other family.

Beloved, the hidden things belong to God but the things that are revealed belong to us and our children forever (Deut 29:29). The revelation God gives you in darkness and trial is for the purpose of bringing increase and blessing to your family and also through you to bless others in many places. If you will rest and trust God in this stony place, you will come to conquer and possess the land that at this time is such a trial to you – and following this period, great increase and blessing is on the way.

Prayer: Father, I want to lay hold of and possess for myself the revelation You have for me in this stony place. Let it not just be a mental enlightenment but a spiritual breakthrough that is brought to me and my family, amen.

Christine Beadsworth

December 13ᵗʰ

Gen 28:15 And, behold, I am with you, and will keep you in every place where you go, and will bring you again into this land. <u>For I will not leave you until I have done that which I have spoken of to you.</u> Gen 28:16 And Jacob awakened from his sleep. And he said, Surely the Lord is in this place, and I did not know. Gen 28:17 And he was afraid, and said, How fearful is this place! This is nothing but the house of God, and this is the gate of Heaven!

God will not leave you and will fulfill every word that He has promised you. He is right there in the dark stony place with you and on every step of the journey ahead of you. The situation which outwardly seems a barren and difficult place is actually the very place where God's presence will become manifestly apparent to you.

This stone you rest your head on is also the appointed gate to your experience of heavenly things. When the dawn comes, you will raise a memorial to the glory of God at this marker in your life journey and all who visit it with you in conversation will acknowledge that this is 'Bethel' -the place where God came to dwell with you! Don't despise the stony pillows God places in your path – they can either be stumbling blocks or stepping stones in your spiritual walk. It depends on what you do with them. Lay your head down and trust God as the night falls.

Gen 28:18 And Jacob rose up early in the morning, and took the stone that he had put for his pillows, and set it up for a pillar, and poured oil upon the top of it. Gen 28:19 And he called the name of that place Bethel (the House of God)

December 14th

Psa 139:7 Where shall I go from Your Spirit? Or where shall I flee from Your presence? Psa 139:8 If I go up into Heaven, You are there; if I make my bed in Sheol, behold, You are there.

There is no place or situation you can find yourself in, where the Spirit of God is not present to minister to you and through you. Even in Sheol – the grave, the place of the dead – His life-giving words can be heard and embraced. Do not be deceived by your natural senses – they will tell you that your situation is so deathly that a God of Life would not deign to presence Himself there. He actually delights in entering the most hopeless situations and overturning them. Did Jesus not march in and take the keys of death from satan himself in his own area of power and influence?

The whole earth is filled with the glory of God and even on the land of the shades of the dead, He causes His dew to fall. The Hebrew word for 'tomb' means 'a stack of sheaves'. Even the place of death becomes the place of fruitfulness as the dew of His light and revelation fall upon your heart. So rest and trust even if you brought down to the grave. Sheaves of wheat are being heaped up to your account. You will see the fruit of the travail of your soul and rest satisfied!

December 15th

Psa 139:11 If I say, Surely the darkness shall overwhelm me, And the light about me shall be night; Psa 139:12 Even the darkness hides not from You, But the night shines as the day: The darkness and the light are both alike to You.

God is light and therefore is unaffected by any outer darkness. We may find ourselves in a situation that appears outwardly dark, yet if we are in Christ, we surrounded by the light that is within Him. So we do not need to fear approaching darkness or the terrors of the night. In the secret place of the Most High there is always light and revelation and wisdom for the occasion.

When the plague of darkness hit Egypt, there was still light within the Israelite's dwellings. Christ is the plumb-line Who divides light from darkness. His presence alone dispels darkness and causes it to flee. To be in Him is to walk in the light of His presence, no matter the hour of the day or the manifestation on the calendar of end-time events. We are the children of the Light. That is why dense darkness may be upon the peoples and the nations but His light and glory arises upon us.

Prayer: Father, the light of Your glorious presence is all I need to guide me through the dark and difficult days ahead. Help me to live my life governed not by the natural light but the supernatural light of heaven, Christ Himself, amen.

December 16th

Psa 46:1   God is our refuge and strength, a very present help in trouble. Psa 46:2   Therefore will not we fear, though the earth be removed, and though the mountains be carried into the midst of the sea; Psa 46:3   Though the waters thereof roar and be troubled, though the mountains shake with the swelling thereof. Selah.

A refuge is a safe place, a place to run to from every threat and danger that looms large on our horizons. God is our refuge. No man has the strength to be a refuge for another human being.

We should not be surprised that men fail us in times of trouble. They were never intended to be our safe place.

Consider the situation described in these verses – mountains plunging into the sea, carrying all that was planted on them into the depths of the churning ocean; this in turn creating a tumultuous wave which crashes on the remaining land. It is a scene which induces terror – yet David that even if this should happen before our eyes, we will not be afraid. What a supernatural response – while others are screaming and crying for fear, God's children are calm and at peace in the midst of chaos. What a testimony; what a signpost to the source of peace that is not of this world!

Now whether the mountain that crashes is the mount of world financial markets or some other natural disaster, we have a place of safety that is unshakable and eternal. Our source of supply is God and not Wall Street.

December 17th

Psa 46:4 There is a river, the streams whereof shall make glad the city of God, the holy place of the tabernacles of the most High.

We are His city, we are His building, the work of His hands and He has built us with a direct unshakable water supply. We drink of the river which flows from under the throne of God. It is the river of Life. God is in the midst of us and in His presence is fullness of joy.

Don't drink of the polluted streams of the world systems. You will be manipulated and controlled from without and your state of mind will follow that of the mountain as it plunges into the sea. Rather drink of the sweet life-giving waters which are always available to the city of God, even when earthly water pipes are broken and sewage is spilling everywhere. You can be full of joy in the midst of world turmoil because you have a different water source! Drink freely and walk in the joy of the Lord!

December 18th

Psa 46:5 God is in the midst of her; she shall not be moved: God shall help her, and that right early.

In the midst of this heavenly city is the almighty presence of the Living God. No wonder the fall of earthly mountains does not affect her! When the shakings take place, that which remains standing afterwards is proved to have Christ as its foundation.

It is the Jerusalem above which is the mother of us all (Gal 4:26) We are not part of earthly systems and organizations. We are registered with the church of the First-Born in heaven and are citizens of another Kingdom. The King of the Universe is uttering His voice and everything that can be shaken will be shaken BUT we who are assembling on Mount Zion are safe in His care.

Psa 46:6 The heathen raged, the kingdoms were moved: he uttered his voice, the earth melted.   The LORD of hosts is with us; the God of Jacob is our refuge. Selah.

Earthly kingdoms will be shaken and fall. Are we not seeing the falling of governments in many countries worldwide at this very time? The nations are in tumult - but don't look at them, look at Him who is in the midst of His city. Far above, in heavenly realms on Mount Zion, the sons of the Kingdom are experiencing peace and joy in the presence of their King.

December 19th

Psa 48:1 <A Song and Psalm for the sons of Korah.> Great is the LORD, and greatly to be praised in the city of our God, in the mountain of his holiness. Psa 48:2 Beautiful for situation, the joy of the whole earth, is mount Zion, on the sides of the north, the city of the great King. Psa 48:3 God is known in her palaces for a refuge.

The city of the living God is the envy of every other city. So great is her beauty and glory that every other earthly city pales into insignificance. Principalities and powers and the kings of the earth gather together against the Lord and His saints but when they see the glory of God radiating forth from mount Zion, they tremble and flee.

Psa 48:4 For, lo, the kings were assembled, they passed by together. Psa 48:5 They saw it, and so they marveled; they were troubled, and hasted away. Psa 48:6 Fear took hold upon them there, and pain, as of a woman in travail. Psa 48:7 You break the ships of Tarshish with an east wind.

Out of Zion, God extends His scepter in righteous judgment and it brings gladness to His saints as recompense is ordered. Judgment is passed in favor of the saints and all iniquity must shut its mouth. 'Let mount Zion rejoice, let the daughters of Judah be glad, because of Your judgments' (Psa 48:11). For those registered in Heaven, a time of great rejoicing is about to be unleashed and they shall go forth as calves let from the stall as God's scepter is extended in the earth on their behalf!

December 20th

Psa 46:8 Come, behold the works of the LORD, what desolations he hath made in the earth. Psa 46:9 He makes wars to cease unto the end of the earth; he breaks the bow, and cuts the spear in sunder; he burns the chariot in the fire. Psa 46:10 Be still, and know that I am God: I will be exalted among the heathen, I will be exalted in the earth. Psa 46:11 The LORD of hosts is with us; the God of Jacob is our refuge. Selah.

When God passes judgment in favor of the saints, He deals with every attack that has been systematically launched against you. He renders desolate the camp of the enemy and burns their chariots in His unquenchable fire of judgment. God is determined for His name to be exalted in the earth and in your life. So you can be still and know that he is God and will bring to pass His every purpose for you.

The work that He executes in the days of judgment and shaking will bring down the strongholds of the enemy and cause your life to be a place of testimony to the greatness of the God you belong to. His name WILL be exalted among the heathen. Lift your head and expect the Lord's mighty hand to move on your behalf. You will again have reason to praise Him because you have walked in the fear of the Lord and not denied His Name!

Isa 66:5 Hear the word of the LORD, you that tremble at his word; Your brethren that hated you, that cast you out for my name's sake, said, Let the LORD be glorified: but he shall appear to your joy, and they shall be ashamed.

December 21st

Psa 50:1 <A Psalm of Asaph.> The mighty God, even the LORD, has spoken, and addressed the earth from the rising of the sun unto the going down thereof. Psa 50:2 Out of Zion, the perfection of beauty, God has shined. Psa 50:3 Our God shall come, and shall not keep silence: a fire shall devour before him, and it shall be very tempestuous round about him.

God is going to shine out of Zion, out of the heavenly city of His saints. He is coming and His fire is coming with Him. As the shakings around us in the earthly kingdoms continue, know that the time of dealing is at the door. He is going to address His people; those dwelling in heavenly places and those who are earthly:

Psa 50:4 He shall call to <u>the heavens</u> from above, and to <u>the earth</u>, that he may judge his people. Psa 50:5 Gather my saints together unto me; those that have made a covenant with me by sacrifice.

There are those who have made a covenant with Him, sealed with the blood of Jesus' sacrifice. Any other transaction holds no weight for only the righteousness of Christ holds up in God's court. No earthly sacrifice is sufficient when God is balancing His ledgers. Self-righteous deeds don't count! Some are placing their hopes in great works of religion and good deeds but in the day when God addresses His people, these will not protect them from His dealings. We must place all our faith in the finished works of the cross. All built with wood, hay and stubble will be consumed by the breath of His mouth.

313

Christine Beadsworth

December 22ⁿᵈ

Psa 50:15 And call upon me in the day of tribulation: I will deliver you, and you shall glorify me.

Those who have a blood covenant with God and have been serving Him in holiness and godly fear, may call upon Him when tribulation and trial threatens and He promises to deliver you with a testimony! However, to those who call themselves people of God, but who are earthly or fleshly, God has a stern rebuke:

Psa 50:16 But unto the wicked God says, What is it to you to declare my statutes, or how can you take my covenant in your mouth? Psa 50:17 Seeing you hate instruction, and cast my words behind you. Psa 50:18 When you see a thief, then you agree with him, and have been partaker with adulterers. Psa 50:19 You speak evil, and your tongue frames deceit... Psa 50:21 These things you have done, and I kept silent; you thought I was altogether like yourself: but I will reprove you, and set them in order before your eyes.

Saints, its audit time for the house of God. These are not unbelievers God is speaking to here, but hypocrites! Those who have been living in a way that is not becoming to a holy people will be dealt with. For because of such behavior, God's name has been dragged through the mud in the world's eyes. Our God is a consuming fire and He is not going to keep silent any longer. It is time to separate the tares from the wheat, the real from the counterfeit! The question is, "Are you completely sure what kind you are?" Examine yourself to see whether you are in the faith and be careful when you think you stand, lest you fall!

December 23rd

Isa 66:10 Rejoice you with Jerusalem, and be glad with her, all you that love her: rejoice for joy with her, all ye that mourn for her: Isa 66:11 That you may suck, and be satisfied with the breasts of her consolations; that you may milk out, and be delighted with the abundance of her glory.

The Jerusalem that we rejoice with is the Jerusalem above. It is the heavenly city that is situated on Mount Zion that will feed the saints with the pure milk of the Word in the end-times. It is this city that will be full of glory because she is the dwelling place of God, a city not built with hands.

Isa 66:12 For thus says the LORD, Behold, I will extend peace to her like a river, and the glory of the Gentiles like a flowing stream: Isa 66:13then shall you suck, you shall be borne upon her sides, and be dandled upon her knees. Isa 66:13 As one whom his mother comforts, so will I comfort you; and you shall be comforted in Jerusalem.

This Jerusalem is the place where those who become as little children will enter the Kingdom and experience righteousness, peace and joy in the Holy Spirit. The Jerusalem above which is our mother is the city where we receive the comfort of a mother, no matter what may be going on in the earthly realm. Let us not attach ourselves to earthly things at this time. They have no ability to succor or offer comfort and peace. The less you are joined to the things of the earthly realm, the less they have the ability to affect you!

315

Christine Beadsworth

December 24ᵗʰ

Isa 66:14 And when ye see this, your heart shall rejoice, and your bones shall flourish like an herb: and the hand of the LORD shall be known toward his servants, and his indignation toward his enemies.

When we see this – when we understand that our source is not in the earthly but in the heavenly – when we grasp the our citizenship is in heaven and that we are not a part of the things that are unfolding in the kingdoms of this world, then we will rejoice! Not only that but our bones will flourish and grow strong because we are being nourished with a diet uncontaminated by worldly additives and 'Christian' junk food. We will be continuously partaking of the feast that is provided upon Mount Zion.

Isa 25:6 And in this mountain shall the LORD of hosts make unto all people a feast of fat things, a feast of wines on the lees, of fat things full of marrow, of wines on the lees well refined.

On mount Zion there is the wine of heavenly revelation reserved for this time, coupled with stored up 'fat things' which speaks of end-time anointing and equipping. Let us no longer waste precious time chewing through the tasteless fast food of fleshly revelation from the unclean kitchens of Babylon. There is a banquet awaiting us on His holy hill and the dinner bell is ringing!

December 25th

Psa 23:4 Yea, though I walk through the valley of the shadow of death, I will fear no evil; for You are with me; Your rod and Your staff, they comfort me. Psa 23:5 You prepare a table for me in the presence of my enemies; You anoint my head with oil; my cup runs over.

He prepares a table for us right in the sight of our enemies. Now if we had been given the option we would have chosen to destroy the enemy first and then have the feast! Oh the audacity of the Father – to organize a table groaning with the best of Heaven's delicacies right under the nose of the enemy troops! This is not a hasty snack for God's soldier from a dehydrated ration pack but a sumptuous carefully prepared meal for the Beloved of God.

Isa 55:1 Ho, every one that thirsts, come to the waters, and he that has no money; come buy and eat; yes, come, buy wine and milk without money and without price. ...Isa 55:3 Incline your ear, and come to Me: hear, and your soul shall live;

This is not only a banquet but a FREE feast! But what are we eating right in front of the enemy? The key is in the last few words -'hear and your soul shall live'. We feast upon the words spoken to us by the Father right in the midst of the difficulty and they are represented by milk and wine. Milk speaks of the pure milk of the Word. Wine represents the spirit-quickened revelation that flows from the water of the Word on the third day of the feast. Bon Appétit!

December 26th

Psa 36:7 How precious is Your loving-kindness, O God! And the sons of men take refuge under the shadow of Your wings. Psa 36:8 They shall be satisfied with the abundance of Your house; and You shall make them drink of the river of Your pleasures.

The reason why you can feast at this table prepared for you is the place it is situated. When we take refuge in Christ we dwell under the shadow of His wings – in this place there is a continual banquet because of the abundance of El Shaddai. We can drink freely of the water of the river of Life which flows from the Throne at any time day or night.

Our earthly situation may be dark and stormy but right in the eye of the storm we find the still small voice which speaks counsel and revelation that nourish and strengthen our inner man. In fact we are able to suck nourishment right out of the midst of the stormy valley path that has been appointed us! Our Father delights in flooding the darkness with the light of heavenly revelation! This is precisely why He allowed us to be led right to this place of threatening shadows.

So take your eyes off the movements in the enemy camp and take your seat at the table prepared for you. As you eat of the meal lovingly prepared for you by the Spirit of Truth, you will taste and see that God is indeed good!

December 27th

Psa 23:5 You prepare a table before me in the presence of my enemies: You anoint my head with oil; my cup runs over. Psa 23:6 Surely goodness and mercy shall follow me all the days of my life: and I will dwell in the house of the LORD forever.

The reason a head was anointed in ancient times, apart from when appointing a king, was in order to prevent excess perspiration and sweat. As you feast upon the banquet of revelation in this valley you are brought to a place of rest from your own fleshly attempts to solve the situation. God doesn't want you to sweat;

He wants you to trust and glean wisdom and understanding from this valley. He will bring to pass His purposes for you and complete them. This valley does not signify a wrong turn in your journey but rather an appointed place of nourishment and equipping for the rest of the journey.

Not only that, but you will come to realize that the shadow of death is only an illusion. When you glance over your shoulder you realize that God has your back covered and goodness and mercy are actually following you! Therefore you never need fear any dark place again. When you make the Lord your refuge and dwell in the secret place of the Most High all the days of your life, it hardly matters where your earthly journey takes you – you are continually in the glorious presence of the Lord anyway!

December 28th

Rev 1:9 I John, who also am your brother, and companion in tribulation, and in the kingdom and patience of Jesus Christ, was in the isle that is called Patmos, for the word of God, and for the testimony of Jesus Christ. Rev 1:10 I was in the Spirit on the Lord's day, and heard behind me a great voice, as of a trumpet

It is during tribulation that we receive the revelation of Christ. When we have been ostracized and shunned because of our Christian stand, then we are in the perfect place to receive a download from heaven.

Mat 5:10 Blessed are they who have been persecuted for righteousness sake! For theirs is the kingdom of Heaven. Mat 5:11 Blessed are you when men shall revile you and persecute you, and shall say all kinds of evil against you falsely, for My sake. Rejoice and be exceedingly glad, for your reward in Heaven is great.

John was persecuted and banished to Patmos, which was intended to be a harsh punishment. However it was the gateway to a great blessing for the island prison was God's appointed place for John to receive a banquet from heaven's kitchen! Persecution is the doorway to revelation of the Kingdom! The more you are reviled for your stand for Christ, the greater the feast of revelation that is assigned to you.

December 29th

Isa 66:15 For, behold, the LORD will come with fire, and with his chariots like a whirlwind, to render his anger with fury, and his rebuke with flames of fire.

Psalm 104:4 tells us that God makes His ministers a flame of fire. When He comes to rebuke in the days ahead, He does not speak in a disembodied voice but will bring forth those who have been lying on the altar of surrender, submitting to His refiner's fire. These burning coals from the altar become the messengers who deliver a Word in season that cleanses unclean lips and impure hearts.

Isa 66:16 For by fire and by his sword will the LORD plead with all flesh: and the slain of the LORD shall be many. Isa 66:17 They that sanctify themselves, and purify themselves in the idol gardens, eating swine's flesh, and the abomination, and the mouse, shall be consumed together, says the LORD.

Using the sword of His unchanging Word, these ministers will rightly divide issues and teach God's people the difference between the clean and the unclean. Those who have been involved in idolatrous practices and all who are fleshly shall find themselves exposed by the plumbline of Truth. Perhaps God has been preparing you upon His altar and it has seemed to you that the refining is never-ending. Be encouraged, burning coal. You will become a flame of fire in the hand of the Master.

December 30th

Isa 4:3 And it shall come to pass, that he that is left in Zion, and he that remains in Jerusalem, shall be called holy, even every one that is written among the living in Jerusalem: When the Lord has washed away the filth of the daughters of Zion, and has purged the blood of Jerusalem from the midst thereof by the spirit of judgment, and by the spirit of burning.

The reason God comes to deal with His Body with fire and the sword is in order to purify, prepare and unleash an army of servant-messengers into all the earth. Among those who come through the fiery dealings of the Spirit in the coming year will be a multitude of willing bond-slaves who will follow the Lamb wherever He goes. They will be used to declare the glory of the Lord amongst the nations:

Isa 66:19 And I will set a sign among them, and I will send those that escape of them unto the nations, to Tarshish, Pul, and Lud, that draw the bow, to Tubal, and Javan, to the isles far off, that have not heard my fame, neither have seen my glory; and they shall declare my glory among the Gentiles.

A great many souls will be brought in as an offering to the Lord. They will come from all the nations of the earth to mount Zion. The Lord's wealth is His people and just as an offering was brought to the Lord in ancient times, so too will many souls be presented to Him as trophies snatched from the realm of the enemy.

Time is short, Beloved. Let the Spirit of burning have its ay unhindered in your heart that you may be of use to the Master.

December 31st

Pro 8:1 Does not wisdom cry, And understanding put forth her voice? Pro 8:2 On the top of high places by the way, Where the paths meet, she stands;

As we stand at the threshold of another year, we are faced with choices - we can choose to venture out into the unknown leaning upon our own understanding and the wisdom of men or we can ask for wisdom for each step we must take. The Spirit of Wisdom offers sound counsel for those who will pause to listen.

Pro 8:14 Counsel is mine, and sound knowledge: I am understanding; I have might. By me kings reign, And princes decree justice. By me princes rule, And nobles, even all the judges of the earth. I love them that love me; And those that seek me diligently shall find me. Riches and honor are with me; Yes, <u>durable wealth</u> and righteousness.

The fruit of Wisdom is better than gold and silver and the currencies of this earth – it is durable wealth which cannot be affected by the stock markets of earth or moth and rust. God desires to fill your treasuries BUT the precondition is that you incline your ear to the voice of Wisdom. That means no impulsive decisions but rather waiting on the Lord until His counsel is spoken. ALL OF THE TREASURES OF WISDOM ARE HIDDEN IN CHRIST.

This is my prayer for you all in the year ahead:

Col 1:9 For this cause we also, since the day we heard, do not cease to pray for you, and to desire that you might be filled with the knowledge of His will in all wisdom and spiritual understanding, that you might walk worthy of the Lord in every way, being fruitful in every work and increasing in the knowledge of God, being empowered with all power, according to the might of His glory, to all patience and long-suffering with joyfulness, giving thanks to the Father, who has made us fit to be partakers of the inheritance of the saints in light.

AMEN

Printed in Great Britain
by Amazon